Taking Action

A volume in
Contemporary Perspectives Through Action Research Across Educational Disciplines
Nancy T. Nasr and Jill A. Perry, *Series Editors*

Contemporary Perspectives Through Action Research Across Educational Disciplines

Nancy T. Nasr and Jill A. Perry, *Series Editors*

Contemporary Perspectives Through Action Research Across Educational Disciplines: The K–12 Classroom (2023)
Nancy T. Nasr and Jill Alexa Perry

Taking Action

Creating Sustainable Change in Student Affairs

edited by

Sara B. Ewell

Northeastern University

Joan Giblin

Northeastern University

Joe McNabb

Northeastern University

INFORMATION AGE PUBLISHING, INC.
Charlotte, NC • www.infoagepub.com

Library of Congress Cataloging-in-Publication Data

A CIP record for this book is available from the Library of Congress
http://www.loc.gov

ISBN: 979-8-88730-395-6 (Paperback)
         979-8-88730-396-3 (Hardcover)
         979-8-88730-397-0 (E-Book)

CONTENTS

Introduction.. vii
Sara B. Ewell, Joseph McNabb, and Joan Giblin

Acknowledgments xiii

1 Understanding the Impact of Student Affairs and Student
Services Directors' Leadership Style on the Undergraduate
Student Experience: An Action Research Study 1
Thomas Tressler-Gelok

2 Investigating the Effects of a Peer Mentorship Program
on Low-Income, First-Generation Students' Access
to Financial Resources 21
Jennifer Bevins

3 Sustaining Engagement Among Student Organizational Leads 37
Brandon Gross

4 Lateral Transfer Students: What Drives their Decision to Leave
and Why Do They Experience Transfer Shock 51
Christopher Collins

5 The Importance of Connections and Collaborations
to Enhance the Successful Graduate Student Experience 67
Kathy Dilks

v

  6 Integrating Mental Health Literacy in Student Affairs
  Master's Programs 87
  Emily Bauer

  7 A Student Centered Approach: Using Systems Theory
  to Improve Community Engagement and Belonging 103
  Joseph Castelot

  8 Understanding and Responding to Career Counseling Needs
  of Chinese International Graduate Students 119
  Lindsey Plewa

  9 A Study of Community College Dropouts: Action Research
  on How a Peer Mentorship Program Through Phi Theta
  Kappa (PTK) Honor Society Can Improve Students'
  Performance 135
  Chunfu Jeff Cheng

  10 Improving Retention of High-Achieving, Generation Z
  Students at a Private, Liberal Arts University 153
  Lars Farabee

  11 Seeing the Unseen: An Action Research Study of First-
  Generation College Student Persistence at a Mid-Size Private
  Institution in the Northeast 167
  Michael A. Urmeneta

  12 HERstory: Giving a Voice to the College Experiences of Black
  Female Students in the New England Area 191
  Nicole Johnson

  About the Editors 215
  About the Contributors 217

INTRODUCTION

The context of contemporary higher education, despite public perception, is dynamic and multifaceted. Trapped somewhere between a public and private good, contemporary higher education faces pressure to redress injustice, prepare the future workforce for jobs that don't yet exist, and engage in innovative research. Tuition costs spiral upwards, information access becomes more instantaneous, and new competitors proliferate as industry certifications emerge. External forces have concerned themselves with higher education since its inception in 1791; Harvard University replied to accusations from the press over its teachings.

Access, equity, purpose, and the role of higher education as a public good have been percolating for over a century, as evidenced in the Morrill Land Grant and in the establishment of HBCUs. Modern conversations and pressure began again when the GI bill put a significant crack into the walls surrounding the impenetrable Ivy Tower. Laws and funding incentives from the federal government, for example, the Higher Education Act, federal work-study programs in 1964, federal student loans in 1965, Pell grants in 1972, and Title IX in 1972 nudged higher education to widen the cracks. Previously excluded populations increasingly accessed higher education institutions. Over the past few decades, Supreme Court decisions on the role of race in admissions decisions regularly swing the pendulum back and forth on issues of equity and access. Unfortunately, as we have learned, mandating access to the physical institution does not guarantee success.

Greater access to higher education laid bare deep societal and infrastructure flaws long hidden. It revealed vast differences in the K–12 system,

Taking Action, pages vii–xii
Copyright © 2024 by Information Age Publishing
www.infoagepub.com
All rights of reproduction in any form reserved.

most often along race and class lines. Higher education institutions found their new students arrived under-prepared through no fault of their own. Today, predictive analytics show that a student's zip code plays a disproportionately large role in their ability to succeed.

Higher education also serves as a battleground for societal issues. Apart from issues of access, the role of higher education in the lives of its students shifted significantly since the 1960s. Contemporary higher education walks a thin line between responsibility for students and their rights as individuals. Colleges no longer stand in locus parentis to students, but still must act enough to protect students from harm. Pressure also exists from changing social mores. Title IX continues to define and re-define, depending on political sensibilities, not only access to institutions but also funding, opportunities, and freedoms for students. The Americans with Disabilities Act not only mandated physical access to classrooms but also to the curriculum and instruction itself. Issues of free speech, affirmative action, and the right to assemble and protest also regularly affect higher education.

CHANGE IN HIGHER EDUCATION

While critics of higher education have remarked on the glacially slow pace of change in higher education, it remains true that glaciers do, in fact, move. And when glaciers move, they make a profound impact on the world around them. The question for those of us in higher education, who care about the quality and purpose of higher education, is how do we change in the most responsible and ethical way possible? External forces continue to push at higher education, forcing large scale change. How do practitioners adapt, improve, and make change within their larger context?

To achieve change, to become a change agent, we need to first identify and understand the problems we are facing, both on a national level and within our local context. Collecting data, verifying assumptions, and solid analysis are all necessary to ensure the change will have the desired results. Applying a rigorous methodological approach to researching and initiating change is important to creating effective change that improves higher education in tangible ways.

While theories of change management often codify the change process into universal and generic steps, genuine change, lasting change, depends on a multitude of interdependent factors, many unique to a specific context. Change at any level in higher education includes navigating esoteric governance structures and building coalitions. All change is local and requires working with stakeholders to design and implement solutions that account for their reality and their understanding of the issue. This leads to lasting change.

ACTION RESEARCH AS A METHODOLOGY

Action research provides a framework for engaging in transformative change. It is both a methodology and a philosophy. Action research aims at helping the action researcher and their professional community identify solutions to real-life problems. Through networks and collaborative relationships, the action researcher can work with participants to find solutions that can create substantial change (Stringer & Ortiz, 2021). Action research can guide the internal work on change that higher education needs today.

The desired outcome of action research is change. To achieve change, to become a change agent, the researcher needs to identify and understand problems within their local context. Change derives from insights taken from the lived experiences of the participants. Action research honors this reality, working with participants to design and implement solutions that account for their reality, their understanding of the issue, with a goal of delivering lasting change. The products of action research are not only written reports but also plans, procedures, models, and other tools that provide the basis for reformulating practices, policies, programs, and services with institutions of higher education (Stringer & Ortiz, 2021).

Action research, unlike traditional research, takes into consideration the social, cultural, and interpersonal factors that affect all human activity. Unlike traditional research, it calls attention to the fact that a study is not done, that work is not complete. Action research is cyclical, acknowledging that change is rarely quick, easy, or neat. If change were these things, higher education would be nimbly adapting to the challenges and issues that it currently faces. Unfortunately, this is not the case.

In the cycles of action research, there is a continuous process of gathering and generating information, analyzing, and interpreting that data, and acting based on that analysis. There are many approaches to action research, but each reflects the diverse ways in which observation, analysis, planning, implementation, and evaluation are described.

For example, in beginning an action research study, the researcher observes what is going on and tries to articulate what it is about the problem that needs improvement. Working with participants and stakeholders, the researcher then gathers relevant information through one or more of the major methods of data collection, for example, interviews, focus groups, and surveys. The researcher then explores and analyzes the data. In collaboration with others, the researcher interprets and explains how or why things are as they are. The next phase involves defining a plan or course of action to address the problem based on this analysis and interpretation. Once the course of action is defined, the researcher implements the plan and evaluates the effectiveness of the actions. At the completion of this cycle, the researcher reviews again, reflects and reanalyzes, and the cycle continues. The action researcher is a reflective practitioner and an intelligent observer of actions and outcomes and acknowledges that change does not happen in one fell swoop, but from a series of often small, incremental steps that can have a long-lasting impact (Johnson & Christensen, 2020).

Action research provides a unique methodological and philosophical approach to improving practice in higher education. As external pressures continue to push higher education, this methodological approach provides a solid framework for higher education practitioners to both identify needed change and to enact that change across a broad range of issues. Within these two volumes, you will see examples of action research to impact seemingly intractable problems, such as implementing formative assessments, bridging practicums with coursework, and tenure-track success efforts at community colleges.

OVERVIEW OF CHAPTERS

All chapters employ an action research approach to impact a diverse set of problems related to student development and support.

Tresselor-Gelok explores the role of leadership styles across student affairs and student directors and how they impact the undergraduate student experience. Leaders in student affairs have great responsibility in supporting the academic, social, and emotional well-being of undergraduate students, but there is little research on the leadership styles that best support them. This study found that there is an opportunity for student affairs leaders to be more innovative, results-driven, and reflective.

Students' understanding of financial resources and supports is critical to their recruitment and retention. Bevins examines the impact of a peer-mentoring program on first-generation students' access to financial resources. The findings indicate peer-mentoring programs offer an opportunity to increase access to financial resources given the mentors are trained and supervised by professional staff. The model promises to decrease the burden on professional staff while increasing access for first-generation students.

The third chapter looks at issues of student engagement among the most involved students, leaders of student organizations. Involvement in co-curricular activities leads to great achievement gains both within higher education and beyond. After first uncovering the root causes for disengagement, Gross demonstrates a model for proactive preparation of students for leadership roles and identifies crucial skills and approaches to improving the engagement of student leaders.

Collins explores how transfer shock impacts lateral transfer students and how they can be best supported in their transition between four-year universities. After discussion of why students transfer and their desire to be more socially connected, the findings indicate it is critical for universities to provide clear, continuous communication on all aspects of integrating into the campus community. Transfer students need immediate social connections, and these are not attainable without the support of university systems.

Student services for graduate students are often an under-resourced area of campus communities that receives little attention. Dilks examines the effectiveness of current graduate student services across five academic colleges. The findings indicate the critical need to create connected opportunities for graduate students that support the social, emotional, academic, and financial needs of graduate students.

The impact of mental health on students on college campuses has never been higher. Bauer's research looks at the importance of integrating mental health literacy into student affairs master's degree programs. The findings indicate it is crucial to redefine the role of student affairs professionals' non-clinical mental health support by integrating theory and practice into graduate programs.

Castelot sought to understand how students' engagement with the on-campus student center shapes their sense of community and belonging. A systems theory approach was used in this study. The findings suggest that the full potential of student centers, as a network of support, has not been fully realized. Improving these networks has the potential to lead to greater connection and community.

Plewa investigated the impact of culturally sensitive individual career counseling on Chinese students studying in the United States. The study found Chinese students faced significant challenges in securing employment in the United States, some of which could be mitigated through support services. The findings support the need for a new higher education model that supports international students across career services, admissions, and student services.

Community college drop-out rates continue to increase and represent the highest level across post-secondary education settings. Cheng investigated the impact of a community college peer mentoring program on student retention at one community college. The findings indicate the peer mentoring program positively impacted students' desire and ability to continue their enrollment because students were able to connect with, encourage, and support one another.

Farabee's research explored the reasons high-achieving students at four-year institutions may not be retained after their freshman year. The findings indicated learning communities show promise increasing interconnectedness among and between students to increase community and ultimately retention of high-achieving students.

First-generation students face unique challenges and research has demonstrated universities fail to retain them at higher levels than other students. Urmeneta's research looked at strategies at one university to track the experiences of first generation students and develop strategies leading to increased retention rates. Urmeneta created *The First-Generation Initiative* that increased first-generation student retention through an increased sense of belonging.

Black female students continue to graduate at lower rates than their counterparts. Johnson's research focused on understanding the experiences of Black female students at a Predominantly White Institution to improve graduation rates. The findings indicated mentorship programs for Black females increase students' sense of belonging and can lead to higher rates of persistence and retention.

—**Sara B. Ewell**
Joseph McNabb
Joan Giblin

REFERENCES

Johnson, R. B., & Christensen, L. (2020). *Educational research: Quantitative, qualitative, and mixed approaches* (7th ed.). SAGE Publications.
Stringer, E. T., & Aragón Ortiz, A. (2021). *Action research* (5th ed.). SAGE Publications.

ACKNOWLEDGMENTS

Many of the chapters in this book were authored by some of the first graduates of the redesigned Northeastern University EdD program. The program was redesigned in 2018 to support social justice change work and we are inspired by all the work our students have done to move the needle forward on equity and justice. We would like to thank our Northeastern University colleagues who have worked tirelessly with us to make the redesigned program a reality. Without their unwavering commitment to our students, curriculum, and social justice, it would not have been possible. We would also like to recognize the work of the Carnegie Project on the education doctorate and Executive Director Jill Perry, for their support and guidance over the years and recognizing Northeastern University as the 2022 EdD Program of the Year.

CHAPTER 1

UNDERSTANDING THE IMPACT OF STUDENT AFFAIRS AND STUDENT SERVICES DIRECTORS' LEADERSHIP STYLE ON THE UNDERGRADUATE STUDENT EXPERIENCE

An Action Research Study

Thomas Tressler-Gelok

Higher education in the United States is being challenged to differentiate, adapt, and revolutionize its services due to a series of external and internal variables that are systematically impacting the sector. These factors include, but are not limited to, the cost of operations, the decline of the traditionally aged college population (18–24), tuition and fee increases, technological

Taking Action, pages 1–20
Copyright © 2024 by Information Age Publishing
www.infoagepub.com

demands, diversification, globalization, social uprisings, and the political dialogue surrounding college accessibility (DeMeyer, 2011; Jenkins, 2019; Kezar & Holocombe, 2017; Wiley Education Services, 2019). Even world-wide pandemics, like COVID-19, are shaping the way higher education operates causing unpredictable and volatile organizational climates (Burke, 2020; Crawford et al., 2020).

At the center of these competing priorities and challenges are the students and their experience. In U.S. higher education, student affairs and student services directors are the individuals tasked with building comprehensive programs and policies while providing developmental support to the students' co-curricular experience (Cochran, 2016; Long, 2012; Martinez, 2018). The leadership displayed by these professionals in their respective discipline can have a direct and paramount impact on the undergraduate student experience; however, there is a gap in the research that understands this impact. This chapter will present an action research study that explores how the leadership style of student affairs and student services directors impact the undergraduate student experience at a small, private college.

BACKGROUND AND CONTEXT

Student affairs and student services divisions in U.S. higher education are responsible for cultivating equitable, engaging co-curricular experiences for their students (Pendakur et al., 2020). With over 4,440 institutions in the United States, each has its own identity, including community colleges, private universities, public colleges and universities, research institutions, art and design schools, for-profit institutions, online universities, technology institutions, HBCUs, tribal colleges, vocational and trades schools, and the liberal arts college (Baldwin et al., 2017; Jacobson et al., 2019; Loo, 2018; Thelin, 2019). Due to these different types of institutions, national organizations emerged to provide holistic guidance and provide guiding best practices. Organizations, like NASPA and ACPA, and seminal documents, like the CAS standards and *Learning Reconsidered,* (2004), emerged as the understood philosophies and values for student affairs and student services professionals (ACPA & NASPA, 2015; Barnes, 2020; Council for the Advancement of Standards in Higher Education, 2015; Hevel, 2016; Roberts, 2007). These examples are highlighted as quintessential best practices that inform professionals in the development of their offices, programs, and services regardless of institution type (Biddix, 2013; Herdlein et al., 2013; Hoffman & Bresciani, 2012; Roberts, 2007).

Although national organizations and competency modules have noted importance, they are currently under scrutiny due to their generality and White, heteronormative foundations in search of more adaptive, nuanced approaches that address micro-needs and campus developments directly (Andersen, 2020; Bazarsky et al., 2020; DeMeyer, 2011; Jenkins, 2019; Kezar & Holocombe, 2017; Pryor, 2019; Roden, 2020; Zenner & Squire, 2020). This inspires a critical review of student affairs and student services experience, particularly as national expectations are critiqued as unsustainable due to the overzealous expectations that require significant output and work to attain (Andersen, 2020; Sallee, 2021). Burnout, anxiety, and sacrifices beyond reasonable expectations for student affairs and student services directors is currently under review especially within times of significant organization turnover (Aldeman, 2021; Andersen, 2020; Sallee, 2021). COVID-19 has only brought a hyperawareness of this perspective and the major departures in the job market (Nietzel, 2021). Student affairs and student services professionals were key stakeholders that involved campus closures as they provided innovation and support to online learning transitions, task force and steering committee managements, positional changes, learning disruptions, refunds, enrollment declines, unexpected costs, new financial burdens, and changing guidance from the federal government (Center for Disease Control and Prevention, 2020, 2021; Koralesky et al., 2020; Prescott, 2021; Rossman et al., 2020; Smalley, 2021).

The liberal arts colleges more so than other institution types felt the impacts of these transitions because it changed the entire nature of the in-person, high touch approach (Garcia-Morales et al., 2021; Rossman et al., 2020). Due to their size and operating budgets, specifically deferred maintenance, new technology, open educational records (OER) reforming costs, debt management, and accessibility, are competing priorities that cause more significant time, attention, and pressure (Brown et al., 2019; Civera et al., 2021; Fowler, 2021; Lewis, 2019; Sullivan & Stergios, 2019; Weis et al., 2017). These variables uniquely impact the way student affairs and student services directors approach their work in this environment because of the variable impact they have on a practitioner's work (Rossman et al., 2020). As they seek to engage students, build their offices, and approach organizational development, understanding eternal pressures and internal reactions is a critical component to the potential impact of their leadership in this environment (Rossman et al., 2020).

The leadership of student affairs and student services directors at a small private liberal arts college can impact the undergraduate student experience. But in a contemporary period of changing demographics, external pressures, and financial insecurity, how can leaders impact the student experience? It is essential to explore this question by examining the leadership style of individuals leading student affairs and student services functions and the impact their particular leadership style can have on the holistic student experience that institutions of higher education aim to provide. The purpose of this study seeks to analyze how the leadership style of student affairs and student services directors impact the undergraduate student experience at a small, private liberal arts college. The identified participant group is full-time student affairs and student services directors working in higher education who are non-tenured and non-unionized.

METHODS

The organization for this action research study is a small, private liberal arts college in the Northeast United States that has been in operation for over 100 years. It is a predominantly White institution. The institution has religious roots but now identifies as non-secular. It is situated in an urban environment and focuses on the liberal arts and sciences. Based on national classification models, the institution is classified as a private, not-for-profit institution that is defined as highly residential and small (Carnegie Foundation for the Advancement of Teaching, 2011). Due to the type of college, it will be referred to with the pseudonym of liberal arts college (LAC).

Participants

In Cycle 1, participation criteria were based on the position of the practitioner at the research site. Individuals had to identify as a director, or equivalent title, of a student affairs and/or student services function. Student affairs and student services directors were selected as participants due to the interdependent work the practitioners do in the small, private liberal arts college. Although other studies may separate these two groups, it was determined to be imperative to the mission of the liberal arts college to study these groups together. Both groups support the mission of liberal arts colleges and the development of co-curricular learning and good practices (Kuh et al., 2010).

To recruit participants, the researcher sent personal outreach. The final participant sample consisted of eight student affairs and student services professionals. Two of the professionals identified as men, while six identified as female. The disciplines represented in Cycle 1 included athletics, student support services, conduct, advising, registration, student accounts, multicultural affairs, and student activities. Individuals were coded based on years in the organization, including new (1 to 3 years of service), seasoned (4 to 7 years of service), and established (8 or more years of service). For Cycle 1, there were three seasoned professionals, four established, and one new.

In Cycle 2, the participation criterion was limited to student affairs and student services directors; eight participated in the coaching session. Five participants from Cycle 1 continued in the coaching series; three new participants joined who were not involved in Cycle 1. Like Cycle 1, the participants were grouped by tenure to protect the identity of new, seasoned, and established. Seven of eight were female-identifying practitioners, while one was male-identifying. There were three seasoned and three established professionals with two new professionals as the smallest tenure group in the sample. The participants worked in security, residential life, business operations, student activities, multicultural affairs, student support services, conduct, and registration.

Data Analysis

Data analysis for this process used methods associated with action research. At the conclusion of the Cycle 1 data collection process, the data was transcribed using the Temi coding software. Upon receipt of the codes, the researcher confirmed the accuracy of the results and coded using a mix of In-Vivo and descriptive coding techniques (Miles et al., 2019; Saldaña, 2016). These codes were reviewed and established five themes. Those themes informed the Cycle 2 action step and the three findings.

Data Collection

Cycle 1 triangulated the data collection process for this study. Semi-structured, individual interviews were used for student affairs and student services directors and for executive leaders. These interviews were between 45 and 60 minutes in length and focused on a person's experience, leadership style, and tools needs to be successful at the research site. Semi-structured focus groups were also used for student affairs and student services directors and undergraduate students. There was one meeting of each focus group. The director focus group discussed organizational culture, shared success or challenges, and difficulties; the student focus group emphasized student experience when working with student affairs and student services directors. The focus group lasted 60 minutes in length. Finally, a quantitative survey was sent to undergraduate students regarding their experience working with student affairs and student services directors. Approximately 70 students responded.

Cycle 2 introduced the development of the Personalized Leadership & Career Coaching tool developed by the researcher. In this cycle, the researcher served as the facilitator for the coaching sessions. This tool used a pre- and post-coaching inventory accompanied by two 1 hour coaching sessions. These coaching sessions used a semi-structured facilitators guide that used self-reflection, leadership style, personality traits, and organizational culture to develop a plan for participants. Cycle 2 also used semi-structured feedback meetings for executive leaders (collaborators) and undergraduate students (stakeholders). These groups provided feedback on the facilitator guide to ensure it was reflective of their experience. These feedback meetings lasted 30 minutes in length.

Trustworthiness and Quality Assurance

This study has followed all provisions and expectations of credible qualitative research, including the adoption of research methods, early familiarity, random sampling techniques, triangulated research design, attempts at participant honesty, and thick descriptions (Lincoln & Guba, 1985; Shenton, 2004). Both Cycle 1 and Cycle 2 used participant, stakeholder, and collaborator voice to ensure value-laden meaning making, aligned with his analysis through analytic memos and research journaling activities. Member check-ins were used to extract further learning from participants as assumptions and findings were made.

FINDINGS

The themes from the Cycle 1 process informed the action step and the findings of this study. This section will briefly present each of the five themes. These five themes were as follows: (a) the student experience is perception-based, (b) institutional awareness is critical, (c) fiscal and human capital resources as an inhibiting factor, (d) personal leadership style, and (e) disconnect. It will then present a graphic representation of the differing impact student affairs and student services directors can have. At the conclusion of the Cycle 1 thematic element discussion, three findings from the action step will be presented including (a) the butterfly effect, (b) burnout, and (c) leadership and self-efficacy.

Cycle 1 Themes

The themes presented in Cycle 1 demonstrate the holistic impact of the undergraduate student experience. The first theme generated from the data analysis was that the *student experience is overwhelmingly perception-based.* This theme connects to this problem as it demonstrates that leadership is not a one-size fits all, but leaders must be willing to adapt to the individual needs of the students. The experience a student has is based on their needed interaction with the particular office and assumptions on the office generate their perceptions. The more positive an interaction, and the topic of that interaction is perceived, the more positive the anticipated experience (and vice versa). The perception based experience was not isolated to the students only. Executive leaders and the directors echoed these sentiments noting that the initial function of their office's identity is a concentric of how students approach the particular office. For example, students having to address billing issues will be more likely to expect a negative experience due to the nature of the problem, while in student activities they expect something more engaging and enjoyable.

The second theme indicates that the *awareness of the organization and the personal relationships* are essential to leaders to be effective. The more aware leaders are of their organization and their leadership style, the more likely they are able to succeed at an LAC. Understanding the social complexities of an organization is an essential need for leaders (Mumby & Kuhn, 2019; Schein & Schein, 2017). Therefore, this establishes evidence that an awareness of the institution is a critical element to a leader's success at the college. However, the awareness of the institution is not isolated and aligns with the third theme of fiscal and human capital resources as an inhibiting factor. This lack of *fiscal and personnel driven resources* were strong influences found within the data collection. The lack of resources was identified as a burden to how student affairs and student services directors can work with undergraduate students. The students noted this in the focus group quite extensively. On three separate occasions, students excused a leader's perceived deficiency because they were aware the organization was missing some form of capital. This included a delay on transcript generation because of an older system, housing posting credits from the closing of the residence halls due to COVID-19, and the lack of large scale programs from the student activities office.

The *awareness of personal leadership style* is the fourth theme through Cycle 1. The more aware a leader was, the more confident they were speaking on their ability to impact the undergraduate student experience. In the quantitative survey, the researcher surveyed approximately 80 undergraduate students who had an opportunity to rank the leadership traits from most effective to least effective according to the descriptions of Bolman and Deal's (2017) typology. The survey provided key stakeholder voice and preference in how a sample of undergraduate students preferred for the leaders of their undergraduate student experience to function. The data demonstrated that 47% of respondents identified the symbolic leadership frame as the type of style that most positively impacted their undergraduate student experience. This provides evidence that although there is not a predominant support for one style over another, the symbolic framework is the preferred type of approach. Table 1.1 demonstrates the responses on preferred leadership style as it relates to Bolman and Deal's (2017) four frameworks. Symbolic leaders were listed as a top selection (47%), followed

TABLE 1.1 Undergraduate Students' Preferred Leadership Style

Field	Min	Max	Mean	SD	Variance	Responses	Sum	Bottom Selection	Top Selection
A good leader is a facilitator and participative manager who supports and empowers others.	1.00	4.00	2.27	1.11	1.23	60	136.00	0.33	0.18
A good leader is someone who thinks clearly, makes good decisions, has good analytical skills, can design structures and systems that gets the job done.	1.00	4.00	2.32	1.02	1.05	60	139.00	0.25	0.17
A good leader is a prophet and visionary, who uses symbols, tells stories, and frames experience in ways that give people hope and meaning.	1.00	4.00	3.13	0.96	0.92	60	188.00	0.07	0.47
A good leader is an advocate and negotiator who understands politics and is comfortable with conflict.	1.00	4.00	2.28	1.13	1.27	60	137.00	0.35	0.18

Note: "Bottom selection" refers to the style that was listed as the least impactful," while "Top Selection" was the style reported most impactful of the four frameworks on the undergraduate student experience.

by a political and human resources leader (18% respectively), and then structural (17%).

The data does not indicate top preference alone, but also that when a person selected a framework other than symbolic (e.g., structural, human resources, and political), the findings demonstrate that the likelihood of ranking the symbolic framework as the least preferred was only 7%. This demonstrates a strong indication that symbolic is a preferred approach in the research site by students.

The final finding theme noted the *disconnect* felt in the organization. The more a student trusts an office, the more effective they believe in the leadership of that office. Student affairs directors were found to be trustworthy from the student perspective, while the student services directors were less trustworthy by the students. Some of this perception can be drawn to previous conversation on the initial interactions with an office. If a student feels they are interacting with the office for a negative or difficult person, they find the office less trustworthy.

Impact Type

The Cycle 1 data collection process supported the validity of the research question. It showed that the impact of student affairs and student services directors' leadership style on the undergraduate student experience is nuanced and widely diversified. The findings determined that there is not a simple linear impact of a leadership student on the undergraduate student experience. Moreover, it demonstrated the interconnectedness of different functions and areas of the impact that student affairs and student services' leaders can have on the undergraduate student experience. Figure 1.1 demonstrates the differing impacts that external and internal variables have on the leadership of student affairs and services directors that were identified from the data collection processes. The four areas include external pressures, personal leadership style, institutional pressures, and the undergraduate student experience.

As seen in the above graphic, the different pressures have a diversified type of impact based on the sectors. Leadership style is directly impacted by the external pressures (e.g., COVID-19, political and social uprisings, federal regulations); external pressures can have a varied impact based on the individual student (e.g., financial aid need, race/ethnicity identification, SES). Additionally, institutional pressures are a factor that can have an interpretive impact on the leaders based on their position, awareness, and trust within the organization. These elements support the acknowledgement of the social constructs of organizations and are important as one serves as a participatory agent in their organization (Clevenger et al., 2019;

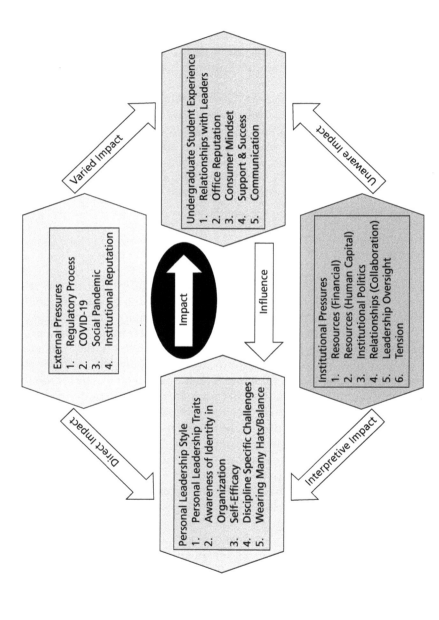

Figure 1.1   Graphic representation of data collection from Cycle 1.

Mumby & Kuhn, 2019; Schein & Schein, 2017). This shows that in order to understand how the leadership style of student affairs and student services directors impacts the undergraduate student experience, there needs to be a holistic, interdisciplinary view of the research site, the organization, and the current needs of the student. This will allow for a true understanding to emerge.

Within this frame of reference, this data collection and analysis process informed the researcher on the Cycle 2 action step which will be described in detail in the next section. Due to the multiple pressures and priorities influencing student affairs and student services directors, Cycle 1 demonstrated that leaders want to adapt to the changing environment of higher education, the undergraduate students, and the institution type but do not have a clear approach to attain this goal. To address this problem, there is a need to provide professional development opportunities that integrate personal leadership style, discipline, and organizational culture that allow practitioners to address these different impeding factors and allow their impact on the undergraduate student experience to be positive

CYCLE 2

The Cycle 2 action step sought to examine ways in which student affairs and student services directors reflect upon their leadership style and the impact they have on their students through meaningful developmental opportunities. Through the feedback from stakeholders and the coaching sessions, the Cycle 2 evaluation process presented the three findings of (a) the butterfly effect, (b) burnout and concerns on the future, and (c) the relationship between leadership style and self-efficacy.

Butterfly Effect

In the coaching sessions, a participant used the butterfly effect as an analogy to describe her work with students stating, "I don't feel like what I do gets to the students. If I am doing something, I can't see the fruits of my labor. I would say, it's more like the butterfly effect. It's passive and they realize the impact later." This example demonstrates, regardless of leadership typology or preference, the work that student affairs and student services directors is best understood in contemporary American higher education as small, gradual, systemic changes to policies, procedures, and actions that have a reciprocal impact on the students. This type of impact also aligns to the findings within Cycle 1. Cycle 1 found that there are four differing types of impacts on the undergraduate student experience that were direct, varied, unaware, and interpretative. Therefore, the coaching experiences examined the positionality of stakeholders, their leadership style, and how they understood the different impacts they could have. The butterfly effect was seen in all cases. Leaders attribute their work to having small, gradual changes that led toward slight adjustments to the undergraduate student experience.

All participants understood, or at least made an attempt to understand, the culture of the institution and how their small contributions have larger opportunities for impact. The directors identified in the study that their work was integral to the student experience but the small efforts and one-on-one connections had a longer impact than involvement in other programming or services efforts. The awareness of the institution and how it functions permits them to make these changes that have long-term impacts. However, the butterfly effect also was discovered to intersect with elements of who the leader is. This section will discuss this in three particular areas: (a) parenthood, (b) interactions, and (c) political maneuvering.

Parenthood

The butterfly effect is not isolated to change and actions, but also has specific correlations to the personality traits of the leader. All of the participants noted that there was some resemblance of their personality in the way they viewed the impact. For example, three participants discussed having paternal instincts and wanting to set up safe communities for students as if they were children. The participants in this study who were also parents indicated that they approached their work with undergraduate students, including how they make small, gradual changes, as they did their parenting style. The goal of their work was to set up their offices, the interactions they had, and their staff in ways they would want their child to be supported.

Personality

Parenthood was not the only personal attribute found in this study, but also intrinsic personality traits. As first seen in Cycle 1, students noted the butterfly effect's impact in the focus group on the coaching tool as it relates to personality. The students agreed that they felt leadership training was important for individuals, but did not feel that a stylistic change would have a big impact. One student in the focus group indicated that he wished more individuals were willing to put in a lot of face time. He specifically criticized other student affairs and student services directors because he felt that they were more willing to do the backend work and fix a problem without involving a student directly. In Cycle 2, the student affairs and student services directors echoed this concern; however, expanded upon it that some of the desire to interact with students is tied to one's personality. It was found that the more comfortable a person was with addressing student concerns or initiating change, the more likely they were to make the small, gradual changes.

Political Maneuvering

All participants understood, or at least attempted to understand, the culture of the institution as a central component to their leadership style. Most particularly, the comfort level the participants had in maneuvering the politics of the organization. In Cycle 1, the terminology "LAC Way" was introduced in the analysis phase as a pseudonym to describe the way the institution functions. It is used throughout the study to describe the frustrations and struggles individuals have working in the research site. It was also used to comically refer to things. For example, participants in the coaching said, "Well that's the LAC way!" and "That's the LAC way, you just roll with it." This knowledge informed participants how they would move throughout the organization.

Participants in Cycle 2 noted that they were comfortable moving within the culture because they "knew the game" and were "comfortable being uncomfortable," while others indicated their struggles in the environment because of their discomfort with politics in the workplace. Overall, this speaks to the idea that if student affairs and student services directors know how to politically maneuver their organization, their work can be more impactful as it relates to the butterfly effect. They can establish small, gradual changes because they are aware of the organizational culture, rites, rituals, and climate.

Burnout and Concern on the Future

The findings from this action step introduced the topic of burnout. Regardless of a person's particular leadership style or their tenure in their position, all participants directly mentioned the impact of COVID-19 as a major source of burnout. The participants discuss burnout directly as a prohibiting factor to them being able to focus on their professional development due to the lack of time and need to continually manage crises.

Burnout cannot be isolated to COVID-19 alone. It would be a simple task to assign that relationship, but COVID-19 is not the only reason for burnout. Current budget deficits (as noted from Cycle 1), institutional politics, and changes in the organization are factors noted that concentrically aligned burnout and concerns for the future. Participants particularly noted that they had student-centered roles but were often taken away from those duties to adhere to organizational politics and internal changes. This included learning to deal with management, balancing new federal and international expectations, and addressing emerging social and political protests. Staffing was a contributing factor to this discussion. Seven of the eight participants mentioned being understaffed and overworked as a result of the pandemic and budgetary restraints.

Leadership Style and Self-Efficacy

The action step supported that there is no best or most preferred leadership style or preferred framework of organizations (Bolman & Deal, 2017). Through memoing, inventory tools, and reflections, the researcher found that there is no best, or dominating, leadership style that has the most prominent impact on the undergraduate student experience by student affairs and student services directors at the small, private liberal arts college. All of the participants noted that they have a general understanding of their approach and that they did not believe they had to commit to a certain leadership ideology. The initial and post-coaching inventory did demonstrate some change after the coaching tool. Based on the consultations, five of eight participants had some movement to another dominant ideology after the debrief with the facilitator. Figure 1.2 identifies the initial responses and post-coaching responses to Bolman and Deal's (2017) typology.

This movement does not speak to the coaching tool changing a person's perception. However, it does indicate that there is development occurring in the sessions. It permits leaders to think more critically about their ability to impact the undergraduate student experience. This endorses the coaching series' approach and the opportunity to provide for leaders to reflect on their stylistic qualities.

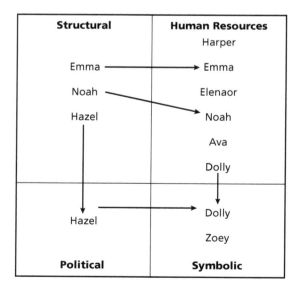

Figure 1.2 Bolman and Deal (2017) typology and leadership style: initial & post-coaching inventory. *Note:* An arrow indicates movement from one typology (initial) to another (post). No movement means there was no change.

Education and Experience

One theme that generated from the coaching was the alignment of education, experience, and a person's belief in their impact on the undergraduate student experience. Within the coaching sessions, a person's education and experience was often relied on as a central understanding of their effectiveness in the organization. Some participants had terminal degrees, others had master's degrees, while others only had bachelor's degrees.

Two participants in particular discussed their lack of advanced degree attainment extensively as a gap in their ability, specifically that they do not have advanced degrees like some colleagues and peers. The discussions presented the idea that a leader of a student affairs or student services discipline cannot be as effective until they have an advanced degree in order to have a stronger impact on the students. This indicates that a change in the conversation is needed as it relates to leaders' education. Education is not a defining factor on a person's leadership ability, but if it becomes one it can result in a negative self-efficacy and potential barrier to a person's success. Their feelings of alienation in their organization can have significant harm.

LIMITATIONS

There are limitations to this study. These limitations do not impact the findings, but they are important to note amongst the elements impacting the reader's perspectives. The natural limitations refer to the nature of how this study was structured and for what purpose. The duration of the study and number of participants serves as a limitation as it exists only within a current state in time. To be more influential and longitudinal, a larger time frame would be more supportive of academic integrity. More time to this study and more stakeholders at different institutions would have permitted the findings to have stronger assertions and transferability to the sector as whole.

The limitations specific to this study also include the number of participants in these roles. Due to the nature of the small private college, many practitioners wear multiple hats. As such, stakeholders do not work in one particular discipline or another. Therefore, there is a potential for the findings to seem too general or too broad as they relate to developing a potential leadership training series. For those not familiar with the institution type, it can seem overly concise or centralized. This study reflects the closeness of the small, private liberal arts college.

Therefore, there is an argument to be made that exploring leadership style is difficult at this point in the organization's workplace because of burnout. Three of the eight participants indicated they were not able to think about their professional development since March 2020 because of the expectations put on them by the organization to pivot, change, and implement their processes and procedures, while supporting the mental health of students in the global pandemic. The other five participants noted that they were feeling a resemblance of burnout because there was an uncertainty as to their long-term tenure within the organization or how their futures might proceed. The impact of COVID-19 and it's relationship with student affairs and student services' directors leadership will need to be studied for years to come.

IMPLICATIONS FOR PRACTICE

Implementing a professional development tool that is reflective of a person's personality, their discipline, and organizational culture is a significant implication for practice as it relates to student affairs and student services directors in contemporary U.S. higher education.

The results for this study indicate that there is an opportunity for student affairs and student services to be more innovative, results-driven, and reflective as it relates to the leaders and their work with undergraduate students. There is a need to continue the work of blending one's leadership style, functional area, and organizational culture to promote how their actions can impact the undergraduate student experience. This new knowledge demonstrates a switch in thinking as it relates to student affairs and student services within higher education organizations. This study shifts thinking from organization-based development to shared interpersonal learning as a critical opportunity for student affairs and student services professionals.

Due to COVID-19, there is a critical opportunity that enables the research site to become leaders in how student affairs and student services directors can impact the undergraduate student experience. One recommendation is the establishment of communities of practice that work with the institution, but also other institutions of similar size, student demographic, and value. This will permit knowledge sharing, personal growth, and best practices to be shared. It will also create an environment that addresses the lack of adaptation that can be found with national organizations. Immediate changes can occur quickly with the practitioners who are part of that process.

Aside from the use of communities of practice, a recommendation from this study is the need to move beyond education as a defining characteristic of a person's persona in U.S. higher education. This study presented active participants' reflections on the lack of educational experience making individuals feel that they are not worthy, or good enough, to hold their positions because they do not have advanced degrees. The organization, and U.S. higher education as a whole, could benefit from rethinking this perspective and cultivating environments where experience and skill can be mentored and developed beyond education. If formal education is a great necessity then organizations should consider ways that they promote individuals getting advanced degrees, but encourage the balancing of personal commitments, providing balance to avoid burnout, and develop sustainable practices. This is not to assert education is not important, it is. However, there is an opportunity to build a workforce that has a heterogeneous group of leaders who come from different perspectives. This can promote innovation especially in times of crisis, chaos, and the unknown facing U.S. higher education, especially the small private liberal arts college.

REFERENCES

Aldeman, C. (2021, March 2). *During the pandemic, "lost" education jobs aren't what they seem*. Brookings. https://www.brookings.edu/articles/during-the-pandemic-lost-education-jobs-arent-what-they-seem/

Andersen, K. (2020). Rethinking college student development theory using critical frameworks. *Journal of College and Character, 21*(3), 234–236. https://doi.org/10.1080/2194587X.2020.1781663

Association of College Personnel Administration, & National Associate of Student Affairs Administrators in Higher Education Professional Competencies Task Force. (2015). *Professional Competencies Areas for Student Affairs Educators.* https://www.naspa.org/images/uploads/main/ACPA_NASPA_Professional_Competencies_FINAL.pdf

Baldwin, D., Towler, K., Oliver II, M., & Datta, S. (2017). An examination of college student wellness: A research and liberal arts perspective. *Health Psychology Open*, 1–17. https://doi.org/10.1177/2055102917719563

Barnes, A. (2020). Higher education and student affairs: Applying expertise in student leadership development and the collegiate context. *New Directions for Student Leadership, 2020*(165), 99–112. https://doi.org/10.1002/yd.20372

Bazarsky, D., Edwards, B. J., Jensen, L., Subbaraman, S., Sugiyama, B., & Travers, S. (2020). Standards of practice: Core competencies for LGBTQIA+ directors and professionals in higher education. *Journal of Diversity in Higher Education, 15*(2), 141–152. http://dx.doi.org/10.1037/dhe0000282

Biddix, J. P. (2013). Directors, deans, doctors, divergers: The four career paths of SSAOs. *Journal of College Student Development, 54*(3), 315–321. https://doi.org/10.1353.csd.2013.0056

Bolman, L., & Deal, T. (2017). *Reframing organizations: Artistry, choice, and leadership* (6th ed.). Jossey-Bass.

Brown, J., Volk, F., & Spratto, E. (2019). The hidden structure: The influence of residence hall design on academic outcomes. *Journal of Student Affairs Research and Practice, 56*(3), 267–283. https://doi.org/10.1080/19496591.2019.1611590

Burke, L. (2020, October 30). *The long haul.* Inside Higher Education. https://www.insidehighered.com/news/2020/10/30/long-term-covid-19-symptoms-have-implications-colleges

Carnegie Foundation for the Advancement of Teaching. (2011). *The Carnegie classification of institutions of higher education, 2010 edition*. https://

www.carnegiefoundation.org/our-work/postsecondary-innovation/carnegie-classifications

Center for Disease Control and Prevention. (2020, December 31). *Considerations for institutions of higher education.* U.S. Department of Health and Human Services.

Center for Disease Control and Prevention. (2021, April 21). *Considerations for institutions of higher education.* U.S. Department of Health and Human Services. https://www.cdc.gov/coronavirus/2019-ncov/community/collegesuniversities/considerations.html

Civera, A., Cattaneo, M., Meoli, M., Paleria, S., & Seeber, M. (2021). Universities' responses to crises: The influence of competition and reputation on tuition fees. *Higher Education, 82,* 61–84. https://eric.ed.gov/?id=EJ1299615

Clevenger, M., MacGregor, C., & Ryan, C.J. (2019). How higher education thinks and behaves. In M. Clevenger & C. MacGregory (Eds.), *Business and corporation engagement in higher education* (pp. 82–94). Emerald Publishing Limited.

Cochran, M. (2016). Student affairs, persistence and the growing need for inquiry. *The Journal of Student Affairs, 2*(1), 1–23.

Council for the Advancement of Standards in Higher Education. (2015). *CAS professional standards for higher education* (10th ed.).

Crawford, J., Butler-Henderson, K., Rudolph, J., Malkawi, B., Glowatz, M., Burton, R., Magni, P., & Lam, S. (2020). COVID-19: 20 countries' higher education intra-period digital pedagogy responses. *Journal of Applied Learning & Teaching, 3*(1), 1–20. https://doi.org/10.37074/jalt.2020.3.1.7

DeMeyer, A. (2011, January–February). Collaborative leadership: New perspectives in Leadership development. *The European Business Review,* 35–40. https://news.smu.edu.sg/sites/news.smu.edu.sg/files/wwwsmu/news_room/smu_in_the_news/2011/sources/EBR_201101_1.pdf

Fowler, D. (2021). Square peg in a round hole: Are small private liberal arts higher education institutions prepared to implement lean operational and organizational methodologies to survive? *Perspectives: Policy and Practice in Higher Education, 26*(1), 8–10. https://doi.org/10.1080/13603108.2021.1944391

Garcia-Morales, V., Garrido-Moreno, A., & Martin-Rojas, R. (2021). The transformation of higher education after COVID disruption: Emerging challenges in an online learning scenario. *Frontiers in Psychology, 11,* 1–10. https://www.frontiersin.org/articles/10.3389/fpsyg.2021.616059/full

Herdlein, R., Riefler, L., & Mrowka, K. (2013). An integrative literature review of student affairs competencies: A meta-analysis. *Journal of Student Affairs Research and Practice, 50*(3), 250–269. https://doi.org/10.1515/jsarp-2013-0019

Hevel, M. (2016). Toward a history of student affairs: A synthesis of research 1965–2005. *Journal of College Student Development, 57*(7), 844–862. https://doi.org/10.1353/csd.2016.0082

Hoffman, J., & Bresciani, M. (2012). Identifying what student affairs professionals value: A mixed methods analysis of professional competencies listed in job descriptions. *Research & Practice in Assessment, 7,* 26–40. https://www.rpajournal.com/dev/wp-content/uploads/2012/07/A2.pdf

Jacobson, M., Levin, J., & Kapur, M. (2019). Education as a complex system: Conceptual and methodological implications. *Educational Researchers, 48*(2), 112–119. https://doi.org/10.3102/0013189X19826958

Jenkins, R. (2019, November 13). *How colleges can survive the coming enrollment crash.* The James C. Martin Center for Academic Renewal. https://www.jamesgmartin.center/2019/11/how-college

Kezar, A. J., & Holcombe, E. M. (2017). *Shared leadership in higher education: Important lessons from research and practice.* American Council on Education.

Koralesky, B., Norin, M., Pitt, S., Seidl, D., & Dobbin, G. (2020, March 20). A marathon sprint: How higher education is responding to COVID-19. *Why IT Matters to Higher Education: DUCASE Review.* https://er.educause.edu/articles/2020/5/a-marathon-sprint-how-higher-education-is-responding-to-covid-19

Kuh, G., Kinzie, J., Schuh, J., Whitt, E, & Associates. (2010). *Student success in college: Creating conditions that matter.* John Wiley & Sons, Inc.

Lewis, E. (2019). Toward a 2.0 company for the liberal arts. *Daedalus, 148*(4), 217–234. https://doi.org/10.1162/daed_a_01768

Lincoln, Y. S., & Guba, E. G. (1985). *Naturalistic inquiry.* SAGE Publications.

Long, D. (2012). The foundations of student affairs: A guide to the profession. In L. J. Hinchliffe & M. A. Wong (Eds.), *Environments for student growth and development: Librarians and student affairs in collaboration* (pp. 1–39). Chicago Association of College & Research Libraries.

Loo, B. (2018, June 12). Education in the United States of America. *World Education News & Review.* https://wenr.wes.org/2018/06/education-in-the-united-states-of-america

Martinez, E. (2018). Changes, challenges, and opportunities for student services at one baccalaureate degree-granting community colleges. *Community College Review, 46*(1), 82–103.

Miles, M. B., Huberman, A. M., & Saldaña, J. (2019). *Qualitative data analysis: A methods sourcebook* (4th ed.). SAGE Publishing.

Mumby, D. K., & Kuhn, T. R. (2019). *Organizational communication: A critical introduction* (2nd ed.). SAGE Publications.

Pendakur, S., Quaye, S. J., & Harper, S. (2020). The heart of our work: Equitable engagement for students in US higher education. In S. J. Quaye, S. J. Harper, & S. L. Pendakur (Eds.)., *Student engagement in higher education: Theoretical perspectives for practical approaches for diverse populations* (3rd ed., pp. 1–16). Routledge.

Prescott, B. T. (2021). Post-COVID enrollment and postsecondary planning, *Change: The Magazine of Higher Learning, 53*(3), 6–13. https://doi.org/10.1080/00091383.2021.1906132

Pryor, J. (2019). Queer advocacy leadership: A queer leadership model for higher education. *The Journal of Leadership Education, 19,* 69–83. https://doi.org/10.12806/V19/I1/R2

Roberts, D. (2007). Preferred methods of professional development in student affairs. *NASPA Journal, 44*(3), 561–577. https://doi.org/10.2202/1949-6605.1836

Roden, P. (2020). Student affairs today: Learning how to meet current challenges. *Journal of College and Character, 21*(4), 329–334. https://doi.org/10.1080/2194587X.2020.1822874

Rossman, D., Wilson, M., Alamuddin, R., Karon, J., Joo, J., & Bond Hill, C. (2020, September 29). *Measuring a liberal education and its relationship with labor market outcomes: An exploratory analysis.* ITHAKA-SR. https://doi.org/10.18665/sr .313872

Saldaña, J. (2016). The coding manual for qualitative researchers. SAGE Publications.

Sallee, M. W. (Ed.). (2021). *Creating sustainable career in student affairs: What ideal work norms get wrong and how to make it wrong.* Stylus Publishing.

Schein, E. H., & Schein, P. (2017). *Organizational culture and leadership* (5th ed.). Routledge.

Shenton, A. (2004). Strategies for ensuring trustworthiness in qualitative research projects. *Education for Information, 22*(2), 63–75. https://doi.org/10.3233/ EFI-2004-22201

Smalley, A. (2021, March 22). *Higher education responses to coronavirus (COVID-19).* National Conference on State Legislatures. https://www.ncsl.org/education/ higher-education-responses-to-coronavirus-covid-19

Sullivan, G., & Stergios, J. (2019, April 1). *A risky proposal for at-risk private colleges: Ten reasons why the board of higher education must rethink its plan* [White paper]. Pioneer Education. https://pioneerinstitute.org/pioneer-research/higher -education-pioneer-research/a-risky-proposal-for-at-risk-private-colleges-ten -reasons-why-the-board-of-higher-education-must-rethink-its-plan/

Thelin, J. (2019). *A history of American higher education.* John Hopkins University Press.

Weis, R., Erickson, C., & Till, C. (2017). When average Is not good enough: Students with learning disabilities at selective, private colleges. *Journal of Learning Disabilities, 50*(6), 684–700. https://doi.org/10.1177/0022219416646706

Wiley Education Services. (2019, November 2). *Top challenges facing U.S. higher education.* Wiley University Services. https://edservices.wiley.com/top-higher -education-challenges/

Zenner, K., & Squire, D. (2020). International student success: Exploring the intercultural competence of academic advisors. *Journal of Student Affairs Research and Practice, 57*(3), 338–351. https://doi.org/10.1080/19496591.2019.1707092

CHAPTER 2

INVESTIGATING THE EFFECTS OF A PEER MENTORSHIP PROGRAM ON LOW-INCOME, FIRST-GENERATION STUDENTS' ACCESS TO FINANCIAL RESOURCES

Jennifer Bevins

For first-generation college students (FGS), an inability to understand and navigate the financial aid (FA) system can pose a significant barrier to degree completion. As of 2018, according to the U.S. Department of Education's National Post-Secondary Study Aid Survey (NPSAS), FGS made up nearly 40% of the U.S. college-going population (U.S. Department of Education, National Center for Education Statistics, 2018). However, only 27% were likely to obtain a 4-year college degree within 4 years (Whitley et al., 2018). FGS are more likely to be female, Hispanic or Black, have children, or come from lower-income families (U.S. Department of Education,

Taking Action, pages 21–35
Copyright © 2024 by Information Age Publishing
www.infoagepub.com
All rights of reproduction in any form reserved.

National Center for Education Statistics, 2018). These characteristics are each associated with lower college completion rates, but being an FGS is itself associated with a lower likelihood of finishing college (Ishitani, 2006; Engle et al., 2006). Eitel and Martin (2009) found that female FGS had low levels of financial literacy, but did not reach out to seek information or support. As the National Association of Student Personnel Administrators ([NASPA], 2017) emphasizes, "The term 'first-generation' implies the possibility that a student may lack the critical cultural capital necessary for college success because their parents did not attend college" (para. 5). Lack of navigational capital can prevent access to information and financial resources and can create significant barriers to college completion for FGS.

The purposes of this mixed methods action research study were to (a) examine the perceptions low-income FGS have about their ability to identify and access financial resources; and (b) describe the impact of a peer mentorship program on mentees' self-efficacy and knowledge for accessing financial resources.

BACKGROUND AND CONTEXT

A review of the current literature surrounding FGS and their access to FA yields three key themes. First, for many FGS, the decision to come to college is economically motivated. Many consider college useful for the material, economic benefits they will reap as the result of obtaining a degree (Ishitani, 2006) and as a path to a better life than their parents (Darling & Scandlyn-Smith, 2007). Second, many FGS lack critical knowledge such as the cost of college, how to apply for FA (Swecker et al., 2013; Kabaci & Cude, 2015; Pascarella et al., 2004; Choy, 2001), and how FA is awarded (Eitel & Martin, 2009). In addition, FGS especially may struggle with unfamiliar financial terminology (Taylor & Bicak, 2020). Finally, FGS often know about support systems but resist them out of a fear or a need to be self-sufficient (Lowery-Hart & Pacheco, 2011); out of a sense of insecurity, unworthiness, or embarrassment (Pratt et al., 2019); or for some Latinx and Asian-American students, out of a fear of losing face, creating conflict, or inviting gossip (Chang et al., 2019).

Three primary theories shape this study's approach to increasing FGS access to financial resources: social cognitive theory (Bandura, 1986), intersectionality (Crenshaw, 1989), and critical pedagogy (Freire, 1970/2018). Viewing this problem through the lens of social cognitive theory would suggest that, due to their lack of college experience, parents of FGS are unlikely to successfully model the behaviors of navigating university systems to pay for college (Horn & Nunez, 2000; McCabe & Jackson, 2016; Mimura et al., 2015). Thus, that student is unlikely to have ever observed the needed behaviors in order to master them. Bandura (1986) also introduces the concept of self-efficacy, or a person's belief that they are able to accomplish a specific task. He (Bandura, 1986) indicates that where there are low levels of self-efficacy, people are less likely to engage in the activities to master those desired skills. If a student possesses low levels of self-efficacy for accessing financial resources, they may not persist in acquiring the skills they need to access FA or may give up trying.

Intersectionality holds that social identities such as race and gender are not independent and that we cannot fully understand their impact if we consider them to be mutually exclusive categories (Crenshaw, 1989). While being first-generation may be one portion of a student's identity, they may also be Asian-American, queer, veteran, female, disabled, or a plethora of other identities. By treating all FGS in the same way, we may miss or misunderstand the reasons why access to financial resources to pay for college can be challenging.

Critical pedagogy centers on educational practices that aim to develop critical thinking skills among students in order to identify and problematize the systemic inequality that keeps them in a state of oppression (Freire, 1970/2018). Critical pedagogy serves as the foundation for this study's intervention. Rather than being handed information about finances from staff members and other people with institutional authority, mentees co-develop and uncover functional knowledge through dialogue and joint problem-solving with their peers.

This study reflects both theory and current literature about FGS in three specific ways: (a) it seeks to address the significant gaps in financial literacy that many FGS display, (b) it creates a support system where students can learn critical navigational skills, and (c) increases their self-efficacy by connecting them with other students who share in their intersectional identities and can demonstrate for them the skills of navigating FA systems to pay for college.

METHODS

This study took place in one of the largest public universities in the United States, located in a major metropolitan area in the Southwest. It will be referred to as Southwest University (SWU). Within SWU, "West College" is located on the downtown campus and contains a wide variety of majors, from social work to criminology to public affairs. Due to this range of majors, it attracts students with diverse interests coming from diverse backgrounds. West College has approximately 5,000 undergraduate students coming from 59 different countries. Of the 17 colleges in SWU, West College holds the highest percentages each of minority students (58%), military veterans (6%), and FGS (29%).

The challenges FGS face nationwide are exacerbated within the local context by the size and structure of the local financial aid department. As they serve over 100,000 students in-person and online, Southwest University's Financial Aid Department utilizes a case-based system that pairs incoming inquiries with the first available staff member for the fastest possible response. Thus, a student may ask for help five times and work with five different staff members. This is problematic for SWU's FGS as it decreases their chance of forming a working relationship with a single trusted staff member to whom they can go with questions and for support. This leads many FGS within the context to believe that they are unable to access the support and resources they need to complete their degree.

Within West College, the student success team conducts informal interviews with exiting students. Many of the FGS dropping out of school have cited a lack of access to financial resources and an inability to navigate the FA system as their primary reason for leaving. In some cases, students simply did not understand how to navigate the massive, impersonal FA system. Some lacked the confidence to reach out and ask for support, so they dropped out. In less severe cases, students did not drop out, but had serious academic consequences resulting from an inability to navigate the system. For example, if a student had an account balance slightly over a certain unpublished threshold that prevented registration, they may miss their opportunity to register for a required class. The fact that a labyrinthine FA system is inhibiting the success of otherwise qualified students of diverse backgrounds was a major concern. Consequently, additional research was needed to clarify what intervention methods could make a positive impact on FGS in West College.

Cycle 1 took place in Spring 2020 and focused on uncovering the challenges FGS face in accessing financial resources and knowledge. Cycle 1 of this study was exploratory. The cyclical nature of an action research approach allowed the researcher to investigate the problem deeply prior to proposing an intervention. The research questions that guided this first exploratory cycle were: (a) "What are low-income FGS' perceptions of their ability to navigate the financial aid system to identify and access the necessary resources to fully support their undergraduate education?"; (b) "How do low-income, FGS interact with peer mentors to increase their access to the range of financial aid available to further support their undergraduate education?"

Two primary sources of data were collected during this phase: individual interviews and a college-wide questionnaire.

Following the results of Cycle 1, an intervention was developed for use in Cycle 2. The additional research questions added for Cycle 2 were: (a) "How and to what extent did mentees' participation in the West First Gen Student

Finances Mentoring Program affect their (i) self-efficacy for accessing financial resources and (ii) knowledge for accessing financial resources?"; (b) "How and to what extent did mentees perceive their experience in the West First Gen Student Finances Mentoring Program as being effective?"

Since participants confirmed in Cycle 1, both through interviews and the questionnaire, that their levels of self-efficacy and knowledge about FA were low, a program to build both their knowledge and their self-efficacy was needed. In Cycle 1, participants expressed hesitation to go to official sources of institutional knowledge, such as the Financial Aid Department. Thus, in Cycle 2 trained peer mentors would support mentees in developing their knowledge about and self-efficacy for accessing financial resources. They would call on the idea of critical pedagogy to jointly investigate solutions to the systemic problems that prevented their accessing aid.

Finally, since several participants in Cycle 1 indicated that their intersecting identities caused unique barriers to access, mentees would be paired with a mentor who shared in some of their intersecting identities and was also a low-income, first-generation student. Mentors were trained and provided with a session protocol that contained topics of conversation and common issues to address. Mentors met with their mentees first for an extended session together, then scheduled check-ins throughout the rest of the fall semester. All mentees completed a retrospective pre- and post-intervention questionnaire to measure their knowledge about and self-efficacy for accessing FA before and after participating in the mentorship program. A retrospective pre-survey was selected over a traditional pre-survey as it asks post-intervention about pre-intervention behaviors (Allen & Nimon, 2007). This method was selected as it increases the likelihood of collecting paired pre- and post-intervention responses for use in statistical analysis, as all responses are collected in a single sitting.

Another round of individual interviews was conducted in Cycle 2, to continue developing deeper knowledge and understanding of the experiences of FGS seeking access to financial resources.

Participants

In Cycle 1, the final participant sample for interviews consisted of 3 females and 1 male; 2 Hispanic, 1 Black, and 1 Asian student. Three participants were seniors and 1 was a junior. Forty-nine students submitted surveys. Of the 44 students who chose to provide demographic information within the survey, 27 were female and 18 were male, 34 were Hispanic, 7 were Black, 2 were White, and 1 was Asian American. Participant criteria included: self- identification as low-income, first-generation college student, sophomore-senior class status, over 18 years old, and having a major within West College. These criteria were used with the understanding that sophomore-senior students, having been at SWU for at least one academic year, would have a greater depth of experience navigating the FA systems at SWU than a first-year student would. Students were recruited via email to either participate in individual interviews or to complete a survey detailing their experiences.

In Cycle 2, the final participant sample for interviews consisted of 4 males, 6 females, and 1 student who identified as gender non-binary; 7 Hispanic, 2 White, 1 Asian American, 2 Black; 3 seniors, 2 juniors, 2 sophomores, and 4 first-year students. Similar to Cycle 1, participant criteria included self-identification as a low-income, first-generation college student, over 18 years old, and having a major within West College. In addition, students participating as mentors needed to be at least in their sophomore year and students participating as mentees needed to be first-year students. The mentors were required to have at least 1 year of experience at SWU so that they could have experience upon which to draw as mentors. The mentees were incoming first-year students as they would have minimal experience navigating the FA system at SWU and the impact of the program on their knowledge and self-efficacy could be better measured. Participants were recruited through email as well as in person at their SWU 101 course. Both mentees and mentors were invited to participate in interviews at the end of the program.

Data Collection

Cycle 1 consisted of two parts: (a) semi-structured individual interviews and (b) a college-wide questionnaire. Each interview, conducted remotely through Zoom, consisted of 15 questions and lasted 20–30 minutes. The interview questions were designed to address RQ1—to shed greater light on the lived experiences of current FGS. Participants were asked about their experiences accessing FA and the degree to which it has been challenging, their sources of financial information and assistance, and the types of people to whom they would be willing to go for help. The college-wide questionnaire was sent out to all low-income, undergraduate FGS within West College. The questionnaire (total complete responses $n = 49$) contained 11 questions that asked about their self-efficacy for accessing FA, their parents' level of education, their primary sources of financial information, and their receptiveness to a possible mentorship program.

Cycle 2 also consisted of three parts: (a) a demographic questionnaire, completed by all Cycle 2 participants ($n = 30$); (b) a retrospective pre- and post-mentorship survey, completed by mentees ($n = 13$); and (c) individual, semi-structured interviews, completed by 11 participants selected at random. The demographic questionnaire was completed immediately after the participants consented to participate in the study. The questions were designed to identify key aspects of their identity and their experiences in college that could be used to pair them with a mentor who shared in some of their intersecting identities. The retrospective pre- and post-survey was intended to capture levels of self-efficacy and knowledge about accessing FA prior to and after participating in the mentoring program. The survey used a series of Likert-type questions about self-efficacy and knowledge where 1 corresponded with low levels of the given construct and 6 corresponded with high levels of the construct. This original measure was developed specifically for this study and was validated during this cycle of research. The Cronbach's alpha values for items about self-efficacy were .747 and .841 for pre- and post-intervention, respectively. The Cronbach's alpha values for items about knowledge were .757 and .809 for pre- and post-intervention, respectively.

Finally, the 11 individual, semi-structured interviews that were conducted through Zoom had 10 questions and lasted 20–40 minutes. The questions focused on their experiences within the mentoring program—what went well, what did not, and their overall perception of its effectiveness.

Data Analysis

Qualitative data was analyzed using the constant comparative method (Creswell & Guetterman, 2019). The researcher then performed open coding to identify the interview-specific concepts that arose in each interview. The open-coded transcript was then returned to the participant for member checking. Next, the transcripts were reviewed in order to group interview-specific concepts into axial codes that arose in multiple interviews. Through this method, three key themes emerged.

Quantitative data was imported into SPSS. Likert scale items were converted into numeric data and missing or incomplete responses were removed. Descriptive statistics and frequency tables were generated. In Cycle 2, paired-samples t-tests were also run to compare means between retrospective pre- and post-intervention data.

FINDINGS

Qualitative Findings

Cycle 1

One theme that arose was the reliance students had upon whichever professional they could establish a relationship with, regardless of whether the professional had any real knowledge of financial policies. Several students continued to refer to high school counselors and mentors for assistance, as they preferred to rely upon that established relationship. Once on campus, they still depended on established relationships for guidance, rather than seeking out the specialists most equipped to support them.

The second theme that arose was the importance of using friends as sources of information. Based on comments they made about what they learned from peers, they did not always get accurate information, but still trusted those peers rather than seeking out official sources of information. For example, one participant held incorrect beliefs about the cost of a graduate program, because a friend had shared that information with her. Even after the researcher provided her with the correct tuition rates, she still continued to express concerns about how she was selecting the more expensive option. This set of interviews highlighted the need for *trained* peers who can use their influence to impart *correct and accurate* financial information.

The final theme was the issue of students' intersecting identities posing a challenge to access. Several participants expressed that their familial obligations made it challenging to seek out financial resources. Two attributed this to their Latina background while one spoke of her identity as a teen mom, and another spoke of his identity as an immigrant.

Cycle 2

There were three major themes that arose as participants spoke of their experiences in the program.

The first major theme that arose was feelings of rejection prompted by specific FA tasks. Several students commented that the FAFSA and FAFSA verification process was a specific pain point. Other students said they stopped applying for scholarships due to the disheartening feeling of rejection when the majority of their applications were unsuccessful. Another student was under the age of 24, so she struggled with the FAFSA classifying her as dependent, despite receiving zero financial support from her parents. She said that, due to lack of parental support and the ways in which this limited her federal FA options, funding college was "basically on me."

Another theme was the importance of relationship building. Since this cycle took place in Fall 2020, when SWU was operating remotely due to the COVID-19 pandemic, both mentees and mentors praised the program simply for its effectiveness in connecting new first-year students with classmates during a time of isolation. Another participant commented that the program should start earlier and include more sessions in order to create the strong relationships they would need in order to help each other through financial challenges. Finally, one mentor commented that, at times, he felt it was more important to focus on the relationship building and just to be there for them.

The final major theme that arose was the idea of the program affecting different students differently, based on their backgrounds. In particular, the level of education of their parents and the type of high school they had attended seemed to make a significant difference. Several of the students who had attended a college prep high school said that they already felt knowledgeable about student finances and that other students might benefit from the program more than them. Similarly, the participants whose parents had some amount of post-secondary education said they liked the program for its social aspect, but already knew much of the information provided about how to navigate FA systems.

Quantitative Findings

Cycle 1

The first source of quantitative data was the college-wide questionnaire, collected in Cycle 1. Most of the participants had a father and mother who received at most a high school diploma. For example, 87% of the respondents reported that their father either did not enter high school, entered high school but did not graduate, or received their high school diploma. 80.4% report the same level of education for their mother. This indicates that the parents of these respondents have relatively low levels of education.

Most students had a medium level of confidence in their ability to identify and access financial resources. On a Likert-type scale ranging from 1–6 with 1 representing a low level of confidence and 6 representing a high level of confidence, participants reported a mean level of 3.65 ($SD = 1.128$). Students indicated that they would be more comfortable talking about their challenges with a trained peer than with a staff member. Using a modified Likert scale with 1 representing a low level of comfort and 6 representing a high level of comfort, there was a mean value of 4.27 for comfort speaking with a staff member and 4.76 for comfort speaking with a trained peer. The students surveyed had a high level of interest in participating in a mentorship program, with 55.1% indicating that they had a high or very high level of interest in participating in such a program.

Cycle 2

The second source of quantitative data came in Cycle 2. Retrospective pre- and post-intervention surveys were sent to the 18 mentorship program participants. Of these, 13 completed the survey. The survey used a series of Likert-type questions about self-efficacy and knowledge where 1 corresponded with low levels of the given construct and 6 corresponded with high levels of the construct. A paired samples t-test was conducted to compare levels of self-efficacy before the intervention and after. There was a significant difference in the scores for self-efficacy before ($M = 3.661$, $SD = .842$) and after ($M = 5.577$, $SD = .507$) participating in the mentorship program; $t(12) = 8.131$, $p = <.001$. A paired samples t-test was also conducted to compare levels of knowledge about accessing FA before the intervention and after. There was also a significant difference in the scores for knowledge before ($M = 4.539$, $SD = .791$) and after ($M = 5.658$, $SD = .412$) participating in the mentorship program; $t(12) = 4.872$, $p = <.001$.

DISCUSSION

Over the course of two cycles of action research, significant findings answered the research questions posed in this study. RQ1 investigated FGS' perceptions of their ability to access financial resources to pay for college. Both the quantitative and the qualitative data from both cycles of inquiry suggested FGS had medium levels of self-efficacy for accessing the financial resources they need to pay for their undergraduate education. Since they have only had limited experiences navigating the FA system, and few opportunities for observational learning prior to college, their confidence in their ability to enact these skills is understandably limited.

RQ2 focused on the interactions between mentors and mentees. Post-intervention survey data and individual interviews with participants suggest that they increased their access to FA both through individual learning sessions and through developing strong relationships. The post-intervention survey data indicated that mentees felt strongly their mentor helped them grow in their ability to navigate the FA system ($M = 5.31$, $SD = 1.032$) and that they felt comfortable talking about student finances with their mentor ($M = 5.62$, $SD = .870$; on a Likert scale where 1—*strongly disagree*, 6— *strongly agree*). Both mentees and mentors emphasized the importance of relationship-building and just knowing that there was someone they could go to for help. This aligns with current literature that suggests FGS may be hesitant to reach out to unfamiliar institutional sources of support (Lowery-Hart & Pacheco, 2011; Pratt et al., 2019; Chang et al., 2019). Rather than putting the onus on the student to reach out to an unfamiliar staff member, a known peer mentor proactively offers support through intrusive advising. Through support offered proactively by known peer mentors who have taken the time to develop a relationship with their mentee, first-generation mentees increased their confidence in their ability to access FA.

RQ3 asked whether participants' self-efficacy for and knowledge about accessing FA increased as a result of participating in the mentoring program. Through examining the results of the paired samples *t*-tests performed on the retrospective pre- and post-survey data measuring participants' level of self-efficacy for and knowledge about accessing financial resources, it is clear that participants experienced significant increases for both constructs as a result of their participation. Bandura (1986) comments that peers serve a critical function in the development of self-efficacy, both in terms of providing competent models of efficacious behavior and in terms of providing validation of the growing capabilities of the learner. In the peer mentoring program, mentors support development of self-efficacy both by modeling advantageous navigational behaviors and by encouraging and validating the growth and development of the mentees.

Finally, RQ4 asked whether participants found the program to be effective. In the post-survey, participants used a six-point Likert scale to indicate their overall perception of effectiveness ($M = 5.615$, $SD = .665$) and their likelihood to recommend the program to a friend ($M = 5.610$, $SD = .650$). This indicates a strongly favorable view of the program's effectiveness. Interview participants also viewed the mentorship program's effectiveness highly, saying that they would "definitely" recommend the program and that it "boosted their confidence."

Implications for Practice

This study yields several implications for practice. Here, a peer mentorship program was an effective way to increase both the knowledge and self-efficacy of participants. The specific financial topics addressed through this program were selected due to (a) being mentioned as challenges by participants in Cycle 1 and (b) through the experience of the researcher as a student services practitioner. These topics included: navigating student-facing information systems, options for paying tuition (including the difference between types of loans), university and external scholarship portals, general financial literacy resources, and the campus student job portal.

Future practice may continue to operate under this peer-led model, as it increased support for FGS without overburdening professional staff. Key to this practice is adequate training and supervision of the peer mentors. Each mentee had one-on-one training with the researcher, where the researcher modeled and narrated an effective mentoring session. Mentors were able to experience a full training session from the perspective of the mentee so that they understood what was expected of them. Documentation and resources were provided to the mentees, ranging from a written mentoring session protocol to a private YouTube channel with tutorial videos to get into greater depth about specific topics in which mentees might be interested. In addition, mentees were required to submit a report after each interaction with their mentees, to capture what topics were addressed and to indicate whether professional escalation of the mentee's concerns was recommended. Mentors in this program were both trained and closely supervised by the researcher, to ensure that they engaged in all of the required elements of the program.

Another implication for practice was the importance of facilitating strong relationships with the people dedicated to serving FGS. Several mentors focused on relationship building over content mastery, but were able to support their mentees with the content later, once open communication had been established. Additionally, several participants said they would hesitate to go to a staff member with their personal problems if they didn't already know them. Both findings suggest that a dedicated "point person" for each first-generation student might result in greater communication about challenges.

Finally, this study suggested the importance of recognizing the intersecting identities of FGS. Rather than treating FGS as a single, homogenous group, we must recognize and address the unique challenges that arise from the many other identities FGS may have. This program paired mentors and mentees based on their responses to an initial demographic questionnaire. The questionnaire featured both standard multiple-choice demographic questions such as gender and ethnicity, as well as free-response questions where participants could identify salient identities not captured through the multiple choice questions (such as being vegan or a K-pop fan). Due to restrictions resulting from COVID, all pairings were made based on the results of the demographic questionnaire, but future efforts might also utilize an in-person "speed-dating" type event where mentors and mentees might have the option to meet in-person prior to assignments being made.

Limitations

Limitations in this study must be acknowledged. Since both cycles of research took place in 2020, during the COVID-19 pandemic, recruiting a representative sample of the population was challenging. Of the 98 low-income, FGS in West College within the downtown campus of SWU, only 17 agreed to participate in the mentoring program. This may also be affected by limited program funding. For Cycle 2, mentors were provided with a $200 stipend for their participation. Several mentors suggested that more FGS may be incentivized to participate if mentees received a stipend as well. Additionally, due to the restrictions put in place due to the pandemic, all mentoring activities had to take place virtually. In-person interactions would likely increase the strength of the relationships between mentees and mentors, and would be preferable in future iterations of the program. Finally, since the researcher served both as a researcher and as the practitioner implementing the program, there may be some bias introduced through these dual roles.

Trustworthiness

Trustworthiness for this study was ensured using several methods. Firstly, triangulation was employed to ensure that, through use of multiple data sources, no one piece of data created a biased picture of the phenomenon. In addition to intervention survey data and interviews, demographic questionnaires were taken, and institutional data was collected for each of the participants. Secondly, interview participants participated in member-checking. They reviewed their transcribed and open-coded transcripts to confirm accuracy of initial interpretations. Thirdly, peer reviews were also conducted. Several peers of the researcher who work in closely related fields reviewed the data and initial findings and engaged with the researcher in conversations about the findings. Finally, the researcher engaged in memoing throughout the grounded theory analysis process, to record and make transparent the development of open codes into larger, central themes.

FUTURE RESEARCH

The findings from this study suggest several avenues for future research. The current iteration of the mentoring program runs only during the fall semester. Expanding the program to run through the spring and summer may continue to help increase self-efficacy and knowledge about funding options during the crucial months when first-year students decide to return for their second year. The other major consideration is expanding the program to be run at a university—rather than a college level. While all of the participants started in the same college, some students changed majors halfway through their first semester. By expanding the program to the university-level, students would not lose their access to a crucial network of support due to changing academic and career interests.

As this study has demonstrated, a peer mentorship program can serve for low-income, FGS as a critical source of personalized coaching that can help to increase their levels of self-efficacy and knowledge about accessing financial aid.

REFERENCES

Allen, J., & Nimon, K. (2007). Retrospective pretest: A practical technique for professional development evaluation. *Journal of Industrial Teacher Education, 44*(3), 27–42. https://files.eric.ed.gov/fulltext/EJ830483.pdf

Bandura, A. (1986). *Social foundations of thought and action.* Prentice-Hall, Inc.

Chang, J., Wang, S. W., Mancini, C., McGrath-Mahrer, B., & de Jesus, S. O. (2019). The complexity of cultural mismatch in higher education: Norms affecting first-generation college students' coping and help-seeking behaviors. *Cultural Diversity and Ethnic Minority Psychology, 26*(3), 280–294. https://doi.org/10.1037/cdp0000311

Choy, S. (2001). *Students whose parents did not go to college: Postsecondary access, persistence and attainment* (No. NCES 2001-126). National Center for Education Statistics. https://nces.ed.gov/pubs2001/2001126.pdf

Crenshaw, K. (1989). Demarginalizing the intersection of race and sex: A Black feminist critique of antidiscrimination doctrine, feminist theory and antiracist politics. *University of Chicago Legal Forum,* (1), 139–167. https://chicagounbound.uchicago.edu/uclf/vol1989/iss1/8

Creswell, J. W., & Guetterman, T. C. (2019). *Educational research: Planning, conducting and evaluating quantitative and qualitative research.* Pearson.

Darling, R. A., & Scandlyn-Smith, M. (2007). First-generation college students: First-year challenges. In M. Stuart Hunter, E. R. White, & B. McCalla-Wriggins (Eds.), *Academic advising: New insights for teaching and learning in the first year* (pp. 203–211). National Resource Center for the First-Year Experience and Students in Transition. https://www.nacada.ksu.edu/portals/0/Clearinghouse/AdvisingIssues/documents/first-gen.pdf

Eitel, S., & Martin, J. (2009). First-generation female college students' financial literacy: Real and perceived barriers to degree completion. *College Student Journal, 43,* 616–630. https://eric.ed.gov/?id=EJ872274

Engle, J., Bermeo, A., & O'Brien, C. (2006). *Straight from the source: What works for FGS–Focus group interviews.* Pell Institute. https://files.eric.ed.gov/fulltext/ED501693.pdf

Freire, P. (2018). *Pedagogy of the oppressed* (50th anniversary). Bloomsbury. (Original work published 1970)

Horn, L., & Nunez, A. (2000). *Mapping the road to college: FGS' math track, planning strategies, and context of support* (NCES 2000153) [Statistical analysis report]. National Center for Education Statistics.

Ishitani, T. T. (2006). Studying attrition and degree completion behavior among first-generation college students in the United States. *Journal of Higher Education, 77*(5), 861–885. https://doi.org/10.1080/00221546.2006.11778947

Kabaci, M. J., & Cude, B. J. (2015). A delphi study to identify personal finance core concepts and competencies of first-generation college students. *Family and Consumer Sciences Research Journal, 43*(3), 244–258. https://doi.org/10.1111/fcsr.12100

Lowery-Hart, R., & Pacheco, G., Jr. (2011). Understanding the first-generation student experience in higher education through a relational dialectic perspective. *New Directions for Teaching and Learning, 127,* 55–68. https://doi.org/10.1002/tl.457

McCabe, J., & Jackson, B. A. (2016). Pathways to financing college: Race and class in students' narratives of paying for school. *Social Currents, 3*(4), 367–385. https://doi.org/10.1177/2329496516636404

Mimura, Y., Koonce, J., Plunkett, S. W., & Pleskus, L. (2015). Financial information source, knowledge, and practices of college students from diverse backgrounds. *Journal of Financial Counseling and Planning, 26*(1), 63–78. https://doi.org/10.1891/1052-3073.26.1.63

National Association of Student Personnel Administrators, Center for First-Generation Success. (2017, November 20). *Defining first-generation* [Web log post]. https://firstgen.naspa.org/blog/defining-first-generation

Pascarella, E. T., Pierson, C. T., Wolniak, G. C., & Terenzini, P. T. (2004). *First-generation college students: Additional evidence on college experiences and outcomes, 75*(3), 249–284. https://doi.org/10.1353/jhe.2004.0016

Pratt, I. S., Harwood, H. B., Cavazos, J. T., & Ditzfeld, C. P. (2019). Should I stay or should I go? Retention in first-generation college students. *Journal of College Student Retention: Research, Theory, and Practice, 21*(1), 105–118. https://doi.org/10.1177/1521025117690868

Swecker, H. K., Fifolt, M., & Searby, L. (2013). Academic advising and first-generation college students: A quantitative study on student retention. *NACADA Journal, 33*(1), 46–53. https://doi.org/10.12930/nacada-13-192

Taylor, Z. W., & Bicak, I. (2020). First-generation college student financial aid: Results from a national financial aid jargon survey. *College Student Affairs Journal, 38*(1), 91–109. https://doi.org/10.1353/csj.2020.0006

U.S. Department of Education, National Center for Education Statistics. (2018). *National postsecondary student aid study-administrative collection: 2018, undergraduates* (NPSAS-AC). https://nces.ed.gov/datalab/powerstats/152-national-postsecondary-student-aid-study-administrative-collection-2018-undergraduates

Whitley, S. E., Benson, G., & Wesaw, A. (2018). *First-generation student success: A landscape analysis of programs and services at four-year institutions.* NASPA: Student Affairs Administrators in Higher Education. https://safesupportivelearning.ed.gov/resources/first-generation-student-success-landscape-analysis-programs-and-services-four-year

CHAPTER 3

SUSTAINING ENGAGEMENT AMONG STUDENT ORGANIZATIONAL LEADS

Brandon Gross

Students at higher education institutions often expand their learning outside of the classroom by participating in co-curricular activities, such as student clubs and organizations (Mikulec & McKinney, 2014). Students who become involved in co-curricular programs are more likely to persist, which benefits both the institution and the student (Tinto, 2017). There are a variety of motivations for joining student groups, as well as various levels of preparation. These organizations are led by student leaders, elected or appointed officers, and are commonly advised by student affairs professionals or faculty members.

Student organization leaders, however, sometimes become disengaged with their role. This disengagement can include not attending meetings, lack of communication, failure to complete tasks, and other neglect of duties. Disengagement can have a detrimental impact on the organization, including loss of membership, failed programming, apathy, and the potential loss of the organization's recognized status on campus. This study is focused

Taking Action, pages 37–50
Copyright © 2024 by Information Age Publishing
www.infoagepub.com
All rights of reproduction in any form reserved.

on providing student affairs professionals with an understanding of how to sustain engagement among student organization leaders.

BACKGROUND AND CONTEXT

Through the years, student groups developed, and co-curricular activities grew in participation and complexity. Existing literature suggests various reasons for a continued focus on co-curricular involvement. For the individual student, academic performance, student development, and persistence (Astin, 1984; Derby, 2006; Foreman & Retallick, 2013; Kuk & Banning, 2010) are among the major outcomes of student involvement. Furthermore, the literature identifies co-curricular involvement as having a consistent positive correlation to student success both inside and outside of the classroom (White, 2012). For the institution, student persistence towards degree completion is paramount among the benefits of student involvement. Co-curricular activities proved beneficial to student success both inside and outside of the classroom as academic performance and overall student development improved.

While student involvement is essential for many reasons, including persistence, the literature suggests various purposes and motivations for student involvement in student groups (Kiersch & Peters, 2017; Phillips et al., 2015; Roulin & Bangerter, 2013; Thompson et al., 2013). Students choose to become involved in student organizations for various reasons, including self-interest and the good of the community. Resume building has often been a primary motivating factor because students perceive these activities as valuable for career aspirations; for example, those looking to enter the labor market sought internships in this area (Roulin & Bangerter, 2013). Students believe this involvement and particularly leadership roles are valued for employability (Thompson et al., 2013). Motivations for involvement often cause students to take part in activities that they may or may not be interested in, but in an effort to look well-rounded to potential employers, they partake in these co-curricular groups (Phillips et al., 2015).

Besides career motivations, some join for the power the position came with. For example, student government leaders perceive a lack of power at the institution and seek these roles to gain such power back for the students (May, 2010). While this may have been for self-interest, many student government officers describe their motivation as for the good of the community (Miles, 2011). A focus on others or external motivation is more common with more actively engaged individuals (Roulin & Bangerter, 2013). Student leaders who regularly attended meetings, took part in club activities, recruited other members, and provided general oversight for the organization are more likely to be focused on the good of the community than individual self-interest. These students are motivated by a desire to contribute to society and the overall community, in addition to developing themselves and their peers (Thompson et al., 2013).

The literature also identifies challenges associated with such roles, including over-involvement, time management struggles, stress management concerns, and the lack of advising or strong mentorship. The literature is replete with examples where colleges, and specifically student affairs professionals, have tried to support students in overcoming these challenges by offering a variety of resources in the area of leadership development. Leadership development programs involved curricular, co-curricular, or extracurricular opportunities throughout higher education (Skalicky et al., 2020). Leadership outcomes have been found through curricular, classroom, and/or out-of-classroom experiences (Foreman & Retallick, 2013). In fact, partnerships between academic affairs and student affairs have proven successful in preparing students to make a positive change in leadership development in college (White, 2012). Many community colleges and four-year institutions have offered student success courses that have assisted in this leadership quality development through the promotion of student engagement and performance (Hoops et al., 2015). Projects that focus on taking ownership of one's work and investigate the influence of servant leadership have proven beneficial in leadership development (Norris et al., 2017). Institutions that offer this resource have provided significant benefits to current and future student leaders. These practices, however, are not endemic in higher education. Further research is required in order to assess how student organization leaders are supported within all colleges and universities. This study is designed to provide student affairs professionals at the research site with an understanding of what engages student organization leaders and how they may become disengaged. This research can offer solutions to ensure the continued success of student organizations and their leaders.

METHODS

This action research study utilized a qualitative research approach designed to interpret research participants' experiences (Ponterotto, 2005). Qualitative research aims to understand social issues from multiple perspectives to gain a better understanding of particular groups (Jencik, 2011). In this case, the study investigated student organization leaders through the lenses of student affairs professionals, student organization advisors, current student organization leaders, and emerging student leaders. The qualitative method was implemented to understand engagement among student organization leaders. The action research approach is a systematic, cyclical methodology focused on relationships, participation, and inclusiveness (Stringer, 2014). This approach offered a localized approach to accomplish a desired resolution to an everyday problem, in this case, student organization leader engagement on the college campus.

Research Site

A predominantly White suburban private research university enrolling over 10,000 undergraduate students and 5,000 graduate and professional students was selected as the site for this study. It is located in an affluent suburb of a major city in the southeast region of the United States. While many of the students come from privileged backgrounds, there is representation from all 50 states and 110 different countries (Institutional Research and Strategic Analytics, n.d.). The student–faculty ratio is 12:1 with 132 bachelor's, 148 master's, and 67 doctoral degree programs. The undergraduate population is 44% White, 25% Hispanic or Latino, 12% Asian/Pacific Islander, 6% Black, with 13% identifying as other or unknown. The university boasts over 300 student clubs and organizations.

Participants

Prior to entering Cycle 1, baseline analysis of engaged versus disengaged student organization leaders was conducted. Current student organization leaders provided insight into their roles, responsibilities, and overall engagement of student organization leaders. These participants were recruited utilizing student organization databases in coordination with the Department of Student Activities and Student Organizations. The participants were traditionally aged undergraduate students involved in a variety of student organizations.

In Cycle 1, student affairs professionals/student organization advisors were the participants. These professional staff members provided both historical and current trends in student organization leadership. Understanding their views regarding their current administrative role on-campus was critical. Additionally, student affairs professionals who oversee student organizations can help coordinate future research and implementation of recommendations outlined in the findings. Participants were recruited utilizing student organization databases in coordination with the Department of Student Activities and Student Organizations. These professional staff members all had master's degrees and above and between 3 and 25 years of experience advising student organizations.

In Cycle 2, emerging student leaders were the primary participants with student affairs staff members serving as collaborators/co-facilitators. A cohort of emerging student leaders was identified through relationships with student affairs professionals. This group participated in a leadership development series to prepare them for future roles as student organization leaders. This group of students was recruited through relationships with student affairs professionals who serve as their advisors. These were traditionally aged college students in the first 2 years of their undergraduate studies. There were 12 students identified with eight who persisted through the leadership development series. The collaborators/co-facilitators, student affairs staff members, assisted in identifying topics, developing curriculum, facilitating sessions, and evaluating results.

DATA COLLECTION

Cycle 1 included data collection from student affairs professionals/student organization advisors at the host institution. Participants were selected to provide insight into the student organizations they advise, student leaders they work with, and current policies, procedures, and resources that exist to support these groups. Semi-structured interviews were conducted with participants in order to provide a guided reflection of their experiences working with student organization leaders. Due to the physical distance, Zoom video conferencing was used to conduct these interviews.

Cycle 2 included several components, including a pre-survey for student participants, individual and group meetings with collaborators, group Zoom sessions with participants inclusive of feedback, individual follow-up with participants, and a closing survey to measure the progress of pre-identified learning objectives.

Student participants were asked to complete the NACA NEXT assessment designed to offer the researchers a starting point for participants as it related to NACE competencies for mastering skills through student involvement in campus activities. Individual and group meetings with collaborators/co-facilitators were essential in determining learning objectives for the leadership development series. This time was used to gather information on the three topics of the program, time management, conflict management, and support systems: mentorship and advising. This information-gathering session was to align with the set learning objectives for each session. Once this information was gathered, PowerPoints were created for an engaging presentation and dialogue with participants. During the series delivery section of the leadership development series, three 1-hour Zoom sessions were hosted on each subject area. Students were asked to identify takeaways at the end of each session and a few minutes with the co-facilitators after each program helped to provide further insight. Lastly, assessment was conducted through individual follow-ups via Zoom, phone calls, or email, and a survey. Five of the eight student participants completed the feedback session and the survey. A facilitator feedback session was also conducted with the three co-facilitators.

DATA ANALYSIS

The data collected was transcribed and analyzed through a coding process where themes and ultimately findings were identified. Each of the three sessions of the leadership development series was recorded and transcribed, with permission from all participants. In conjunction with the field notes, the transcript helped identify themes from each session utilizing NVivo Qualitative Research Software. Direct quotes relevant to the emerging themes were sorted until general findings were cataloged. Member checking and utilizing the survey results assisted in verifying and drawing conclusions during the data analysis. To analyze the action steps, participants completed a self-assessment, measuring their perceptions of learning objective attainment. Additionally, the feedback from collaborators/co-facilitators confirmed the analysis and offered additional insight. The learning objectives analyzed were student persistence at the institution, thriving student organizations, a positive impact on the campus climate and community overall, student organization leader sustained engagement, and the future success of the student leader beyond college. Individual session learning objectives were also assessed. A barrier to measuring the longitudinal success of the leadership development series on sustained engagement among student organization leaders is that the emerging leader cohort that took part in this study has not yet taken on future leadership roles. A recommendation of this study was to continue to monitor this cohort to further measure the success of the program on long-term sustained engagement in leadership roles on campus and beyond.

TRUSTWORTHINESS AND QUALITY ASSURANCE

Lincoln and Guba (1985) defined credibility as having confidence in the "truth" of the findings. To establish credibility, the authors suggested prolonged engagement, persistent observation, and member checking. These were three important components utilized from series development to delivery and ultimately assessment of results.

Prolonged engagement was related to spending enough time in the field of research in order to understand the culture, setting, and context of the topic of interest (Lincoln & Guba, 1985). While prolonged engagement provides scope, persistent observation provides depth by helping to identify characteristics most relevant to the problem of practice (Lincoln & Guba, 1985). Within this particular study, scope and depth were both met. The researcher was a student and later a staff member at the host site, spending a total of 14 years at the institution. This included interactions and developing personal rapport with the collaborators. That said, there were no prior interactions between the primary researcher and the student cohort. During the time at the host site, the researcher served as a student leader and student affairs professional consistently engaged with student organizations as either a member or advisor. The researcher has continued their work related to the problem of practice in a similar role at a large, public institution today. This prolonged engagement with the site and subject of the research should have provided both credibility and trustworthiness.

Finally, member checking was an important factor in trusting the research. Member checking provided the researcher with an opportunity to review their interpretations of the findings with participants. As Lincoln and Guba (1985) described, the participant was provided an opportunity to correct errors and validate interpretations outlined by the researcher. In this study, after the data was analyzed, the researcher contacted each participant requesting direct one-on-one feedback, a survey, and result validation to provide an overarching look at the findings of the study.

FINDINGS

A primary finding of this study is that sustained engagement can be maintained among student organization leaders by proactively preparing students for their leadership roles. Student participants and collaborators/co-facilitators identified a voluntary, selective, cohort-based model with in-person components, strategically timed, and focused on one engaging topic per session as the best format for this type of program moving forward. Results of this study led to ways to meet the overall learning objectives: student persistence at the institution, thriving student organizations, a positive impact on the campus climate and community overall, student organization leader sustained engagement, and the future success of the student leader beyond college. Strategies that emerged which led to continued engagement are discussed below.

Time Management

To enhance student organization leader engagement, skill development in the area of time management is essential. There was unanimous recognition of this necessary skill set among student participants and collaborators/co-facilitators. Several students identified time management as a struggle whether they were aware of it at the beginning of the series or learned about the challenges through the session.

Conflict Management

A deeper understanding of conflict and how to manage it is key to student organization leader development. It became evident that defining conflict is an essential aspect. By focusing on communication and compromising, students began to understand the benefits of conflict and ways to manage it. Time needs to be dedicated to multiple areas of conflict management including defining conflict, developing an awareness of resources, and strategizing to de-escalate intense situations. It is also important to understand and appreciate the potential benefits of conflict.

Support Systems: Mentorship and Advising

Mentors and advisors can help keep student organization leaders engaged in their roles. Support systems can include mentors and advisors that help to guide student leaders in their roles as well as in their lives. This was the final topic of the leadership development series that was intended to bring the learning together by offering structured guidance and support.

Overall

Generally, survey results indicated that students felt engaged with the leadership development series. They found it to be a valuable use of their time (80%), stated they would recommend it for others (80%), and that it helped them to grow as a leader (80%). Student participants commented on the knowledge acquisition offered by qualified facilitators. Students are more engaged with roles they are passionate about.

The leadership development series offered emerging student leaders the opportunity to develop skill sets in key competency areas including time management, conflict management, and support systems: mentorship and advising.

DISCUSSION

This study makes significant contributions to improving engagement among student organization leaders at colleges and universities. Engagement was defined as sustained active participation within the leadership role. Student affairs professionals are better informed as to best practices for engaging student organization leaders.

Sustaining Student Engagement Through Proactive Preparation

Sustained engagement can be maintained among student organization leaders by proactively preparing students for their leadership roles. Through a review of existing literature and through this study, it was revealed that leadership can be developed and improved through a focus on proactive training in key competency areas (Caza & Rosch, 2014; Hamid & Krauss, 2013; Hoops et al., 2015; Skalicky et al., 2020). The leadership development series was the primary action step that led to this finding. Hamid and Krauss (2013) described several factors that contributed to leadership readiness including student leadership opportunities. Skalicky et al. (2020) discussed purposeful leadership opportunities that revolve around the holistic student experience and how that can have a positive impact on higher education. This study took those findings and identified not only the impact on higher education, but also the individual student. This purposeful series led to sustained engagement as challenges in the competency areas of time management, conflict management, and support systems: mentorship and advising were addressed and strategies to overcome were offered.

Strategically Designing a Student Leadership Development Series

Student participants and collaborators/co-facilitators identified a voluntary, selective, cohort-based model with in-person components, strategically timed, and focused on one engaging topic per session as the best format for this type of program moving forward. As Hensley et al. (2018) explained, it is essential to focus on well-designed college success courses by engaging students in the process. That is precisely what was done in evaluating this study. Student participants offered their take on challenges involved with sustained engagement during early cycles of data collection. Their feedback/lived experiences/suggestions were then used as the foundation for the leadership development series. Working with collaborators/co-facilitators, these themes were turned into a series of 1-hour workshops that offered leadership development opportunities for a group of emerging student organization leaders. Feedback from the participants and collaborators/co-facilitators then turned into findings related to a strategically designed leadership development series.

Developing Skill Sets in Time Management, Conflict Management, and Utilizing Support Systems

Time management, conflict management, and support systems: mentorship and advising are essential in enhancing student organization leader engagement. The three focus areas for this leadership development series were found to positively impact the emerging student leader cohort in preparation for major leadership roles on campus.

Time Management

To enhance student organization leader engagement, skill development in the area of time management was essential. Among the three focus areas of this leadership development series, this topic was perhaps most aligned with the literature (Foreman & Retallick, 2013; Häfner et al., 2015; Hensley et al., 2018). Participants and collaborators/co-facilitators unanimously recognized time management as a necessary skill set in leadership development. Häfner et al. (2015) described effective time management as helpful in clarifying goals, developing strategies, and overcoming obstacles. Perceived stress decreased and perceived control of time increased after training, all while demand remained unchanged. Time management training can result in successful outcomes for undergraduate students (Hensley et al., 2018).

Conflict Management

Time needs to be dedicated to multiple areas of conflict management. Defining conflict by highlighting both the positive and negative implications was important and effectively executed during the leadership development series. That said, a focus on developing an awareness of resources and how to de-escalate intense situations was also defined as critical. The assessment indicated that more time needed to be devoted to the latter.

Support Systems: Mentorship and Advising

Support systems can help students remain engaged in their leadership roles. In college, these support systems are often in the form of a mentor or advisor. Rosch and Nelson (2018) described how student organization advisors are among the most powerful avenues in providing student members with holistic leadership development. Miles (2011) explained that advisors are in a unique position to provide opportunities for students to learn on their own while also being there to prevent significant failure. Students and advisors must work collaboratively to accomplish the goals of the organization while also assisting in the overall leadership development of the student leader and organization members.

Mentors and advisors can help keep student organization leaders engaged in their role. They do so by offering guidance to student leaders both inside and outside the classroom (Yarbrough, 2002), in their organizational roles, as well as in their lives.

Implications for Practice

At colleges and universities today, significant focus is placed on leadership development. In fact, many mission statements at various institutions across the country specifically focus on the development of the world's future leaders (Foreman & Retallick, 2013; Skalicky et al., 2020). Co-curricular activities are highlighted by student organizations. Derby (2006) found that students who are involved on campus by participating in clubs and organizations were more likely to persist and complete their degrees than uninvolved students. Rosch and Nelson (2018) expanded upon this as their findings demonstrated increased academic performance, grades, retention, and overall satisfaction with the institution by those involved in these activities and leadership roles. All of these studies emphasized Astin's (1984) theory of student involvement.

Persistence at the institution, thriving student organizations, positive impact on campus climate and the community overall, sustained student organization leader engagement, the future success of the leader, and support for student affairs professionals were the outcomes sought through the leadership development series delivered during this study. Through this study, it became clear that some students were simply unprepared or underprepared for their leadership roles. The proactive approach recommended by this study should lead to sustained engagement as students will know what they are getting themselves into and are more prepared for challenges that will inevitably arise.

LIMITATIONS

There were a select number of limitations with this research. In this study, the number of participants was one of those areas. The site of study was home to over 300 student organizations. Further research may be conducted assessing student organization leadership by organization type and by a broader participant selection process. Additionally, a change agent has the skill to facilitate and coordinate a change effort that can transform a community (Luenburg, 2010). While this research intended to transform the community at the site university, a mid-sized, private, predominantly White institution, applying the findings to other institutions will require further study.

Conducting research during a worldwide pandemic cannot be overlooked as a limitation for a variety of reasons. COVID-19 has forced significant changes within higher education and student leadership. While the intent of this research was always to utilize Zoom, the reality of online learning fatigue was one that certainly impacted the study. A virtual study prevented the researcher from some natural observation opportunities. While there were certainly some benefits to the virtual approach including flexibility, recording capabilities, and more, there were some challenges as well.

Lastly, the student affairs professionals that served as collaborators and co-facilitators as well as the primary researcher all had a significant strain on their work-life due to COVID-19 that impacted time that could be dedicated to the program. Most of this was overcome by strategic planning and expectation-setting conversations, but the impact must be considered.

All research studies have limitations that are intended to provide opportunities for further study on the topic. While these are limitations of this study, the research provided valid and tested opportunities to enhance student organization leader engagement locally with hopes that its application can have further impact more globally.

REFERENCES

Astin, A. W. (1984). Student involvement: A developmental theory for higher education. *Journal of College Student Personnel, 25*(4), 297–308. https://psycnet.apa.org/record/1985-18630-001

Caza, A., & Rosch, D. M. (2014). An exploratory examination of students' pre-existing beliefs about leadership. *Studies in Higher Education, 39*(9), 1586–1598. https://doi.org/10.1080/03075079.2013.801434

Derby, D. C. (2006). Student involvement in clubs and organizations: An exploratory study at a community college. *Journal of Applied Research in the Community College, 14*(1), 45–51. https://eric.ed.gov/?id=EJ774410

Foreman, E. A., & Retallick, M. S. (2013). Using involvement theory to examine the relationship between undergraduate participation in extracurricular activities and leadership development. *Journal of Leadership Education, 12*(2), 56. https://doi.org/10.12806/V12/I2/R4

Häfner, A., Stock, A., & Oberst, V. (2015). Decreasing students' stress through time management training: An intervention study. *European journal of psychology of education, 30*(1), 81–94. https://doi.org/10.1007/s10212-014-0229-2

Hamid, J. A., & Krauss, S. E. (2013). Does university campus experience develop motivation to lead or readiness to lead among undergraduate students? A Malaysian perspective. *Journal of Student Affairs Research and Practice, 50*(2), 208–225. https://doi.org/10.1515/jsarp-2013-00015

Hensley, L. C., Wolters, C. A., Won, S., & Brady, A. C. (2018). Academic probation, time management, and time use in a college success course. *Journal of College Reading and Learning, 48*(2), 105–123. https://doi.org/10.1080/10790195.2 017.1411214

Hoops, L. D., Yu, S. L., Burridge, A. B., & Wolters, C. A. (2015). Impact of a student success course on undergraduate academic outcomes. *Journal of College Reading and Learning, 45*(2), 123–146. https://eric.ed.gov/?id=EJ1089045

Institutional Research and Strategic Analytics. (n.d.). *University of Miami 2019–2020 common data Set.* https://irsa.miami.edu/_assets/pdf/cds1920.pdf

Jencik, A. (2011). Qualitative versus quantitative research. In J. T. Ishiyama & M. Breuning (Eds.), 21st century political science: A reference handbook (pp. 506–513). SAGE Publications.

Kiersch, C., & Peters, J. (2017). Leadership from the inside out: Student leadership development within authentic leadership and servant leadership frameworks. *Journal of Leadership Education, 16*(1). https://doi.org/10.12806/V16/I1/T4

Kuk, L., & Banning, J. (2010). Student organizations and institutional diversity efforts: A typology. *College Student Journal, 44*(2), 354–361. https://eric.ed .gov/?id=EJ917226

Lincoln, Y. S., & Guba, E. G. (1985). *Naturalistic inquiry.* SAGE Publications.

Luenburg, F. (2010). Managing change: The role of the change agent. *International Journal of Management, Business and Administration, 13*(1), 1–6. http://national forum.com/Electronic%20Journal%20Volumes/Lunenburg,%20Fred%20C. %20Managing%20Change%20The%20Role%20of%20Change%20Agent%20 IJMBA,%20V13%20N1%202010.pdf

May, W. P. (2010). The history of student governance in higher education. *College Student Affairs Journal, 28*(2), 207. https://eric.ed.gov/?id=EJ965985

Mikulec, E., & McKinney, K. (2014). Perceived learning outcomes from participation in one type of registered student organization: Equestrian sport clubs. *Journal of the Scholarship of Teaching and Learning, 14*(3), 93–109. https://doi .org/10.14434/josotl.v14i3.4168

Miles, J. M. (2011). Reflections of student government association leaders: Implications for advisors. *College Student Journal, 45*(2). https://www.semanticscholar .org/paper/Reflections-of-Student-Government-Association-for-Miles/26deb f386a5dd066b04c6ecd932f67c485c6f781

Norris, S., Sitton, S., & Baker, M. (2017). Mentorship through the lens of servant leadership: The importance of accountability and empowerment. *NACTA Journal, 61*(1), 21–26. https://www.proquest.com/docview/1884957139

Phillips, J. A., McLaughlin, M. M., Gettig, J. P., Fajiculay, J. R., & Advincula, M. R. (2015). An analysis of motivation factors for students' pursuit of leadership positions. *American Journal of Pharmaceutical Education, 79*(1). https://doi .org/10.5688/ajpe79108

Ponterotto, J. G. (2005). Qualitative research in counseling psychology: A primer on research paradigms and philosophy of science. *Journal of counseling psychology, 52*(2), 126–136. https://doi.org/10.1037/0022-0167.52.2.126

Rosch, D. M., & Nelson, N. E. (2018). The differential effects of high school and collegiate student organization involvement on adolescent leader development. *Journal of Leadership Education, 17*(4). https://doi.org/10.12806/V17/I4/R1

Roulin, N., & Bangerter, A. (2013). Extracurricular activities in young applicants' résumés: What are the motives behind their involvement? *International Journal of Psychology, 48*(5), 871–880. https://doi.org/10.1080/00207594.2012.692793

Skalicky, J., Warr Pedersen, K., van der Meer, J., Fuglsang, S., Dawson, P., & Stewart, S. (2020). A framework for developing and supporting student leadership in higher education. *Studies in Higher Education, 45*(1), 100–116. https://doi.org/10.1080/03075079.2018.1522624

Stringer, E. T. (2014) *Action research*. SAFE Publications.

Thompson, L. J., Clark, G., Walker, M., & Whyatt, J. D. (2013). 'It's just like an extra string to your bow': Exploring higher education students' perceptions and experiences of extracurricular activity and employability. *Active Learning in Higher Education, 14*(2), 135–147. https://doi.org/10.1177/1469787413481129

Tinto, V. (2017). Through the eyes of students. *Journal of College Student Retention: Research, Theory & Practice, 19*(3), 254–269.

White, J. V. (2012). Students' Perception of the Role of Reflection in Leadership Learning. *Journal of Leadership Education, 11*(2). https://journalofleadershiped.org/wp-content/uploads/2019/02/11_2_White.pdf

Yarbrough, D. (2002). The engagement model for effective academic advising with undergraduate college students and student organizations. *The Journal of Humanistic Counseling, Education and Development, 41*(1), 61–68. https://eric.ed.gov/?id=EJ648457

CHAPTER 4

LATERAL TRANSFER STUDENTS

What Drives their Decision to Leave and Why Do They Experience Transfer Shock

Christopher Collins

Higher education enrollment managers are looking at transfer students as integral pieces to achieve institutional strategic plans. While most in enrollment management are familiar with vertical transfer students (those that attend a 2-year or community college and transfer to a 4-year university), lateral transfer students (those that transfer from one 4-year university to another 4-year university) make up a large demographic on university campuses. Universities focus their resources on vertical transfer students by creating efficient advising plans, providing guaranteed admissions programs, and visiting various community college campuses, though this population makes up only 43% of transfer students on a campus (Kirk-Kuwaye & Kirk-Kuwaye, 2007).

Transfer students can experience what is known as transfer shock, which can be described as a decrease in students' grades in their first semester

Taking Action, pages 51–65
Copyright © 2024 by Information Age Publishing
www.infoagepub.com
All rights of reproduction in any form reserved.

after transferring to a 4-year university (Ishitani, 2008). Resources are needed for transfer students as they transition into a 4-year university to limit the damage transfer shock can cause, especially for those lateral transfer students who typically do not receive any assistance until enrollment.

Transfer students experience this transfer shock for unique reasons but understanding them will be how we can implement the necessary resources to ease the transition. The purpose of this study is to understand lateral transfer students' perspectives through their transition to a state land grant university in the southeast and how to limit the transfer shock they experience.

BACKGROUND AND CONTEXT

Transfer enrollment is stated within the site institution's most recent strategic plan, but programming, including scholarship programs, is exclusively geared toward students from one of the 58 community colleges in the state. The state system policy for each member institution (public, 4-year universities within the state system) is to display baccalaureate degree plans (BDPs), which are 2 + 2 detailed advising plans for interested vertical transfer students. No such advising plans exist for those coming from another 4-year university. A dual-admission, dual-enrollment program was created for transfer students but is limited to only those attending certain community colleges. There is no guaranteed admission or articulated transfer plan for those attending a 4-year university looking to transfer.

Lateral transfer students seek to transfer due to the lack of social and academic connection to their home institution. With academic failure not being a primary reason for transferring, these students desire a stronger connection to their institution both inside and outside the classroom. Lateral transfer students left their home institution for an improved fit at another institution or the opportunity to study a different curriculum that aligns better with their educational goals (Ishitani & Flood, 2018). Students view their original institution as a stepping-stone to a better or more prestigious university (Shealy et al., 2013). Students felt their original institution did not fit their needs academically and therefore sought another institution that was more challenging or offered a diverse curriculum. Those who change or desire to change their major are viewed as more likely to transfer out along with students who saw an academic "misfit" (Ishitani & Flood, 2018). Additionally, a recent study revealed that students decided to leave their home institutions for reasons such as social circumstances, relocation, fit, proximity to home, and strategic moves (Choi et al., 2019). Lateral transfer students decided to leave their original institution for that social connection potentially closer to home or strategically aligning with a new academic interest.

As students transfer from one institution to the next, they experience transitional difficulties as they try to settle into their new environment. Otherwise known as transfer shock, students struggle socially and academically to adjust in their first semester after transferring. Hills (1965) was the first to document transfer shock as a phenomenon of GPA decline in the first semester after transferring. Students, especially in STEM (science, technology, engineering, and math) majors saw academic difficulties due to their inability to understand the demands these specific majors required (Scott et al., 2018). Whether the coursework is more rigorous, the expectations are higher, or being unprepared, transfer students struggle academically in their first semester at their new institution. It is also consistent through literature that students rebound and see their grades level back out in their second semester (Hills, 1965; Ishitani, 2008). Those students who persist to a second semester adapt to their new environment by creating new study habits or figuring out the demands of the new academic institution, thus resulting in their GPA bouncing back. Gaining quality studying habits was found to be a factor in lowering the risk of difficulty in adjustment (Laanan, 2007).

Socially transitioning into a new environment is important for transfer students to connect to the institution. Prominent levels of involvement on campus and degree engagement are direct correlations to student success (Ivins et al., 2017). On top of dealing with difficulties adjusting academically, institutions are forcing transfer students to socially connect and figure out campus on their own.

Attending a new institution means transfer students will be interacting and utilizing new technologies. Without proper introduction and training of new systems and technologies, transfer students are left frantically searching for resources instead of acclimating to campus. Institutions assume transfer students come in with the intimate knowledge of daily functions, such as accessing e-mail or navigating the online learning management system (Chin-Newman & Shaw, 2013). Instead of introducing themselves to high-impact activities, transfer students are struggling to figure out tasks such as registering for courses, especially when it comes to new technology not used at their prior institutions (Zilvinskis & Dumford, 2018). While transfer students are not new to college life itself, institutions neglect the fact that simple daily functions that are routine can be foreign to these students. In place of institutions preparing transfer students for these adjustments, students seek outside help from family or friends to provide a better chance of a successful transition (Chin-Newman & Shaw, 2013). Transfer students seek precise, detailed information regarding their transfer process, which usually is absent throughout their transition (Alpern, 2000).

The lack of information adds barriers to the already difficult transition transfer students face during their change to a new institution.

METHODS

This study was conducted at a public, R1, land-grant university located in the Southeast. The institution is one of 16 public university members of the state system, in which schools are independent, but their strategic management is overseen externally. With around 35,000 total students and just over 24,000 undergraduates. Around 1 in 5 graduates did not originally start at the institution, while 50% of each incoming transfer class in the fall are students outside the community college system. Founded in 1887, the institution focused on mechanics (now known as engineering) and agriculture. Today, it is known as a university for the citizens of its state and is known for its STEM programs with nationally ranked engineering and natural resources programs. While STEM is a strong focus, 43% of each freshman class enters an academic program outside of STEM.

PARTICIPANTS

Cycle 1 data was collected by identifying lateral transfer students who were beyond their first semester at the institution and the key staff members who interact daily with them. Once these participants were selected, a semi-structured interview protocol was performed in person. The interview protocol explored their experiences at their previous institution, the enrollment process, and finally, the transitional period for the lateral transfer students. The staff members discussed their personal experiences with lateral transfer students, what is being done at the institutional level, and what could be done to ensure their successful transition. Three current students and three staff members were selected and participated in Cycle 1.

The participants for Cycle 2 were lateral transfer students in their first semester at the university. The lateral transfer students who acted as mentors were not only participants but also collaborators. These mentors assisted in the creation of the programming and necessary discussion topics throughout the Fall 2020 semester. These student populations are also internal stakeholders since the future success of this implementation will directly impact them. The members of the transfer success committee also acted as collaborators in this implementation phase. They helped identify colleges and departments that fit the criteria of this study and assisted in developing integral discussion topics throughout the semester for mentors and their mentees. Since many of these members have daily interactions with lateral transfer students, they were also internal stakeholders as they are on campus and will see firsthand the program's outcomes. In Cycle 2, there were six mentees selected and five mentors selected. A data request for current students who previously transferred from another 4-year institution yielded the emails for a recruitment campaign to find the mentees. A similar data request was submitted except for lateral transfer students who would be starting their first semester at the institution These recruitment campaigns yielded the 11 students who would participate in Cycle 2.

DATA COLLECTION

Cycle 1 data was collected with a semi-structured interview protocol that was performed in person. The interview protocol explored their experiences at their previous institution, the enrollment process, and finally, the transitional period for the lateral transfer students. The staff members discussed their personal experiences with lateral transfer students, what is being done at the institutional level, and what could be done to ensure their successful transition.

Cycle 2 data collection was done through the usage of pre- and post-meeting surveys, pre- and post-semester surveys, and field notes and memos that were generated from the start of the cycle until the conclusion. The field notes and memos were created from the initial meetings with stakeholders, academic departments, and the identified mentors prior to recruitment. Field notes and memos were also created during the recruitment process of mentors and mentees. These meetings took place online either through email, Zoom, or Google Video. Once the mentees were identified, an initial survey was sent to them via Google Forms, utilizing questions created from previous cycle analysis and the discussions with stakeholders.

Before each meeting, a survey would be sent to the mentee, asking if there are any specific topics they wish to discuss. After each meeting, the mentor sent an email to the researcher to summarize what was discussed and any recommendations for the rest of the semester. Once a month, the researcher reached out to the mentors to check on their progress and ask if they wished to discuss anything. All communication via email was saved for analysis. At the end of the program, a post-survey was sent to the mentees that evaluated their integration into the campus and whether they felt the mentor program was integral. There was also a post-survey with the mentors about their overall feeling of the program's effectiveness and any recommendations for future iterations of the program. These two post-qualitative data collections were important in evaluating the program's effectiveness and what would need to happen for this to be implemented on a larger scale.

The final data collection was the academic integration from the student. As seen in literature and Cycle 1, transfer shock showed that students performed poorly in their first semester compared to their previous institution. The pre-semester survey sent to mentees asked what their GPA was at their previous institution and what GPA they expected to have in their first semester at their current institution. After the Fall 2020 semester was completed and final grades were posted, the researcher accessed the final GPA through a record request from the registrar's office.

Due to COVID-19, all interactions were virtual, which was a barrier to analyzing the data. By not sitting in the room and soaking up the interview environment, the nonverbal observations were difficult to note. These nonverbal indicators were integral in analyzing themes in Cycle 1 and therefore lacked in evaluating the action steps. The mentors and mentees were also meeting virtually, which hindered the bond necessary to forge a trusting relationship. Furthermore, COVID-19, in general, presented new problems in the analysis that were not present during previous cycles. Once the institution went fully virtual and asked students to leave campus, mentors and mentees were more difficult to reach for updates on meetings. This lack of connection also resulted in only two mentees filling out the post-survey even after multiple requests.

DATA ANALYSIS

Miles and colleagues (2014) have suggested two major stages (first cycle and second cycle) to coding qualitative data (p. 65). The first cycle of coding utilized the in vivo method through which the researcher pulled out keywords or phrases from the participants' own language that acted as codes (Miles et al., 2014, p. 65). These codes were in some form of relation to the overarching research questions. The second cycle of coding took the in vivo codes and condensed them into thematic code categories that helped put the bigger picture into focus (Miles et al., 2014, p. 79–80).

Finally, an important step to data analysis is to verify and draw conclusions based on the extracted data on hand. Utilizing Miles et al.'s (2014) 13 tactics of analyzing qualitative research, the researcher noted patterns and themes that arose from the previous two steps of data analysis. This tactic was useful as looking through the in vivo codes and the thematic code categories allowed for the identifications of patterns and themes based on the observations of cyclical phenomena (Miles et al., 2014, p. 275). It was important to receive feedback from participants to verify or check that the interpretations followed their mindset. This "member-checking" process was used in order for one of my participants to evaluate the thematic findings observed and whether the participant viewed the data the same or in a different way (Miles et al., 2014, p. 303). This process was a reflection step in the analysis phase that provided integral feedback into the major themes derived from the qualitative data.

The GPAs were collected by utilizing questions on the pre-survey and a data request to the registrar's office on campus. The GPAs listed for the previous institution and the expected first semester were compared and analyzed as to whether they were higher or lower. The GPA pulled from the data request was the final GPA for Fall 2020 and was compared once again to those listed on the pre-survey. The final GPA was put into each student's context utilizing the other forms of data collection (surveys, electronic correspondence, and field notes).

TRUSTWORTHINESS AND QUALITY ASSURANCE

Guba (1981) surmised that four main criteria were necessary for a qualitative study to live up to the expectations of positivist critics:

- credibility
- transferability
- dependability
- confirmability

To address the credibility of a study, Stringer (2014) discussed a method of member checking where participants are allowed the opportunity to review and verify the data analysis. After Cycle 1 data analysis, I provided the themes and quotes from the data collection for participants to verify that the research represented their perspectives and experiences. While the study was performed at one research site, the experiences are transferable for professionals at other institutions. The themes derived from the data analysis in Cycle 1 were grounded in literature, including other studies on transfer shock. If institutions allow transfer students into their enrollment classes, this study is transferable. Detailed notes, journals, and other artifacts were kept for the study to be audited and confirmed as just. In-depth reports and executive summaries were developed to ensure the study is dependable and trustworthy.

Inherently, I have a bias in the research process as my job forces me to remain close to transfer students. I am immersed in the field and understand that there will be bias throughout the process. Action research is cyclical, which provides the researcher the opportunity to step back and reflect on the process. After each data collection cycle, I wrote a reflection of the process to ensure my bias did fully guide the direction of the study. This reflexive process allowed the study to be grounded in the methodology, data collection, and data analysis.

FINDINGS

This section interprets the Cycle 2 findings by discussing how they relate to the evaluation process. The extent to which these findings were successful in achieving the purposes of the action steps is also discussed.

Successful Academic Adjustment

Utilizing the pre-semester survey, the previous institution GPA and the expected first-semester GPA was collected and compared to the final posted first-semester GPA. These calculations are presented in Appendix E. Five of the six students filled out the survey, three of whom expected to have a lower GPA than at their previous institution. Instead of entering the semester full of confidence, these students expected to run into academic challenges greater than they had previously experienced. Student 1 stated, "The classes will be more rigorous," as the single biggest worry about starting the semester. Student 2 listed on their pre-semester survey that they would like "advice on how to handle my engineering classes." These students lacked confidence in themselves. Student 2 expected to have a drop of over 0.5 points in their GPA compared to their previous institution. Students 1–4 participated in the mentorship program by initiating contact with their mentors and holding at least one meeting. Three out of the four students who participated as mentees had GPAs higher than expected by an average of 0.26 points. Student 3 was the only student to have a lower than expected GPA (by 0.20 points), bringing the total average to an increase of 0.14 GPA points. Regarding their GPA at their previous institution compared to their first semester actual GPA, only one of the four students who were active in the mentorship program saw their GPA rise (Student 1 at 0.23). Overall, the four students saw an average decrease of 0.08 from what their GPA at their previous institution.

While their GPAs dropped less than 0.1 point on average from their previous institutions, 75% of the students received a higher first semester GPA than expected. It can be concluded that for those students who were active in the program, the implementation of virtual meetings throughout the semester was successful regarding their academic performance. Student 1's mentor discussed how, during their first meeting, topics "such as navigating Moodle, tutoring for her stats/chem class" were important to help set her up for a successful semester. The mentor discussed how establishing a tutor early on for stats and chemistry can prevent struggles that would be inevitable later in the semester. Later in the semester, Student 1 mentioned struggling with the long readings in a history course, and they worked together on "designating Monday as her history reading day." Student 2, during the stressful mid-term exam period, was able to have a check-in with their mentor on "how classes and exams are going so far as well as a few extra ways to get help." Meetings at the beginning of the semester were important for setting the mentee up for academic success, and the periodic check-ins that helped mentees like Student 2 find the help they needed to be successful on their mid-term exams.

Once all courses went online, new lateral transfer students had to quickly navigate a new learning management system and virtual learning environment. Student 4 "expressed frustration with Moodle because [they] were used to Canvas" and requested a meeting with their mentor to understand the system. Their mentor said that in this meeting, Student 4's main frustration was "not all assignments showed up in advance, but I let him know about invisible assignments that you must unlock to see." Instead of allowing the frustration to grow and potentially miss assignments, Student 4 was able to understand that "some professors have been posting all assignments at once, while others have been doing it on a weekly basis." When courses switched to online, students were left to adapt without much assistance.

Therefore, these periodic meetings helped new lateral transfer students understand how their weekly assignments would work moving forward. However, it was discovered that assignments were not the only grading mechanism employed by professors. Student 4 once again grew frustrated with another piece of technology called TopHat. A quick meeting request and their mentor "explained it is often used for attendance at the beginning of class, and that questions appear that you can respond to via text or online [while] some professors also use it for homework." The mentor went on to state that they "recommended looking at his syllabus for more details on how his class uses TopHat and emailing his professor in case he has missed anything or isn't enrolled correctly on TopHat." Instead of simply going online and learning what the technology was and how it was used, having a mentor meant that mentees could receive personalized action items to ensure full credit would be received.

By pairing up mentors and mentees based on major, the mentors prepared the mentees for specific classes and the expected workload as the semester was starting. The mentors experienced the often difficult academic adjustment to a new institution before and were aware of the specific courses required by their common major. In preparation for scheduling next semester's courses, Student 1 reached out to their mentor "after finding out via text I'm taking biological psychology a few days ago," she wanted to ask a few questions about this course because she's considering taking it next semester and wanted to see how hard it was. Instead of blindly signing up for a course without knowing details, such as the professor and the rigor of the class, mentees were prepared to set up their course schedule. Four mentors filled out the post-semester survey, and three of them listed classes as the most discussed topic during their meetings with mentees. These conversations and the increased expected GPA show that the mentorship program positively influenced the academic adjustment for lateral transfer students.

Difficult Social Adjustment

The purpose of the mentor–mentee relationship was to provide each mentee with someone familiar with their journey of transferring to a new institution and provide an established connection to campus from Day 1. This relationship was specifically designed around the reliance on the familiarity derived from the Cycle 1 data analysis. During a virtual meeting with one of the mentors before the semester starts, she said, "I really, really wish I had this," when the details and purpose of the program were discussed. She went on to say that just knowing someone was there if she needed them would have been extremely beneficial to her first semester and transition to the institution. A second mentor explained, "I just really wish I had something like this. At [previous institution], I never had to use a degree audit to assist in scheduling courses, but here it was just assumed we knew how important the tools were." Since this mentor did not have any established connections on campus when they transferred, they were left to navigate the journey alone. These mentors understood the power of having an established connection to campus and its effect on a transfer student's transition to a new environment.

Student 5 did not join any club or organizations during the first semester but stated on their post-semester survey that having a mentor meant, "I knew that I always had someone to answer questions that I had." Student 4 shared a similar sentiment, stating that it was "great to have someone to talk to." The mentees knew that at any point during the semester if they were lost or needed guidance, their mentor was there to help answer any questions. Instead of sorting through websites or previous emails, simply having someone quickly answer a question put their mind at ease. When the transfer students were trying to transition and connect to their new campus, just having someone to talk to or lean on when classes were challenging or course registration opened was beneficial to their adjustment.

The Fall 2020 semester was carried out at the institution under unique circumstances. COVID-19 caused the Spring 2020 semester to move online after spring break (mid-March), but the campus community had not felt the true effects of this global pandemic until the fall. Once courses moved fully online a week into the semester, Student 4 stated, "I'm not going to lie, but I signed up for peer mentoring because I thought the campus would be back in-person, but now since it's permanently online, I don't really have any concerns." The fears of social adjustment left students' minds as they were no longer physically a campus community member. Student 4's mentor confirmed this feeling by saying COVID-19 affected their program experience because "once learning went remote, my mentee felt that he didn't need much help any longer since he wasn't going to campus." COVID-19 prevented these students from immersing themselves in the campus culture and caused them to treat their college-going experience as transactional.

While the peer-mentor program was virtual from the beginning of the semester, the campus shift to fully virtual created significant barriers for the program and the mentees transitioning to campus. Student 1's mentor explained that "internet troubles like extremely bad connection when we met sometimes led to meeting less." Student 2 also missed meetings due to "technical issues during the day the meeting was planned" and rescheduled for a later date. Unreliable technology not only hindered the program because meetings were less frequent or had to be rescheduled but added to the frustration and anxiety of a first-semester transitional experience. Rescheduling meetings grew to be a tough task as the virtual shift caused mentees and mentors to become busier. Student 3's mentor told the researcher that going virtual was difficult because "online classes people are a lot busier, and our schedules didn't line up." This was a common theme and not just for the peer-mentorship program. The institution is not known for remote learning as they only offer one online degree. When speaking with students outside the peer-mentorship program, they discussed feeling "detached" from being a college student and did not have any free time outside work or academic work.

Constant communication between the researcher and mentors also became challenging due to busy schedules. Student 2's mentor emailed the researcher, saying, "I'm really sorry I haven't been in touch; lately, school has been very hectic. Unfortunately, I was not able to meet with [Student 2] last week, nor this week, due to both our schedules conflicting." Student 1's mentor sent a meeting summary over a week after the meeting took place with the reasoning, "The last week of school has been the time where assignments start popping out like crazy, so I got a little behind!" The peer-mentorship program's focus was on the new lateral transfer student, but the unprecedented global pandemic showed that even the mentors themselves were socially detached this semester.

DISCUSSION

The primary purpose of this study was to investigate lateral transfer students' experiences of transfer shock, and how an institution can assist in limiting transfer shock. Lateral transfer students explained that a lack of connection and lack of familiarity at their home institution was a primary reason for transferring. They sought to transfer to an institution they had grown up spending time at or where family members attended. They need-ed a familiar support system in place, such as a sibling or high school friend that would help them on their journey to achieve their academic aspira-tions. As D'Amico and colleagues (2010) stated, lateral transfer students decided to transfer out for social circumstances and proximity to home. All three students interviewed discussed the desire to either come closer to home or to a place they felt more comfortable. A sense of familiarity in their minds was needed to allow for success.

Transfer shock is a real phenomenon and the data collected showed that both socially and academically, a difficult transitional period exists. Due to a gap in communications after admittance, lateral transfer students found themselves lost or uncertain regarding next steps. Simple daily functions, such as buying a parking pass or obtaining a student ID, were lost in transla-tion and became an addition to an already overwhelming process. Not ev-ery institution uses the same learning management system or student infor-mation system, and if students are not introduced to these systems prior to enrolling, they will spend their time figuring out how to access class mate-rial instead of forming social connections to campus. Academically students could fall even further behind if they are focusing time trying to navigate a course shell online, when this material was taught to their native classmates as freshman. Chin-Newman and Shaw (2013) discussed this in their study, stating that institutions just assume these students are familiar with daily technology functions and do not include this in transitional assistance.

Students found information regarding joining clubs and organizations to be scarce or not clear, and therefore did not get involved early on. This further distanced themselves from integrating in a new environment.

Looking back, the students understood the importance of getting in-volved early and that by not doing so, they found themselves lost on cam-pus. If the information is not pushed out directly and continuously to these students, they do not understand why they need to find a social connection. Townsend's (1995) study revealed that the information on how to get in-volved on campus was not easily attainable for transfer students. If they are unable to quickly or easily find what is necessary, students will skip over it in order to work on removing another success barrier that stands in their way.

Performance inside the classroom is where lateral transfer students showed the most experience of transfer shock. The students stated that the transition inside the classroom forced them to re-learn how to study and were unable to just rely on what they had done previously. By not un-derstanding the different expectations and rigor at a new institution, these lateral transfer students struggled and felt lost in their courses. Hills (1965) tagged the term transfer shock to identify the GPA drop for transfer stu-dents, and all participants spoke on how their struggles in the first semes-ter resulted in a lower GPA compared to previous work. By the time they realized they needed assistance, tutorial services were at capacity, or they had to research and find information on where to find help. At every turn these students face another barrier in place.

Limitations

This study had several limitations throughout the research process. Cycle 1 of this study included three lateral transfer students and three full-time staff/faculty members. The research site has over 24,000 undergraduate students and 10,000 employees, meaning the sample size is much smaller in comparison. While the study is to be trusted, a larger sample size in the future is recommended. Initially, for Cycle 1, a participant was to be lateral transfer students in their first semester at the new institution, but no one volunteered, and due to the time constraint of the study, I shifted toward the staff/faculty perspective. This means that the student perspective was limited to students who were not currently dealing with the transitional problems and only could be reflected upon. Finally, starting in March 2020, COVID-19 struck the world and caused universities to go online. Cycle 2 action steps were forced online as a result of the COVID-19 pandemic. This limited the recruitment efforts of mentors and mentees, on-campus participation in the action steps, and student's involvement in the program.

Implications for Practice

At the institution, 50% of transfer students do not come from community colleges within our state. The remainder of students who do are given benefits prior to transferring, such as a state-wide articulation agreement guaranteeing the award of transfer credits and baccalaureate degree plans (BDPs) that create advising plans to provide students two plus two pathways. Four-year universities make up four of the top six transfer applicant feeders, meaning lateral transfer students represent a large part of the transfer pool. While this statistically does not label them a minority, lateral transfer students are not acknowledged or viewed legitimately on our campus. As a member of the transfer success committee, it is seen that faculty speak their preference for students who leave high school to attend a community college versus those who move from a 4-year university due to the convenience of easier academic advising plans. Vertical transfer students represent the power class within the hierarchy of enrollment management. Social justice speaks about the unconscious benefits populations receive, and these students receive these perks simply just by transferring from a community college (McIntosh, 2010). These students do not inherently understand their position of power, because this oppression has unconsciously been drilled in their psyche since taking ACA 122 (transfer success) their first semester at the community college (Bell, 2007). That means it takes just one change agent to develop the knowledge to disperse to those decision-makers to fully understand that a student population is not only being ignored locally, but nationally.

With most of the state educational policy dealing with linear transfer policy, the researchers suggest that policymakers need to understand that student behavior will not always follow that of linear flow (D'Amico et al., 2010). Most state schools have some sort of agreement or articulation with community colleges to ensure a pipeline of students are transferring in. Researchers that have examined this conclude that vertical transfer students are typically prepared for transfer shock, whereas lateral transfer students receive no guidance in navigating this phenomenon; lateral transfer students often did not give thought to the changes or differences a new college campus might provide (Kirk-Kuwaye & Kirk-Kuwaye, 2007).

This study sought to break down the barrier lateral transfer students face in their initial transition to a new institution. The findings showed that transfer students should not be thought uniformly, and instead be valued individually based on their unique experiences. Throughout this study, the primary researcher found that lateral transfer students were left to fend for themselves, and persistence would be up to their self-reliance. It also became clear that lateral transfer students who had an on-campus support system were able to get ahead and not be lost in the system.

REFERENCES

Alpern, B. E. (2000). *Factors that influence community college transfer students' satisfaction with their baccalaureate institutions* (ProQuest 9963735) [Doctoral Dissertation, University of Michigan]. https://www.proquest.com/docview/304627965

Bell, L. A. (2007). Theoretical foundations for social justice. In M. Adams, L. A. Bell, P. Griffin (Eds.), *Teaching for diversity and social justice* (pp. 1–16). Routledge.

Chin-Newman, C. S., & Shaw, S. T. (2013). The anxiety of change: How new transfer students overcome challenges. *Journal of College Admission, 221*, 14–21. https://www.rti.org/publication/anxiety-change

Choi, A. N., Curran, G. M., Morris, E. J., Salem, A. M., Curry, B. D., & Flowers, S. K. (2019). Pharmacy students' lived experiences of academic difficulty and tinto's theory of student departure. *American Journal of Pharmaceutical Education, 83*(10), 2150–2160. https://doi.org/10.5688/ajpe7447

D'Amico, M. M., Giani, M. S., Taylor, J. L., & Jain, D. (2010). The multiple dimensions of transfer: Examining the transfer function in american higher education. *Community College Review, 45*(4), 273–293. https://doi.org/10.1177/0091552117725177

Guba, E. (1981). Criteria for assessing the trustworthiness of naturalistic inquiries. *ECTJ, 29*(2), 75–91. https://www.jstor.org/stable/30219811

Hills, J. R. (1965). *Transfer shock: The academic performance of the junior college transfer.* Distributed by ERIC Clearinghouse. https://eric.ed.gov/?id=ED010740

Ishitani, T. T. (2008). How do transfers survive after "transfer shock"? A longitudinal study of transfer student departure at a 4-year institution. *Research in Higher Education: Journal of the Association for Institutional Research, 49*(5), 403–419.

Ishitani, T. T., & Flood, L. D. (2018). Student transfer-out behavior at 4-year institutions. *Research in Higher Education: Journal of the Association for Institutional Research, 59*(7), 825–846. https://eric.ed.gov/?id=EJ1192826

Ivins, T., Copenhaver, K., & Koclanes, A. (2017), Adult transitional theory and transfer shock in higher education: Practices from the literature. *Reference Services Review, 45*(2), 244–257. https://doi.org/10.1108/RSR-08-2016-0048

Kirk-Kuwaye, C., & Kirk-Kuwaye, M. (2007). A study of engagement patterns of lateral and vertical transfer students during their first semester at a Public Research University. *Journal of the First-Year Experience & Students in Transition, 19*(2), 9–27. https://eric.ed.gov/?id=EJ798196

Laanan, F. S. (2007). Studying transfer students: Part II: Dimensions of transfer students' adjustment. *Community College Journal of Research & Practice, 31*(1), 37–59. https://doi.org/10.1080/10668920600859947

McIntosh, P. (2010). White privilege: Unpacking the invisible knapsack. In P. S. Rothenberg (Ed.), *Race, class and gender in the United States: An integrated study* (pp. 188–192). Worth Publishers.

Miles, M., Huberman, A. M., & Saldaña, J. (2014). *Qualitative data analysis: A methods sourcebook* (4th ed.). SAGE Publications.

Scott, T. P., Thigpin, S. S., & Bentz, A. O. (2018). Transfer learning community: Overcoming transfer shock and increasing retention of mathematics and science majors. *Journal of College Student Retention, 19*(3), 300–316. https://doi.org/10.1177/1521025115621919

Shealy, E., Brawner, C., Mobley, C., & Layton, R. (2013, June). *A descriptive study of engineering transfer students at four institutions: Comparing lateral and vertical transfer pathways* (Paper presentation). 2013 ASEE Annual Conference and Exposition, Atlanta, Georgia. https://doi.org/10.18260/1-2—19053

Stringer, E. (2014). *Action research: A handbook for practitioners* (4th ed.). SAGE Publications.

Townsend, B. K. (1995). Community college transfer students: A case study of survival. *The Review of Higher Education, 18*(2), 175–193. https://www.proquest.com/docview/304627965

Zilvinskis, J., & Dumford, A. D. (2018). The relationship between transfer student status, student engagement, and high-impact practice participation. *Community College Review, 46*(4), 368–387. https://doi.org/10.1177/0091552118781495

CHAPTER 5

THE IMPORTANCE OF CONNECTIONS AND COLLABORATIONS TO ENHANCE THE SUCCESSFUL GRADUATE STUDENT EXPERIENCE

Kathy Dilks

Institutions of higher learning have a mission to educate, serve, and prepare all students personally and professionally. The need for well-trained student affairs professionals, orientations, and services dedicated to the post-baccalaureate learner have not always kept pace with the growth of the graduate population (Evans et al., 2018; Pontius & Harper, 2006). This research-site university established the centralized Office of Graduate Student Affairs. As the site's understanding of their "typical" graduate student developed, the role of student affairs evolved to accommodate unique demands in developing meaningful experiences and supports in serving myriad graduate

Taking Action, pages 67–85
Copyright © 2024 by Information Age Publishing
www.infoagepub.com
All rights of reproduction in any form reserved.

student constituencies (Bain et al., 2010; Cox et al., 2015; Pontius & Harper, 2006; Poock, 2004).

The purpose of this action research study was to examine the effectiveness of current graduate student services and examine ways to foster a collaborative, student-centered community. Forty-five volunteer graduate-student, faculty, and administrator participants across five academic colleges were interviewed over two cycles. An action step of a modified, collaborative orientation series was implemented after the first set of interviews, and subsequently became the foundation for future student–leader/academic/student affairs collaborations. This qualitative action report includes research related to student services, understanding the value of connections and engagement leading to enhanced confidence and success, and the characteristics of the post-baccalaureate learner to provide context, background, and support to the study.

BACKGROUND AND CONTEXT

Existing literature indicates mental health, emotional well-being, and stress reduction have become major foci within higher education to support student success and safety (Evans et al., 2018; Veilleux et al., 2012). With their balance of work, family, research, or clinical commitments, graduate students are faced with intensified pressures in and out of the classroom (Grady et al., 2014; Hyun et al., 2006; Pain, 2018). The academic demands, especially for those with career licensure or board exams, can be overwhelming (McKinney, 2017; Novotney, 2014; K. S. Shaffer et al., 2017). Self-efficacy within the education setting can be affected while judging one's own capabilities. Self-efficacy determines their reactions to outside influences, level of stress management, self-debilitating negative behavior responses, goal development, and educational or career pursuits (Bandura, 1982; McDowell et al., 2015). Impostor syndrome, feelings of fraudulence when comparing oneself to peers, can hamper student success (Bothello & Roulet, 2019; Clance & Imes, 1978). Offering student support systems to help identify and appreciate individual talents, minimize competition among peers, and foster trust and communication between students and their mentors or colleagues, can help alleviate impostorism and anxiety, allowing for a more fulfilling graduate experience (Cohen & McConnell, 2019).

The importance of student engagement has been well studied, documented, and discussed at the undergraduate level. Far less focus and resources have been placed on understanding how to build a community to engage the post-baccalaureate learner (Kinzie & Kuh, 2004; Kuh, 2001; Pontius & Harper, 2006; Quaye & Harper, 2015). Fostering an inclusive and involved environment for graduate students takes university effort (Duranczyk et al., 2015). Graduate students are immersed in research, evaluations, classes, and internships. It can be an isolating experience adding stress to their already busy work and family life (Erichsen & Bolliger, 2011; Flores-Scott & Nerad, 2012; Grady et al., 2014; Irani et al., 2014). Connecting graduate students with peers who understand the pressures of graduate school is integral for reducing anxiety and creating meaningful collegial and career connections (Lehker & Furlong, 2006; Pontius & Harper, 2006).

Connections with faculty reduce feelings of isolation and demoralization (Grady et al., 2014; Irani et al., 2014). Faculty who treat their students with respect as future colleagues create open dialog and help diminish feelings of failure, perceived or real. This dialogue allows the student to feel more confident in their skills (Boyle & Boice, 1998; Curtin et al., 2013). These early connections can increase the feeling of belonging, also encouraging a more confident entrance into the profession (Curtin et al., 2013; Major & Dolly, 2003; Suh et al., 2018).

Research suggests academic departments or student affairs professionals with expertise in orientation onboard graduate students, however, graduate students benefit highly from currently enrolled students to provide insight and peer-mentoring (Coulter et al., 2004; Cox et al., 2015; Mears et al., 2015). Connection to the campus, faculty, and fellow students initiates the socialization process transitioning from their previous educational environment to a new, advanced degree program (Poock, 2004; Ward-Roof, 2010). With more programs being offered in an online or hybrid format, offering an online equivalent orientation will prepare students academically and emotionally (Berry, 2018; Bozarth et al., 2004; Britto & Rush, 2013) and is imperative in building a social environment for collaboration and moral support (Milman et al., 2015; Schroeder & Terras, 2015).

International students with varied cultural belief systems represent another subset of the graduate population who need purposeful support (Cavusoglu et al., 2016; Erichsen & Bolliger, 2011; Pavlik, 2016; Zenner & Squire, 2020). International students uniquely need to understand not only the ethos of their new institution, but also learn the culture of American higher education. Orientation beyond explaining visa regulations familiarize the international learner and create a milieu where students can voice their questions or concerns. This space is essential as often faculty and staff misinterpret students' understanding of academic or university requirements, timing, and level of commitment needed to be successful (Cokley et al., 2013; Curtin et al., 2013; Erichsen & Bolliger, 2011). Cultural differences concerning group work, self-directed learning, academic integrity, and the level of faculty attentiveness also exist (Ward-Roof, 2010). Orientations can alleviate these known issues.

Serving a graduate student population in an undergraduate-dominant culture requires strong faculty and student affairs collaboration (Gardner & Barnes, 2007). There can be great victories in student affairs and academic partnerships, as long as there is mutual agreement to share responsibility for developing student success (Colwell, 2006; Doyle, 2004; Kezar, 2003; Kinzie & Kuh, 2004). For universities concerned with developing or enhancing graduate academic programs, student affairs professionals provide an additional resource with an understanding of universitywide functions in areas such as aid, career, counseling, housing, technology, and support-services. These professionals assist academic departments in mitigating problems that could be unfamiliar, reduce faculty anxiety in working with new students, and strengthen the graduate student experience (Cho & Sriram, 2016; Cassuto, 2015; Gansemer-Topf et al., 2006; Pruitt-Logan & Isaac, 1995; White & Nonnamaker, 2008).

METHODS

This research institution is a medium sized, Carnegie classified doctoral/professional university (D/PU). Approximately one third of the undergraduate population enrolls at the post-baccalaureate level. The research site is beginning to understand and acknowledge the needs of their diverse graduate student population. Action research is the appropriate model to capture the graduate student voice on this campus. Action research is an iterative practice of collecting data, reviewing, applying a corrective plan, and then researching again to inform and test the recommended solutions (Herr & Anderson, 2015; Stringer, 2014). Cycle 1 data determined common factors influencing confidence, needed preparation for graduate school as well as necessary dedicated graduate student services. From this initial study, a modified and extended orientation to focus on building self-efficacy, creating a socially connected environment, and including greater faculty and peer-mentor connections at the onset, was implemented and evaluated.

Cycle 1 Participants

The participants were divided into three groups: (a) current graduate students who had attended a different institution for their bachelor's degree, (b) current graduate students who had attended the same institution for their bachelor's degree as their current graduate university, and (c) faculty and key administrators who taught or had knowledge of the graduate school experience. Volunteer student participants consisted of 16 students ranging in age from 22–52. Six of the participants identified as male,10 identified as female. Four of the participants identified as Black, 10 identified as White, 1 identified as Middle Eastern, and 1 as Hispanic. Participants included members of 13 different academic programs; 4 attended part-time, while 12 attended full-time. The group of volunteer student participants varied by program, college, age, course-load, and ethnicity, and organically corresponded demographically to the total graduate population. Ten faculty and administrators volunteered, and it was a theoretical sample by their knowledge of student experiences across multiple academic disciplines. Faculty and administrator participants were organically diverse (Miles et al., 2019).

Cycle 2 Participants

The participants were divided into three groups: (a) students just beginning their graduate career at the research-site institution; (b) current graduate students who had attended the previous orientation format, and also participated in the new orientation series; and (c) faculty and key administrators who taught or had knowledge of the graduate school experience. Student participants included 12 students who ranged in age from 22–54. Four identified as male, 8 identified as female. One identified as Black, 9 identified as White, and 2 as Hispanic. Student participants were members of nine different academic programs; 5 attended part-time while 7 attended full-time, which corresponded to the total graduate population. This group included various academic programs. Seven faculty and administrators, who spanned multiple academic disciplines and had experience in graduate orientations also participated. Overall, participants included representatives from all colleges serving graduate students across multiple programs, and were representative of the self-identified gender, age, and ethnic diversity of the institution for both cycles (Miles et al., 2019).

Cycle 1 Data Collection

Cycle 1 research consisted of 26 semi-structured interviews. The interviews investigated what would make students feel more confident, satisfied, and successful. From the results of the Cycle 1 data collection and analysis, notions for enhanced preparation-services emerged. Faculty and administrators demonstrated a greater understanding of the concept of services; however, they needed more clarification on the concept of student *confidence* as it could relate to potential support services.

Cycle 2 Data Collection

Building on the results from the Cycle 1 research, an action step was developed. This action step took the form of implementing a modified orientation. Cycle 2 data collection focused on the effectiveness of the action step to (a) expand the scope of the orientation to be more academic and program specific; (b) create a social engagement component; and (c) incorporate areas of improvement that were discovered in Cycle 1 such as academic development, building confidence, creating a sense of community, and highlighting graduate focused services. Data collection took the form of semi-structured interviews with 12 initial questions to probe participants' viewpoints of self-confidence, satisfaction, success, and engagement.

Data Analysis

Every subject was given a pseudonym and a unique identifier. Once all recordings were transcribed, the transcripts were reviewed several times resulting in over 800 in vivo codes. Additional patterns, themes, and sub-themes emerged. A small number of participants reviewed the themes and sub-themes for verification, and subsequently, outcomes were presented to participants and stakeholders (Miles et al., 2019).

TRUSTWORTHINESS AND QUALITY ASSURANCE

One faculty member and one student in Cycle 1, and one academic administrator in Cycle 2 uniquely contradicted topics that others mentioned were highly important, however, their contributions enriched the research and served to support the need for diversified preparation services. The data between interview recordings, notes, and codes between both cycles of research were triangulated and cross-checked for additional understanding and confirmation of themes. This researcher also applied referential adequacy by archiving some of the Cycle 1 data to then go back and code the remaining data to test the validity of the initial findings (Lincoln & Guba, 1985; Patton, 2001).

CYCLE 1 RESULTS

Factors Influencing Confidence and Success in Graduate School

Participants identified a lack of self-efficacy and feelings of fraudulence as common causes which impacted their success. Even when participants attained success, they did not always believe that they deserved it. Reassurance that participants possessed the requisite level of intelligence and ability needed to handle the coursework was discussed. Participants noted that addressing this earlier in their college career may positively affect their self-efficacy and diminish feelings of fraudulence. Interactions and relationships to peers, faculty, and fellow graduate students also emerged as beneficial and necessary to building confidence and success. Participants noted establishing clear connections in and out of the academic program as integral, and if this need is not satisfied, students then began to have feelings of isolation, and the lack of belonging can hinder one's ability to feel confident.

Graduate-Specific Preparation

Student participants expressed a desire to understand graduate-specific resources. Some participants expressed concern that graduate students were viewed as less important than their undergraduate counterparts. Graduate student participants also noted the need for explicitly addressing increased academic and professional expectations. Independent and self-directed learning at the graduate level proved a difficult adjustment for most. Mitigating the shock and understanding the differences between undergraduate and graduate rigor is necessary. Student participants also described feeling lost and unprepared to handle the pressures of heading into their new professional experiences, and identified workload and work/life imbalance as a common theme which required learning new time management and coping skills.

Needed Graduate Student Services and Amenities

Participants valued social engagement and socialization and felt this should be included within tuition. Participants also noted they are entitled to these services as a member of the greater university community. Participants felt excluded because of their age or academic level from much of campus life. Stress relief, connectivity, socialization, support, or an alternative way to gather information, allows the student a purposeful respite from the intensity of their graduate work. Participants mentioned the ability to connect outside of their program to avoid the scrutiny of their faculty and peers within a highly competitive program, and taking a moment to decompress from the pressures of a busy schedule. Graduate students reported feeling more anxious and sought methods to nurture positive mental health. Graduate students felt isolated when told the counseling center served undergraduates first.

Faculty participants indicated they are not prepared to handle certain non-academic issues as they arise, such as mental health concerns. Faculty were also genuinely surprised at the level of additional tutoring, training, and support graduate students needed. Ongoing writing, research, and academic integrity services emerged as a theme of remarkable importance.

Whether it was peer-to-peer, faculty-to-student, or guidance from a professional, the connections were important to help orient and transition. Student participants noted they were not conditioned in their undergraduate experiences to do as much academic research or have the level of awareness to avoid academic integrity issues.

ACTION STEPS

Informed by Cycle 1 results, a new program-specific orientation series replaced the traditional single, multi-program, one-day orientation. Converting the single-day orientation into a series of multiple orientations for each academic cohort allowed for shorter, more frequent touchpoints with the greater ability to sustain students' interest, as well as align necessary material closer to when new graduate students could appreciate and use the information. The following are the main features of the expanded series launched over the summer:

1. *Early-engagement pre-orientation events.* These events were intended to be short social engagement opportunities as a precursor to orientation. These sessions incorporated some of the necessary information concerning relocation services, financial aid, university procedures, and registration. The pre-orientation events also sought to build self-efficacy and imposter syndrome awareness to help mitigate self-sabotaging feelings, increase confidence, and highlighted the value of support services provided to the graduate student. The gatherings were via Zoom providing greater accessibility. These began once the majority of the individual cohorts or programs were registered over the summer. The use of trivia software was implemented to create a speedy, engaging, and novel approach.

2. *Enhanced main student orientations.* The focus of the main student orientation became working more closely with individual departments or small colleges which allowed for increased faculty and student–leader involvement as opposed to the large, mass orientations with multiple programs in attendance. Sessions during the main orientation allowed for further depth, since basic information was removed and covered in the prior, smaller, pre-orientation

gatherings. Use of the trivia software and anonymous polling were introduced to increase engagement and to alleviate potential embarrassment while asking questions or reviewing material.

CYCLE 2 RESULTS

Importance of Making Earlier Connections

One hundred percent of the participants identified the importance of making early connections as positively influencing student confidence, satisfaction, and success. Creating an earlier collaborative community helped eliminate the mystique of returning to college and further supported engaging with peers. Participants also valued the connections with their orientation peer mentors, current graduate students who became an integral channel of support, guidance, and comfort throughout the summer leading into the term. Participants noted the value in creating a mutual, knowledgeable, and welcoming experience. Current students shared their insider's perspective and gave credence to the information disseminated by faculty and staff, which was valued by participants. Connections made with university employees, and the affiliation with their program and institution, were also found to be highly important and transformative. Student participants noted they felt a connection and trust with the staff and faculty during the orientation, a deeper connection they had not felt during their prior educational experiences. Participants identified connections made during orientation as a factor in their potential future achievement, continuation in the program, and increased academic self-efficacy at the graduate level.

Social Engagement Enhanced Graduate Experience

Social engagement is defined as interactions outside of the academic or classroom setting. There have been notable assumptions that graduate students lack the inclination and the time to add social engagement and interactions to their already busy schedules. This research shows, however, regardless of program, class-load, distance from the university, or age of the student, if engagement services are offered, graduate students will value the experience, and if not offered, note the absence. Planned and organized gatherings are welcome if aligned appropriately with interest and class timings, however, organic gatherings among peers is also fostered by a sense of community created at the onset.

Increased Confidence Reduced Anxiety

Having comfort or assurance in a situation can mitigate feelings of doubt or anxiety. Between addressing concerns, clarifying offerings, and creating a comfortable and engaging environment, participants indicated the modified orientation series further eased the natural tension and doubt that students in transition experience. A common theme throughout Cycle 1 was the presence of low self-efficacy and imposter syndrome. Though confronting complex emotions and constructs can be intimidating at the start of a new academic experience, overall, most appreciated the open and safe dialog introducing these concepts to help sustain confidence. The casual pre-orientation gatherings coupled with the collaborative main-orientations gave participants the comfort that they could reach back to their peer-mentors, faculty, or staff, also increasing confidence that they have support if needed. Cycle 2 seemed to effectively address self-efficacy concerns.

DISCUSSION

The newly created centralized Office of Graduate Student Affairs entered an established system that was traditionally focused on a full-time, traditional-aged, predominantly residential, undergraduate population. When graduate programs rose from less than 15 to more than 40, and the population increased from less than 800 to more than 3,000 across multiple campuses and delivery systems, an enhanced focus on the post-baccalaureate student became necessary, particularly with concern to orientation and services provided. The following findings from the study are situated in the context of the extant literature.

Connections Are Foundationally Essential

This study supports current literature that for adult graduate populations, connectedness or feeling connected to peers, faculty, and the institution, is not only necessary, but critical in assimilation and retention (Irani et al., 2014; Lambert & Felten, 2020; Lawson et al., 2011; Tinto, 2012). Relationships made with other students, their faculty, and the sense of program affiliation have a greater influence on students' satisfaction than facilities and services, potentially influencing students' willingness to persist with heightened satisfaction (Strahan & Credé, 2015). According to Lambert and Felten (2020),

> Decades of research demonstrate that peer-to-peer, student–faculty, and student–staff relationships are the foundation of learning, belonging, and achieving in college. Students' interactions with peers, faculty, and staff positively

influence the breadth and depth of student learning, retention and graduation rates, and a wide range of other outcomes, including critical thinking,
identity development, communication skills, and leadership abilities. (p. 5)

This researcher attempted to understand tangible services and resources,
but what it unearthed was the importance of making appropriate, foundational, and meaningful connections that were not only at the heart of student satisfaction, but also fostered greater feelings of confidence. Building
confidence and self-efficacy, reducing thoughts of fraudulence, and supporting students through services, also increases success (McDowell et al.,
2015; Mears et al., 2015; Suh et al., 2018). Additionally, a fostered sense of
belonging can not only be satisfying, it also increases confidence (Bain et
al., 2010; Curtin et al., 2013; Duranczyk et al., 2015; Gopalan & Brady, 2020;
Holloway-Friesen, 2021; Zenner & Squire, 2020). The confident connections created early in the student's graduate career often spark the desire
to further engage socially, which has implications for heightened feelings
of satisfaction, also cycling back to enhanced success and persistence (M.
Cohen & Greenberg, 2011; Rovai, 2002; Strahan & Credé, 2015).

As a result of the Cycle 2 research, the act of making positive connections is the nucleus for all facets of the positive graduate student experience: (a) engagement, (b) confidence, (c) satisfaction, and (d) success.
These areas not only function independently, but also influence each other
and are foundationally intertwined. Few align this concept at the graduate
level, especially programs that have a siloed and focused goal of student
academic advancement, and not the entire student experience holistically.
This interconnection is displayed in Figure 5.1.

Figure 5.1 Interconnections. Results from Cycle 2 Research.

Gamification Facilitates Engagement and Preparation

The use of games within the orientation was found to facilitate the themes of preparation, confidence, engagement, connections, and success. In the process of innovating orientations by offering additional smaller sessions and increasing touchpoint engagement opportunities, thus reducing the amount of information offered in a singular session, gameplay and anonymous polling surveys were employed to boost entertainment and efficiency. Though research questions were not geared toward assessing the use of games or an anonymous digital component, this finding emerged as a result of the inductive data analysis process. 100% of participants volunteered that the use of games was one of the most successful and engaging additions. Participants commented that using the trivia game to introduce key aspects of the university, pertinent deadlines, relevant services, and key terminology, queried in a multiple-choice format, allowed confident recollection from previous emails and conversations concerning these topics. Participants played, engaged, and discussed answers together. Student participants indicated they felt greater connections with each other, greater confidence that they were prepared to embark on their next educational journey, and identified having a greater desire to engage in the future, supporting the themes in both Cycles 1 and 2. Because students could select an in-game-name, the play was anonymous, so the learning removed feelings of shame if answers were incorrect, and allowed student participants to be self-motivated to recall solutions and use reasonable deduction in answering questions, also linking the theme of increasing confidence and making connections (All et al., 2016; Le Hénaff et al., 2015; D. W. Shaffer et al., 2005). Game-based learning or gamification employs gameplay with specific learning objectives in mind with the balance of learning with play as the goal. Clear rules and goals, immediate feedback, appropriate levels of increasing challenge, relatable information, and a sense of personal control are key for the adult learner (Plass et al., 2015; Whitton, 2010).

Continuous Training and Services Necessary

Cycle 1 demonstrated previous orientations that offered too much information for one session. Likewise, faculty participants voiced that they did not always appreciate or understand student's concerns or issues until students voiced frustration, failed out, or left the university. Faculty noted they desired assistance in serving their graduate students. These findings support literature identifying the following: (a) more frequent connections and touchpoints (Lambert & Felten, 2020; Pontius & Harper, 2006); (b) clear understanding of services throughout the life of the student (Blimling, 2013; Britto & Rush, 2013; Gansemer-Topf et al., 2006; Lehker & Furlong,

2006); and (c) a collaborative environment focused on the student (Gulley, 2017; Pontius & Harper, 2006) are all necessary for students' healthy transition to graduate school, and their continued success and satisfaction (Mears et al., 2015; Pavlik, 2016; Ward-Roof, 2010).

Synergy of Divisions Aids Student Transition

Collaborations between student affairs and academic affairs supported the literature concerning these partnerships, and further expanded research in the area specific to the graduate population. The need for a synergy of ideas to support graduate students begins prior to orientation. With a collaborative model, institutional knowledge gaps can be identified and addressed with greater services for master's and doctoral students (Commodore et al., 2018; Jackson & Ebbers, 1999; Kezar, 2003; Tompkins et al., 2016). "Student life" or more aptly termed as student engagement, has been identified in both cycles as necessary for students' health and sense of satisfaction. Faculty participants in this study have acknowledged that engagement outside of class is integral for the mental health of their students, and it additionally opens the door for further collaborations to include co-curricular professional development, continued training, orientation beyond the initial series, and earlier notification when students are in distress (Pain, 2018; Pontius & Harper, 2006; Wyatt & Oswalt, 2013).

LIMITATIONS

The limitation to qualitative research, while allowing participants to express themselves freely in their own words, may not offer the study a large enough sample to be viewed as representative of the population (Jencik, 2011). Much of the university's research participants can be considered homogenous with concern to ethnic diversity, however, that is actually the representative body as this institution still strives to attract faculty and students of color. While this researcher tried to understand what is needed in a successful student experience, one must realize that though the Office of Graduate Student Affairs is intended to be centralized across more than 45 disciplines, continued in-depth research by individual program, delivery system, and campus location is recommended to dedicate appropriate services toward each unique population (Miles et al., 2019).

IMPLICATION FOR THE PRACTICE

There is limited research concerning centralized graduate student services and the importance of creating a graduate community, however, this research can enhance the narrow existing body of knowledge. Reflective of the process and outcomes of this study, higher education must adapt as graduate students' needs and expectations increase exponentially over time. Support is now more broadly defined to include emotional feelings, not just tangible services, or events. Connectedness and a sense of belonging should now be viewed as institutional goals. Socialization into graduate education, the program, and the profession are equally valuable. Customer service is not merely finding solutions, but also about creating a meaningful experience. Likewise, engagement programming is not only for entertainment; it is also a way to build confidence and success when connections are made with others.

Universities seeking to expand post-baccalaureate offerings should incorporate all university stakeholders to assure equitable resources. An internal audit of their current writing and research support for graduate students emerged deficit by both faculty and students in this study. Universities should undertake this audit proactively to ensure proper support. Mental health and support emerged in both cycles of research. Literature supports these results as a growing concern across American colleges and universities, particularly for master's and doctoral students. Free and accessible counseling services to a university's graduate population and graduate student representation on behavioral assessment teams are recommended.

For existing graduate programs, universities should consider the positive effects of peer-mentoring programs to enhance confidence and influence socialization. Research on peer-affinity groups also has implications for positive transition and retention of graduate students, as they do with their undergraduate counterparts. As more programs are offering online delivery options, it is crucial to understand the non-cohorted, part-time, remote population with concern to support, reducing feelings of isolation, and building institutional loyalty to assure success and retention. Equitable services and amenities in relation to their undergraduate counterparts, yet suitable and dedicated to the post-baccalaureate consumer, will assist graduate student success.

REFERENCES

All, A., Nuñez Castellar, E. P., & Van Looy, J. (2016). Assessing the effectiveness of digital game-based learning: Best practices. *Computers & Education, 92–93*, 90–103. https://doi.org/10.1016/j.compedu.2015.10.007

Bain, S., Fedynich, L., & Knight, M. (2010). The successful graduate student: A review of the factors for success. *Journal of Academic and Business Ethics, 3*(7), 1–9. https://www.aabri.com/manuscripts/10569.pdf

Bandura, A. (1982). Self-efficacy mechanism in human agency. *American Psychologist, 37*(2), 122–147. https://doi.org/10.1037/0003-066X.37.2.122

Berry, S. (2018). Building community in an online graduate program: Exploring the role of an in-person orientation. *The Qualitative Report, 23*(7), 1673–1687. Academic Search Ultimate. https://doi.org/10.46743/2160-3715/2018.3299

Blimling, G. S. (2013). Challenges of assessment in student affairs. *New Directions for Student Services, 2013*(142), 5–14. https://eric.ed.gov/?id=EJ1014894

Bothello, J., & Roulet, T. (2019). The imposter syndrome, or the mis-representation of self in academic life. *The Journal of Management Studies, 56*(4), 854–861. https://doi.org/10.1111/joms.12344

Boyle, P., & Boice, B. (1998). Best practices for enculturation: Collegiality, mentoring, and structure. *New Directions for Higher Education, 1998*(101), 87–94. https://doi.org/10.1002/he.10108

Bozarth, J., Chapman, D., & LaMonica, L. (2004). Preparing for distance learning: Designing an online student orientation course. *Journal of Educational Technology & Society, 7*(1), 87–106. https://citeseerx.ist.psu.edu/viewdoc/download;jsessionid=06524ED99B6FCE9DC8AD65BDDCA55116?doi=10.1.1.108.3700&rep=rep1&type=pdf

Britto, M., & Rush, S. (2013). Developing and implementing comprehensive student support services for online students. *Journal of Asynchronous Learning Networks, 17*(1), 29. https://files.eric.ed.gov/fulltext/EJ1011371.pdf

Cassuto, L. (2015). *The graduate school mess: What caused it and how we can fix it?* Harvard University Press.

Cavusoglu, M., White, W., James, W. B., & Cobanoglu, C. (2016, November 6–8). *Factors Associated With International Graduate Students' Academic Performance: A Comparative Analysis between the First Semester and the Subsequent Semester in the U.S.* [Conference paper]. American Association for Adult and Continuing Education (AAACE), Commission for International Adult Education (CIAE) Annual Pre-Conference, Albuquerque, NM.

Cho, A. R., & Sriram, R. (2016). Student affairs collaborating with academic affairs: Perceptions of individual competency and institutional culture. *College Student Affairs Journal, 34*(1), 56–59. https://doi.org/10.1353/csj.2016.0003

Clance, P. R., & Imes, S. A. (1978). The imposter phenomenon in high achieving women: Dynamics and therapeutic intervention. *Psychotherapy: Theory, Research & Practice, 15*(3), 241–247. https://doi.org/10.1037/h0086006

Cohen, E. D., & McConnell, W. R. (2019). Fear of fraudulence: Graduate school program environments and the impostor phenomenon. *The Sociological Quarterly, 60*(3), 457–478. https://doi.org/10.1080/00380253.2019.1580552

Cohen, M., & Greenberg, S. (2011). The struggle to succeed: Factors associated with the persistence of part-time adult students seeking a master's degree. *Continuing Higher Education Review, 75*, 101–112. https://files.eric.ed.gov/fulltext/EJ967811.pdf

Cokley, K., Mcclain, S., Enciso, A., & Martinez, M. (2013). An examination of the impact of minority status stress and impostor feelings on the mental health of diverse ethnic minority college students. *Journal of Multicultural Counseling and Development, 41*(2), 82–95. https://doi.org/10.1002/j.2161-1912.2013.00029.x

Colwell, B. W. (2006). Partners in a community of learners: Student and academic affairs at small colleges. *New Directions for Student Services, 2006*(116), 53–66. https://eric.ed.gov/?id=EJ760935

Commodore, F., Gasman, M., Conrad, C., & Nguyen, T.-H. (2018). Coming together: A case study of collaboration between student affairs and faculty at Norfolk State University. *Frontiers in Education, 3.* https://doi.org/10.3389/feduc.2018.00039

Coulter, F., Goin, R., & Gerard, J. (2004). Assessing graduate students' needs: The role of graduate student organizations. *Educational Research Quarterly, 28*(1), 15–26. https://www.proquest.com/docview/216182731

Cox, W. C., Wingo, B., & Todd, A. J. (2015). How we transitioned to a comprehensive professional and graduate student affairs office. *Medical Teacher, 37*(5), 417–421. https://doi.org/10.3109/0142159X.2014.929100

Curtin, N., Stewart, A. J., & Ostrove, J. M. (2013). Fostering academic self-concept: Advisor support and sense of belonging among international and domestic graduate students. *American Educational Research Journal, 50*(1), 108–137. https://www.jstor.org/stable/23319709

Doyle, J. (2004). Student affairs division's integration of student learning principles. *NASPA Journal, 41*(2), 375–394. https://eric.ed.gov/?id=EJ746534

Duranczyk, I. M., Franko, J., Osifuye, S., Barton, A., & Higbee, J. L. (2015). Creating a model for graduate student inclusion and success. *Contemporary Issues in Education Research, 8*(3), 147–158. https://doi.org/10.19030/cier.v8i3.9346

Erichsen E. A., & Bolliger D. U. (2011). Towards understanding international graduate student isolation in traditional and online environments. *Educational Technology Research and Development, 59*(3), 309–326. https://doi.org/10.1007/s11423-010-9161-6

Evans, T. M., Bira, L., Gastelum, J. B., Weiss, L. T., & Vanderford, N. L. (2018, March 6). *Evidence for a mental health crisis in graduate education* [Comments and Opinion]. Nature Biotechnology.

Flores-Scott, E. M., & Nerad, M. (2012). Peers in doctoral education: Unrecognized learning partners. *New Directions for Higher Education, 2012*(157), 73–83. https://doi.org/10.1002/he.20007

Gansemer-Topf, A. M., Ross, L. E., & Johnson, R. M. (2006). Graduate and professional student development and student affairs. *New Directions for Student Services, 2006*(115), 19–30. https://eric.ed.gov/?id=EJ760924

Gardner, S. K., & Barnes, B. J. (2007). Graduate student involvement: Socialization for the professional role. *Journal of College Student Development, 48*(4), 369–387. https://doi.org/10.1353/csd.2007.0036

Gopalan, M., & Brady, S. T. (2020). College students' sense of belonging: A national perspective. *Educational Researcher, 49*(2), 134–137. https://doi.org/10.3102/0013189X19897622

Grady, R. K., La Touche, R., Oslawski-Lopez, J., Powers, A., & Simacek, K. (2014). Betwixt and between: The social position and stress experiences of graduate students. *Teaching Sociology, 42*(1), 5–16. https://eric.ed.gov/?id=EJ1020494

Gulley, N. (2017). Mission-driven collaboration between academic and student affairs in community colleges. *Journal of College Student Development 58*(3), 463–468. https://doi.org/10.1353/csd.2017.0035

Herr, K., & Anderson, G. L. (2015). *The Action Research dissertation: A guide for students and faculty.* SAGE Publications, Inc.

Holloway-Friesen, H. (2021). The role of mentoring on Hispanic graduate students' sense of belonging and academic self-efficacy. *Journal of Hispanic Higher Education, 20*(1), 46–58. https://doi.org/10.1177/1538192718823716

Hyun, J. K., Quinn, B. C., Madon, T., & Lustig, S. (2006). Graduate student mental health: Needs assessment and utilization of counseling services. *Journal of College Student Development, 47*(3), 247–266. https://doi.org/10.1353/csd.2006.0030

Irani, T., Wilson, S., Slough, D., & Rieger, M. (2014). Graduate student experiences on- and off-campus: Social connectedness and perceived isolation. *Journal of Distance Education = Revue de l'Enseignement a Distance (Online), 28*(1), 1–16. https://www.ijede.ca/index.php/jde/article/view/856

Jackson, J. F. L., & Ebbers, L. H. (1999). Bridging the academic-social divide: Academic and student affairs collaboration. *College Student Journal, 33*(3), 380. https://www.researchgate.net/publication/324065118_Bridging_the_Academic-Social_Divide_Academic_and_Student_Affairs_Collaboration

Jencik, A. (2011). *Qualitative versus quantitative research.* SAGE Publications, Inc., https://doi.org/10.4135/9781412979351

Kezar, A. (2003). Enhancing innovative partnerships: Creating a change model for academic and student affairs collaboration. *Innovative Higher Education, 28*(2), 137–156. https://doi.org/10.1023/B:IHIE.0000006289.31227.25

Kinzie, J., & Kuh, G. D. (2004). Going DEEP: Learning from campuses that share responsibility for student success. *About Campus, 9*(5), 2–8. https://doi.org/10.1002/abc.105

Kuh, G. D. (2001). Assessing what really matters to student learning: Inside the national survey of student engagement. *Change, 33*(3), 10–17. https://doi.org/10.1080/00091380109601795

Lambert, L. M., & Felten, P. (2020). *Relationship-rich education: How human connections drive success in college.* Johns Hopkins University Press. https://doi.org/10.1353/book.78561.

Lawson, T. J., Kleinholz, S. A., & Bodle, J. H. (2011). Using Facebook to connect alumni, current students, and faculty: A how-to guide. *Teaching of Psychology, 38*(4), 265–268.

Le Hénaff, B., Michinov, N., Le Bohec, O., & Delaval, M. (2015). Social gaming is inSIDE: Impact of anonymity and group identity on performance in a team game-based learning environment. *Computers & Education, 82*, 84–95. https://doi.org/10.1016/j.compedu.2014.11.002

Lehker, T., & Furlong, J. S. (2006). Career services for graduate and professional students. *New Directions for Student Services, 2006*(115), 73–83. https://doi.org/10.1002/ss.217

Lincoln, Y. S., & Guba, E. G. (1985). *Naturalistic inquiry.* SAGE Publications.

Major, C., & Dolly, J. (2003). The importance of graduate program experiences to faculty self-efficacy for academic tasks. *The Journal of Faculty Development, 19*(2), 89–100. https://eric.ed.gov/?id=EJ720287

McDowell, W., Grubb, W. C., III, & Geho, P. (2015). The impact of self-efficacy and perceived organizational support on the imposter phenomenon. *American Journal of Management, 15*(3), 23–29. http://www.m.www.na-businesspress.com/AJM/McDowellWC_Web15_3_.pdf

McKinney, B. (2017). Associations among social support, life purpose and graduate student stress. *Virginia Journal, 38*(2), 4–9. https://link-gale-com.sacredheart .idm.oclc.org/apps/doc/A542801438/AONE?u=alberta_envlib&sid=google Scholar&xid=6fca4303

Mears, D. P., Scaggs, S. J. A., Ladny, R. T., Lindsey, A. M., & Ranson, J. W. A. (2015). Successful transitions to graduate school: Using orientations to improve student experiences in criminology and criminal justice programs. *Journal of Criminal Justice Education, 26*(3), 283–306. https://doi.org/10.1080/105112 53.2015.1018914

Miles, M. B., Huberman, A. M., & Saldana, J. (2019). *Qualitative data analysis: A methods sourcebook.* SAGE Publications.

Milman, N. B., Posey, L., Pintz, C., Wright, K., & Zhou, P. (2015). Online master's students perceptions of institutional supports and resources: Initial survey results. *Online Learning, 19*(4). https://doi.org/10.24059/olj.v19i4.549

Novotney, A. (2014). Students under pressure. *American Psychological Association, 45*(8), 36. https://www.apa.org/monitor/2014/09/cover-pressure

Pain, E. (2018, March 6). *Graduate students need more mental health support, study highlights.* Science. https://www.science.org/content/article/graduate-students-need -more-mental-health-support-new-study-highlights

Patton, M. Q. (2001). Evaluation, knowledge management, best practices, and high quality lessons learned. *American Journal of Evaluation, 22*(3), 329–336. https://doi.org/10.1177/109821400102200307

Pavlik, A. (2016). Adopt 3 ideas for supporting international graduate student success. *Enrollment Management Report, 20*(9), 1–5. Education Research Complete. https://doi.org/10.1002/emt.30236

Plass, J. L., Homer, B. D., & Kinzer, C. K. (2015). Foundations of game-based learning. *Educational Psychologist, 50*(4), 258–283. https://doi.org/10.1080/00461 520.2015.1122533

Pontius, J. L., & Harper, S. R. (2006). Principles for good practice in graduate and professional student engagement. *New Directions for Student Services, 2006*(115), 47–58. https://doi.org/10.1002/ss.215

Poock, M. C. (2004). Graduate student orientation practices: Results from a national survey. *NASPA Journal, 41*(3), 470–486. https://doi.org/10.2202/ 1949-6605.1356

Pruitt-Logan, A. S., & Isaac, P. D. (1995). *Student services for the changing graduate student population.* Jossey-Bass.

Quaye, S. J., & Harper, S. R. (Eds.). (2015). *Student engagement in higher education: Theoretical perspectives and practical approaches for diverse populations* (2nd ed.). Routledge.

Rovai, A. P. (2002). Sense of community, perceived cognitive learning, and persistence in asynchronous learning networks. *The Internet and Higher Education, 5*(4), 319–332. https://doi.org/10.1016/S1096-7516(02)00130-6

Schroeder, S. M., & Terras, K. L. (2015). Advising experiences and needs of online, cohort, and classroom adult graduate learners. *NACADA Journal, 35*(1), 42–55. https://files.eric.ed.gov/fulltext/EJ1069233.pdf

Shaffer, D. W., Squire, K. R., Halverson, R., & Gee, J. P. (2005). Video games and the future of learning. *Phi Delta Kappan, 87*(2), 105–111. https://doi.org/10.1177/003172170508700205

Shaffer, K. S., Love, M. M., Chapman, K. M., Horn, A. J., Haak, P. P., & Shen, C. Y. W. (2017). Walk-in triage systems in university counseling centers. *Journal of College Student Psychotherapy, 31*(1), 71–89. https://doi.org/10.1080/87568225.2016.1254005

Strahan, S., & Credé, M. (2015). Satisfaction with college: Re-examining its structure and its relationships with the intent to remain in college and academic performance. *Journal of College Student Retention: Research, Theory & Practice, 16*(4), 537–561. https://psycnet.apa.org/record/2015-14790-004

Stringer, E. T. (2014). *Action research* (4th ed.). SAGE Publications.

Suh, S., Veronica Crawford, C., Hansing, K., Fox, S., Cho, M., Chang, E., Lee, S., & Lee, S. (2018). A cross-cultural study of the self-confidence of counselors-in-training. *International Journal for the Advancement of Counselling, 40*(3), 255–266. https://doi.org/10.1007/s10447-018-9324-4

Tinto, V. (2012). *Completing college: Rethinking institutional action.* The University of Chicago Press.

Tompkins, K. A., Brecht, K., Tucker, B., Neander, L. L., & Swift, J. K. (2016). Who matters most? The contribution of faculty, student-peers, and outside support in predicting graduate student satisfaction. *Training and Education in Professional Psychology, 10*(2), 102–108. https://doi.org/10.1037/tep0000115

Veilleux, J. C., January, A. M., VanderVeen, J. W., Reddy, L. F., & Klonoff, E. A. (2012). Perceptions of climate in clinical psychology doctoral programs: Development and initial validation of the graduate program climate scale. *Training and Education in Professional Psychology, 6*(4), 211–219. https://doi.org/10.1037/a0030303

Ward-Roof, J. A. (Ed.). (2010). *Designing successful transitions: A guide for orienting students to college.* University of South Carolina, National Resource Center for the First-Year Experience and Students in Transition. https://files.eric.ed.gov/fulltext/ED558878.pdf

White, J., & Nonnamaker, J. (2008). Belonging and mattering: How doctoral students experience community. *NASPA Journal, 45*(3), 350–372. https://eric.ed.gov/?id=EJ819179

Whitton, N. (2010). *Learning with digital games: A practical guide for engaging students in higher education.* Routledge.

Wyatt, T., & Oswalt, S. B. (2013). Comparing mental health issues among undergraduate and graduate students. *American Journal of Health Education, 44*(2), 96–107. https:doi.org/10.1080/19325037.2013.764248

Zenner, K., & Squire, D. (2020). International student success: Exploring the intercultural competence of academic advisors. *Journal of Student Affairs Research and Practice, 57*(3), 338–351. https://doi.org/10.1080/19496591.2019.1707092

CHAPTER 6

INTEGRATING MENTAL HEALTH LITERACY IN STUDENT AFFAIRS MASTER'S PROGRAMS

Emily Bauer

Mental health impacts on college campuses are on the rise. According to the National College Health Assessment (NCHA), students reported increased depression and anxiety symptoms that overwhelmed their studies. Recent NCHA data show that 1 in 6 undergraduates felt too depressed to function, 1 in 5 felt overwhelming anxiety, and 1 in 15 seriously considered suicide. Counseling centers are unable to meet the current demand and campuses are increasingly concerned about the effect of the COVID-19 pandemic (Gorczynaki et al., 2017). With high percentages of depression, anxiety, and suicide ideation, it is imperative to assist college campuses in intervening in the current mental health crisis (Rafal et al., 2018). How can campuses prepare a safety net of non-clinical mental health support to best assist students?

The purpose of this action research study was to enhance the skills and confidence of graduate students in student affairs master's programs in the area of mental health literacy. Specifically, this focused on addressing mental health impacts through the training of non-clinical college/university staff (known as the field of student affairs) during their master's programs. This population of front-line practitioners must gain literacy, skills, and knowledge which are crucially needed.

Use of mental health literacy assists in framing this problem. Mental health literacy focuses on elements that, if known, would improve individual mental well-being and reduce community impacts of mental illness (Spiker & Hammer, 2019). Ultimately, mental health literacy can provide a powerful tool for non-clinicians in addressing mental health issues on college campuses.

BACKGROUND AND CONTEXT

Mental health literacy has been found to be an effective measure of community health and a method for intervention. Elements of mental health literacy include problem-recognition, professional help and effective treatment, self-help strategies, and mental health support (Jorm et al., 2006).

Application of Mental Health Literacy

Studies confirm that the use of mental health literacy concepts can result in lessening of mental health impacts in the adolescent population (Attygalle et al., 2017; Gorczynski et al., 2017; Lubman et al., 2017; Skre et al., 2013). Successful application of mental health literacy allows for the measurement of mental health knowledge and help-seeking behavior. It creates a common language and set of concepts to compare populations and understand mental health impacts. Ultimately, gauging and helping to increase the level of mental health literacy in adolescents can be accomplished. Gorczynski et al. (2017) found a general lack of sufficient mental health literacy among college students. This low level of mental health literacy is coupled with high mental health impact. These findings illustrate that many students are struggling.

In addressing the mental health literacy of college students, focus on increasing help-seeking behavior as well as lowering stigma around mental health treatment are paramount. Jorm (2012) notes that help-seeking behavior is sometimes needed in order to maintain or restore mental well-being. Ultimately, knowledge of resources as well as positive attitudes toward help-seeking yield better long-term outcomes for individuals (Jorm, 2012).

Research identified obstacles to help-seeking in college populations. These included self-reliance and embarrassment (Lubman et al., 2017), being unsure of when to seek help (Gagnon et al., 2017), stigma (Fröjd et al., 2007), and lack of problem recognition (Coles & Coleman, 2010). These findings point to a need for basic problem identification and work related to reducing negative perceptions, or stigma, around mental health on campus. If stigma can be lowered, college students will be more likely to seek help when an issue is emerging and before it becomes severe.

With mental health concerns come an inherent risk of suicide ideation or action. Literature found various campus implications for preventing suicide. Burns and Rapee (2006), found a lack of mental health professional referrals for those experiencing signs of suicide ideation. Cukrowicz et al. (2011) found that there exists a level of suicidal ideation in those with subclinical depression (Cukrowicz et al., 2011). This means that potential suicidal students are not at the level of being diagnosed with depression but are still in danger. Awareness of the signs and symptoms of depression become paramount in identifying those in need of intervention.

College campuses should be mindful of populations at high risk for negative mental health impacts. Literature points to specific sub-populations with increased risk of negative consequences, including suicide. These populations include racial/ethnic minorities (Cheng et al., 2013; Horwitz et al., 2020), gender/sexual minorities (Canady, 2019), male students (Goodwill & Zhou, 2020), and traditional-aged college students (Goodwill & Zhou, 2020).

The Importance of Student Affairs in Addressing Campus Mental Health Needs

Multiple studies provide insight into addressing mental health on college campuses. Reynolds and Altabef (2015) note the growing amount of mental health concerns on campus. They state that support for students in distress must not belong solely to counseling centers (Reynolds & Altabef, 2015). Gorczynaki et al. (2017) note the inability of college counseling centers to keep up with increasing mental health demands. Reavley et al. (2014) note educational institutions as valuable, unique locals for preventing and intervening in mental health problems. Reynolds and Atlabef (2015) claim student affairs as an important partner in addressing growing mental health concerns.

The concept of mental health literacy can be applied to non-clinical staff on college campuses. Identifying and specifically training on concepts of mental health literacy can arm college campuses with a broad workforce ready to help students without solely relying on counseling professionals.

Currently, there is a need for updated training around mental health issues in student affairs preparation programs. Reynolds and Altabef (2015) state that

> given the growing awareness of college student mental health concerns ... and the limited attention they receive in preparation program courses, more work is needed to ensure that newly trained student affairs professionals are effectively prepared to respond to such challenging issues. (p. 230)

Student affairs graduate preparation programs become a potential starting point for spreading mental health literacy on college campuses.

METHODS

Multiple research sites were utilized for this study. Cycle 1 research took place with 11 large, public universities across the United States. Cycle 2 research took place at one large, public, research university located in the Northeastern United States.

Participants

Cycle 1 consisted of individual interviews with 11 student affairs program faculty across the nation. Selection criteria included current teaching faculty in student affairs programs at large, public universities in the United States. Participants were from six geographic regions across the United States: the Northeast, the South, the Midwest, the West Coast, the Southwest, and the Northwest. Participants were 2/3 male. There was an even mix of new to moderate faculty experience (1–9 years) mixed with extensive faculty experience (10–20 years).

Cycle 2 consisted of a collaborative learning community at one institution's master's program. Participants at the Cycle 2 site included (a) teaching faculty in the student affairs preparation program, (b) student affairs practicum/assistantship supervisors at the site, and (c) mental health experts. Targeted recruitment through campus project leads yielded 10 participants, selected through their roles on campus and ties to the subject of the study.

Data Collection

Online interviews were used in Cycle 1 to set the stage for the Cycle 2 action step. Cycle 1 themes were used to identify common skills and knowledge desired in the graduate student population; frame the desired roles related to mental health assistance, as well as the limitations of non-clinical roles; and identify needed competence areas that are currently not addressed in these programs.

Cycle 2 research culminated in a collaborative learning community (CLC) at one university and the creation of an ideal curricular and co-curricular model for that graduate program. Anderson (2013) describes CLC as places for shared ownership and transformative dialogue. The CLC model was identified as the culminating location for exploring, discussing, planning, implementing, and evaluating mental health educational opportunities for graduate students. Participants were viewed as experts in their work and potential collaborators for future work around the topic. Analysis resulted in specific desired skills, knowledge, and practice of graduate students.

Data Analysis

Cycle 1 Results

Four major findings resulted from analysis of the interview transcripts with faculty members. The four findings included a lack of awareness of mental health literacy, the importance of aligning foundation courses to practice, the need to better prepare students in mental health areas, and the desire to update their programs through integration of mental health literacy concepts.

Participant 8 linked her lack of awareness of important mental health information to a need for future practitioners to get "language for that . . . if they run into something new, they have the capacity to make sense of it." Participant 8's sentiments were shared by all interviewees.

Participant 9 spoke of the need to tie student development theory courses to actual practice, "giving them opportunities to gain practical skills and then to engage with students in concrete ways" (Participant 9). Thus, applying foundational courses to practice is important for developing the appropriate student affairs core.

Many participants spoke about graduates as underprepared practitioners. Participant 1 stated, "Grad students are really dealing with a lot of mental health concerns . . . and I don't know that they always feel equipped . . . they don't feel prepared to have a conversation or how to approach the situation." Participant 3 discussed the need for graduate programs to better prepare their students around mental health.

> I think there are certain types of things that get lost that we should try to help them better work on. For example, I don't have a good sense of how our

students are leaving the program with particular types of what I would call helping skills. (Participant 3)

All participants shared a desire to update their graduate program around mental health literacy.

This finding included items needed to address mental health specifically. These were broken into six areas: essential knowledge needed around mental health and wellness, essential skills needed around mental health and wellness, various lenses that impact how one reacts to mental health issues, appropriate roles of new practitioners in the field, the importance of practice in the graduate student experience, and thoughts on the ideal design of a master's preparation program to address mental health literacy. For example, one important lens shared by research participants is the use of a justice framework. Participant 2 discussed embedding a framework of justice to student wellness. He stated that there are "implicit biases that people bring based upon the narratives around mental illness . . . we want to ensure a just outcome and a fully humanizing experience for all students." The use of lenses allows for additional knowledge and application to be discussed with graduate students.

Cycle 1 takeaways included focus on graduate student education and practice, that this research is needed and important, and the questioning of the appropriate role of student affairs practitioners in addressing mental health as non-clinicians. The idea of mental health integration throughout the curriculum can be found in all interviews.

The use of mental health literacy helped participants in framing their mental health and wellness concerns. It gave a common language by which to view program curriculum or lack of curriculum. Positive reaction to the concept of mental health literacy resulted in adoption of an overarching mental health literacy framework for Cycle 2 research. It also confirmed that mental health literacy is not currently covered in master's programs, and that program change is warranted.

Cycle 2 Action Step

One institution from Cycle 1 was selected as the site for the Cycle 2 action step. This took place through a CLC to discuss and develop educational enhancement opportunities for graduate students.

Research objectives included (a) utilizing the collaborative learning community environment, (b) identifying problematic mental health impacts and developing strategies to address these through the use of a mental health content expert from the JED Foundation, (c) utilizing student affairs practitioners to develop educational enhancement for use in the practicum/assistantship/internship setting, (d) utilizing student affairs teaching faculty to develop educational enhancements for their graduate students, and (e) combining the expertise of both areas to create a synergistic learning opportunity for graduate students.

Success of the CLC was measured through specific participant outcomes. These outcomes evolved from Cycle 1 findings and included (a) knowledge of mental health literacy, (b) awareness of the impact of mental health concerns at the host institution and in the undergraduate student population in general, (c) empowerment to take action to alleviate mental health concerns, and (d) confidence in addressing mental health concerns in a nonclinical way. Specifically, the work of the CLC was intended to positively impact the host institution by providing resources and strategies for their use. The resulting educational enhancement of graduate students was intended to positively support their development as emerging student affairs practitioners and their future work with undergraduate students.

Cycle 2 Results

Collaborative learning Community members were invited to participate using purposeful sampling. Participants were asked to share their experiences, expertise, and personal understanding of the phenomena at five online CLC meetings. Meetings 3 and 4 were separated into faculty and staff. Discussion and consensus were used to identify issues of concern around mental health and to create a pilot educational enhancement for graduate students. Ultimately, a pilot model for curricular/co-curricular education was created for Fall 2021 implementation at this site.

After analyzing the transcripts from CLC meetings and individual evaluation interviews, three findings emerged specifically, the importance of addressing mental health on college campuses, the value of CLC as a process for problem identification and solutions generation, and the effectiveness of outcomes of the CLC process. The three overarching findings are described below.

Addressing mental health on campus was noted by all as needing entire campus engagement. Participant 7 echoed themes that resonated throughout the interviews:

> Anymore, the whole campus has to pitch in. And that's where the change is. I don't want to view it from a deficit perspective, "Well, why don't we do this? We've been ignoring this issue. I just think it's heightened in such importance, now more than ever before. And the structure we have on most campuses, just can't work."

Thus, realizing that change is needed to adequately address the emerging mental health crises is the start of this work.

The finding on the value of CLC included participant reflection on the CLC process itself, thoughts around potential practice/field application, and potential curriculum/class application. This finding takes the need to address mental health on campus and focuses on this need through a lens of potential solution application. Participants found the thought process built into the framework helpful for problem identification and solution generation. This involved taking a step back from everyday issues, brainstorming together, thinking about the bigger picture, diving deep, and letting the importance of the issue speak for itself. Participant 9 shared, "I think this whole opportunity, to think about many layers that need to be in place to make a successful series of learning objectives for the students, is great." This was put another way by Participant 5, "You forced us to sort of sit down and look at it and dissect things, deconstruct it to see how best to put it back together." This CLC process, which utilized the specific ideas of faculty and student affairs field supervisors, provided a synergistic opportunity for problem solving.

The positive and substantive CLC outcomes finding included participant reflection on impact and effectiveness, desired content, and the overall outcomes.

Based on these findings, student affairs pilot elements for implementation were identified for professional development committees, student affairs supervisors, and graduate student learning groups. Faculty pilot elements identified for implementation included short-, medium-, and long-term actions.

Professional development committees will be given a guiding document developed by the CLC team with notes, resources, strategies, and considerations. Student affairs supervisors will be given a module for applying mental health literacy into their work with higher education administration graduate students. Graduate student learning groups who work for these supervisors will have a debriefing group to explore their own mental health, mental health literacy, and appropriate skills for working with students around mental health. Exercises will include journaling, self-assessment, discussion, and guest lecturers.

In the short-term, faculty will incorporate mental health into current class case studies, scenarios, guest lecturers, or discussion prompts; raise awareness of mental health literacy/mental health impacts within college programs; conduct a student needs survey for graduate students in the higher education administration program.

In the medium-term, faculty professional development programs will address mental health literacy; faculty will pilot a special topics course on mental health; and faculty will embed mental health in their courses. In the long-term, based on professional development programs and assessment of the special topics course and integration of mental health within their courses, the curriculum will be revised and updated.

DISCUSSION

Four findings stood out when looking at the data through the lens of literature. These include (a) the effectiveness of mental health literacy, (b) the need for high-risk population awareness, (c) the synergy of using a practice and theory combination, and (d) that the role of student affairs staff in working with mental health issues needs to be redefined.

Finding 1: Effectiveness of Mental Health Literacy

A foundation of mental health literacy will effectively impact college student mental health needs. This study finding supports literature from psychology and counseling journals. This includes Jorm's (Jorm, 2012; Jorm et al., 2006) seminal work as well as multiple others supporting and furthering the study of mental health literacy in the adolescent population.

Both literature and research participants support the finding that a foundation of mental health literacy will effectively impact college student mental health needs. This confirms literature on the use of mental health literacy elements to result in lessening of mental health impacts in the adolescent/college-aged population (Attygalle et al., 2017; Burns & Rapee, 2006; Fröjd et al., 2007; Gorczynski et al., 2017; Lubman et al., 2017; Skre et al., 2013; Yarcheski et al., 2011). Spiker and Hammer (2019) concur and share that mental health literacy can improve the compounding effects of mental health issues overall.

This study resulted in participant consensus on the importance of including mental health literacy in their work with graduate students. Having this baseline of knowledge was seen as paramount, as the mental health impacts of the COVID-19 pandemic could raise mental health concerns on campus exponentially. Study findings are consistent with Jorm's (2012) elements of mental health literacy.

Participants identified problem recognition and help-seeking as important areas of knowledge to ground graduate students' work. Problem recognition and help-seeking benefits include identifying the problem at hand, reduced delay in help-seeking, reduction in poorer outcomes, and reduction in long-term severity of mental health issues (Jorm, 2012).

Participants confirmed findings in the literature on the importance of getting students to effective professional help. Professional help and effective treatment benefits include stigma reduction, increased help-seeking beyond informal sources, an increase in effective treatment, and increased recovery of those who experience mental health issues (Jorm, 2012).

Participants in both research cycles confirmed the importance of self-care for students. This confirms the literature which notes that mild symptoms and ongoing maintenance can be addressed through supportive means (Jorm, 2012). Noted self-help strategy benefits include maintenance of well-being, view of strategies as positive and more acceptable, and decreased severity of mental health outcomes (Jorm, 2012).

Mental health support benefits include increased ability to help self and others, increased professional help-seeking, increased openness about mental health, and stigma reduction (Jorm, 2012). Participants noted the importance of similar components to the literature including ongoing social support, encouragement, and openness about mental health to lessen help-seeking stigma. This component confirms that educating people on risk factors and early warning signs arms them with tools and talking points for when they notice someone becoming unwell (Jorm, 2012). Participants confirmed the importance of prevention as they discussed the context of need. They confer that this element of mental health literacy is a needed and effective piece of addressing mental health on campus.

Finding 2: High-Risk Population Awareness

The negative mental health impacts of high-risk groups are so severe that they must be focused on intentionally and separately beyond the main concepts of mental health literacy. This finding supports literature on the ways in which specific populations are at higher risk for suicide and other negative mental health impacts. Participants identified trauma-informed care as the way to best address diverse student populations around mental health.

Participants noted the potential negative mental health of racial/ethnic minority students given the events of 2020 and ongoing racial trauma. Racial and ethnic minority students are considered to be at high-risk for mental health impacts throughout the literature (Cheng et al., 2018; Horwitz et al., 2020; Lipson et al., 2018).

Literature identifies extreme risk for gender minority and sexual minority students. Canady (2019) confirms the high risk of this population by noting three to four times the presence of suicide ideation, plans, and attempts, two times the level of depression, anxiety, non-suicidal self-injury, and eating disorder rates, higher lifetime suicide rates, and that transgender students are four times more likely to experience mental health problems overall.

The potential fit of trauma-informed care practices for work with student mental health was found in both Cycle 1 and Cycle 2 data. Specifically, it came up as a possible lens to view work with students as well as a method for addressing racial trauma and diversity issues. Thus, trauma-informed care becomes a skill for student affairs grads that extends beyond mental health literacy, while assisting in increasing mental health literacy at the same time.

Finding 3: Synergy of Theory and Practice Combination

Student affairs master's programs should utilize a theory and practice combination to effectively prepare graduate students for mental health support. Participants spoke often about the use of both a knowledge-based and practical application approaches with graduate students.

Recommended graduate student preparation in the theory component includes areas of knowledge as well as methods for imparting that knowledge. Participants confirmed support for Pinto-Foltz et al. (2011), who highlighted a need for long-term, ongoing education as well as personal reflection in learning mental health literacy. Literature mirrors this study's discussion of the importance of graduate student reflection and processing and a need to remain flexible in delivery.

Recommended graduate student preparation in the practice component includes applying knowledge to practice and developing desired skills. This finding supports Young (2019), who discussed the importance of supervised practice in student affairs preparation programs. Ultimately, this finding supports the importance of practicing to build skills and confidence.

Reynolds and Altabef (2015) point out the need for updated training around mental health issues in student affairs preparation programs. This study supports this through a combination of theory and practice approaches.

Finding 4: Redefining Roles

The role of student affairs professionals in providing non-clinical mental health support needs to be discussed and redefined as a whole. The focus of this study is graduate students; however, this role must be agreed upon and expanded by the field for this work to be impactful.

This study showed an acute awareness that student affairs practitioners are not mental health professionals. However, this is combined with the notion that the entire campus must engage in supporting student mental health. Ultimately, this finding is based on the notion that student affairs practitioners must change their traditional pattern on not engaging with students around mental health issues. The field must identify appropriate methods to engage in non-clinical/non-crisis support.

CONCLUSION

Research findings include the effectiveness of a foundation of mental health literacy, needed understanding and support of high-risk populations, recommended graduate student preparation, and a need to redefine roles of Student Affairs practitioners around mental health support. The overarching conclusion is that the field of student affairs must redefine its role around non-clinical mental health support. This should be done by integrating a theory/practice approach founded in mental health literacy into master's preparation programs.

Implications

This pilot provides methods for applying mental health literacy to non-clinical mental health support on college campuses. When graduate students are provided a curriculum based in mental health literacy, and ways to practice needed skills around this, they will be better prepared to address mental health issues of students they will work with throughout their careers.

Two overall implications tie directly to practitioners in student affairs. These are the notion of non-clinical mental health support and the use of trauma-informed care practices. The traditional view of student affairs staff addressing mental health concerns, is one of "I am not qualified, here is a referral to counseling." The updated notion of non-clinical mental health support shows that staff can support students in many ways outside of crisis counseling and diagnosis. Ultimately, there is a middle ground for non-clinical mental health support that lies between the practitioner and the counseling center. In this, mental health literacy is a ready and effective framework.

High-risk populations should be a consideration in response planning. The use of trauma-informed care can provide supportive environments for all students. If students can openly discuss issues that are less severe, learn that they are treatable, and feel support for help-seeking behavior, they will be more likely to take care of emerging issues before they become severe.

The main takeaway for practitioners is empowerment to address mental health issues as non-clinicians. This project exemplifies a starting point and resources to assist individual practitioners in this work. Specific information on components of mental health literacy and data from the literature ground potential action in a proven and effective way. Ultimately, practitioners can use this study for its resources and approach in working with others and for its content and resources in applying those to individual practice.

FUTURE RESEARCH

Trauma-informed care has been found successful in working with diverse populations and cultural backgrounds. According to Carello and Butler (2015), a trauma-informed approach focuses on understanding where someone is coming from and "applying that understanding to design of systems and provisions of services so they accommodate trauma survivors' needs and are consonant with healing and recovery" (Carello & Butler, 2015, p. 264). Trauma-informed care should be further explored as a vehicle to accommodate mental health discussions on college campuses. Specifically, what are examples that practitioners can use in everyday interactions with students?

An ongoing use of mental health literacy and the measuring of its impact on college campuses can have many impacts. This includes continued expansion of student affairs roles in addressing mental health impacts. It can also build a repository of known and effective training and interventions. Ultimately, further research can continue to empower change around non-clinical mental health support. This can be done in a way that lessens mental health impacts on college campuses.

REFERENCES

Anderson, H. (2013). Collaborative learning communities: A postmodern perspective on teaching and learning. In B. Irby, G. H. Brown, R. LaraAiecio, & S. Jackson (Eds.), *Handbook of Educational Theories* (pp. 515–547). Information Age Publishing.

Attygalle, U. R., Perera, H., & Jayamanne, B. D. W. (2017). Mental health literacy in adolescents: Ability to recognise problems, helpful interventions and outcomes. *Child and Adolescent Psychiatry and Mental Health, 11*(1), Article 38. https://doi.org/10.1186/s13034-017-0176-1

Burns, J. R., & Rapee, R. M. (2006). Adolescent mental health literacy: Young people's knowledge of depression and help seeking. *Journal of Adolescence, 29*(2), 225–239. https://doi.org/10.1016/j.adolescence.2005.05.004

Canady, V. (2019). Gender-minority students face large mental health disparities. *Mental Health Weekly, 29*(33), 5–6. https://doi.org/10.1002/mhw.32035

Carello, J., & Butler, L. D. (2015). Practicing what we teach: Trauma-informed educational practice. *Journal of Teaching in Social Work, 35*(3), 262–278. https://doi.org/10.1080/08841233.2015.1030059

Cheng, H., Kwan, K. Karl, & Sevig, T. (2013). Racial and ethnic minority college students' stigma associated with seeking psychological help. *Journal of Counseling Psychology, 60*(1), 98–111. https://doi.org/10.1037/a0031169

Cheng, H., Wang, C., Mcdermott, R. C., Kridel, M., & Rislin, J. L. (2018). Self-Stigma, mental health literacy, and attitudes toward seeking psychological help.

Journal of Counseling & Development, 96(1), 64–74. https://doi.org/10.1002/jcad.12178

Coles, M. E., & Coleman, S. L. (2010). Barriers to treatment seeking for anxiety disorders: Initial data on the role of mental health literacy. *Depression and Anxiety, 27*(1), 63–71. https://doi.org/10.1002/da.20620

Cukrowicz, K. C., Schlegel, E. F., Smith, P. N., Jacobs, N. P., Van Orden, K. A., Paukert, A. L, Pettit, J. W., & Joiner, T. E. (2011). Suicide ideation among college students evidencing subclinical depression. *Journal of American College Health, 59*(7), 575–581. https://doi.org/10.1080/07448481.2010.483710

Fröjd, S., Marttunen, M., Pelkonen, M., Pahlen, B., & Kaltiala-Heino, R. (2007). Adult and peer involvement in help-seeking for depression in adolescent population. *Social Psychiatry and Psychiatric Epidemiology, 42*(12), 945–952. https://doi.org/10.1007/s00127-007-0254-4

Gagnon, M. M., Gelinas, B. L., & Friesen, L. N. (2017). Mental health literacy in emerging adults in a university setting: Distinctions between symptom awareness and appraisal. *Journal of Adolescent Research, 32*(5), 642–664. https://doi.org/10.1177/0743558415605383

Goodwill, J., & Zhou, S. (2020). Association between perceived public stigma and suicidal behaviors among college students of color in the U.S. *Journal of Affective Disorders, 262*(1), 1–7. https://doi.org/10.1016/j.jad.2019.10.019

Gorczynski, P., Sims-Schouten, W., Hill, D., & Wilson, J. C. (2017). Examining mental health literacy, help-seeking behaviours, and mental health outcomes in UK university students. *The Journal of Mental Health Training, Education and Practice, 12*(2), 111–120. https://doi.org/10.1108/JMHTEP-05-2016-0027

Horwitz, A., Mcguire, T., Busby, D., Eisenberg, D., Zheng, K., Pistorello, J., Albucher, R., Coreyell, W., & King, C. A. (2020). Sociodemographic differences in barriers to mental health care among college students at elevated suicide risk. *Journal of Affective Disorders, 271*(1), 123–130. https://doi.org/10.1016/j.jad.2020.03.115

Jorm, A. F. (2012). Mental health literacy: Empowering the community to take action for better mental health. *American Psychologist, 67*(3), 231–243. https://doi.org/10.1037/a0025957

Jorm, A. F., Barney, L. J., Christensen, H., Highet, N. J., Kelly, C. M, & Kitchener, B. A. (2006). Research on mental health literacy: What we know and what we still need to know. *Australian and New Zealand Journal of Psychiatry, 40*(1), 3–5. https://doi.org/10.1080/j.1440-1614.2006.01734.x

Lipson, S., Kern, A., Eisenberg, D., & Breland-Noble, A. (2018). Mental health disparities among college students of color. *Journal of Adolescent Health, 63*(3), 348–356. https://doi.org/10.1016/j.jadohealth.2018.04.014

Lubman, D. I., Cheetham, A., Jorm, A. F., Berridge, B. J., Wilson, C., Blee, F., & Proimos, J. (2017). Australian adolescents' beliefs and help-seeking intentions towards peers experiencing symptoms of depression and alcohol misuse. *BMC Public Health, 17*(1). https://doi.org/10.1186/s12889-017-4655-3

Pinto-Foltz, M., Logsdon, M. C., & Myers, J. A. (2011). Feasibility, acceptability, and initial efficacy of a knowledge-contact program to reduce mental illness stigma and improve mental health literacy in adolescents. *Social Science & Medicine, 72*(12), 2011–2019. https://doi.org/10.1016/j.socscimed.2011.04.006

Rafal, G., Gatto, A., & Debate, R. (2018). Mental health literacy, stigma, and help-seeking behaviors among male college students. *Journal of American College Health, 66*(4), 1–8. https://doi.org/10.1080/07448481.2018.1434780

Reavley, N., McCann, T., Cvetkovski, S., & Jorm, A. (2014). A multifaceted intervention to improve mental health literacy in students of a multicampus university: A cluster randomised trial. *Social Psychiatry and Psychiatric Epidemiology, 49*(10), 1655–1666. https://doi.org/10.1007/s00127-014-0880-6

Reynolds, A. L., & Altabef, D. (2015). Addressing helping competencies in student affairs: Analysis of helping skills course syllabi. *Journal of Student Affairs Research and Practice, 52*(2), 220–231. https://doi.org/10.1080/19496591.2015.1018268

Skre, I., Friborg, O., Breivik, C., Johnsen, L. I., Arnesen, Y., & Wang, C. E. A. (2013). A school intervention for mental health literacy in adolescents: Effects of a non-randomized cluster controlled trial. *BMC Public Health, 13*, Article 873. https://doi.org/10.1186/1471-2458-13-873

Spiker, D. A., & Hammer, J. H. (2019). Mental health literacy as theory: Current challenges and future directions. *Journal of Mental Health, 28*(3), 238–242. https://doi.org/10.1080/09638237.2018.1437613

Yarcheski, A., Yarcheski T., & Mahon, N. (2011). Stress, hope, and loneliness in young adolescents. *Psychological Reports, 108*(3), 919–922. https://doi.org/10.2466/02.07.09.PR0.108.3.919-922

Young, D. G. (2019). Supervised practice experiences and professional preparation of graduates from student affairs master's programs. *Journal of College Student Development, 60*(3), 290–306. https://doi.org/10.1353/csd.2019.0027

CHAPTER 7

A STUDENT CENTERED APPROACH

Using Systems Theory to Improve Community Engagement and Belonging

Joseph Castelot

The student center on many college campuses serves as the center of campus community. Its primary function is to serve the student population through various resources, support, and programs, and is designed to help students succeed academically, socially, and in preparing for their life outside of college by providing educational opportunities focused on student leadership and building community. Just as every college campus is different from the next, each student center functions and is structured differently.

Using the student center as a sample of the campus community, this research sought to understand how engagement with the student center shapes a student's sense of community and belonging. With each area serving a different audience, the relationship among the parts is the opportunity for students to engage with and see how their contributions are valued

Taking Action, pages 103–117
Copyright © 2024 by Information Age Publishing
www.infoagepub.com
All rights of reproduction in any form reserved.

by the overall student center community, and in turn, develop a sense of belonging at the institution.

The student center in this study is lacking a cohesive community. Each department or organization supports a different population, resulting in engagement being limited to individual organization membership and students representing one aspect of their identity at a time. The founding principle of this student center was to support students of all walks of life, with no limiting factors such as financial status or athletic ability, circumstances that limited social life for the student center donor. As the demand for the student center increased, so did the available space. From one building to two buildings, to its current iteration of multiple facilities, the student center has adapted to the needs of the student population.

BACKGROUND AND CONTEXT

The student center, or student union, is a building or set of buildings on a college campus that houses resources primarily intended for students in supporting the educational mission of the college outside of academics. It is a place that focuses on student engagement through student support staff, programs, events, programs, and social spaces. Student engagement is the time and effort students put in to have meaningful interactions with the staff, students, resources, and programs that make up the student center.

Finding community on a college campus is one of the most impactful experiences a student will have in their academic career, including being the deciding factor for if a student decides to stay at a college or university (Tinto, 2012). As colleges continue to provide additional resources to adapt to a more diverse population, many areas of campus are beginning to work in silos. Students are finding communities, but that does not mean they feel valued and respected as part of the overall campus community (Cheng, 2004). This comes at a time when college administrators are looking for ways to engage their campus communities, especially those in underrepresented populations.

Student center spaces are highly desired on college campuses, but have specific expectations to meet, specifically the needs of the student population, and even more specific, the needs of students whose needs are not being met elsewhere. The student center is not just another building on campus, but it could easily be turned into one if the community is not tended to. Increasing engagement with the student center community strengthens the student voice by uniting individual student experiences under a singular student center community. Students wouldn't be limited to engaging with individual departments but have them serve as entry points to the other student center experiences. The result is a student population that has a willingness to engage with the community, utilizes resources housed within student center spaces, has a stronger sense of belonging to the overall institution, and further engages in educational experiences (Kuh, 1995). Community, belonging, and engagement are all interlocked when it comes to the student experience on a college campus, each one strengthening the others.

As for the student center community, that has expanded as well. Being the first space on campus without fees associated, a specific skill set needed, or academic criteria, the student center became the administrative support for students focused on multiculturalism, well-being, and other student experiences outside the classroom. As the institution expanded its support for these areas by creating departments and hiring staff, the direct connection with the student center was severed. The various populations that made up the student center communities became their own individual communities, focusing on supporting their own population with their own identity. Subcultures often develop because students are not represented in the overall culture of the community (Harper, 2008; Quaye & Harper, 2015). These subcultures within this student center are representative of student life on campus, but not representative when it comes to engagement with the student center community.

Theoretical Framework

A systems theory approach informed the design of this study, looking at the student center as a system rather than individual parts. This student center has all its parts, but they are not working together. Russell Ackoff (1971) encourages us to look at each individual part and how they work together, understanding the separate parts of an organization working together produce a much greater product. "In an imperfectly organized system even if every part performs as well as possible relative to its own objectives, the total system will often not perform as well as possible relative to its objectives" (Ackoff, 1971, p. 661).

Ernest Boyer's (1990) six principles of community and the National Survey of Student Engagement ([NSSE], 2015) engagement indicators were used to inform the action step, along with how each participant's experience shapes their perception of community within the student center. A systems theory lens looks at these experiences as the relationship each participant has with the student center, forming a sense of community, or lack thereof. Engagement in outside the classroom experiences contributes to a student's sense of community and belonging (Elkins et al., 2011), and the student center is the center of campus community (Smyth, 2016). With each area serving a specific audience, engagement with the student center community is the opportunity for students to see how their contributions are valued by the campus community.

METHODS

The research site is a small, private, 4-year institution of higher education in the Northeast region of the United States. The institution has a long history that predates student affairs practices that shape life on college campuses today. This research study focused on the student center community and how engagement with the various departments, student organizations, and programs contributes to a student's sense of community and belonging.

The student center in this study is made up of several departments that support various aspects of student life. The departments focused on throughout this study support student organizations and programs; Greek life, multicultural advising, Native American programs advising, outdoor programs advising, student activities, student center operations, and student wellness. Excluded from this study were departments that do not advise or support student organizations, or support activities that occur primarily outside of the student center.

Cycle 1 data was collected through interviews with nine participants. The participants in Cycle 1 were students involved in the student center through various offices housed in the physical plant of the student center, representing four student center programming and advising offices. Participant 9 described two involvements, but within two separate buildings of the student center spaces. Seven out of the nine participants in Cycle 1 were members of Greek letter organizations, but none connected their Greek letter experience with the student center.

Cycle 2 had 11 participants during the action step, with nine of those 11 participants participating in the data collection process, representing six departments. Cycle 2 data was collected through a survey and interviews with nine participants. The participants for Cycle 2 were all students or recent graduates who were engaged in departmental or student organization programming within the student center.

To meet recruitment goals, purposeful sampling was used in both Cycles 1 and 2. Student organization advisors were given the requirements for participants, including that the students should be leaders in organizations and have been involved in programming, events, or leadership positions in the student center. All participants had completed at least 1 year at the research site institution and were at least 18 years of age.

Action research methodology was chosen due to the goal of shifting the perception of community, engagement, and belonging that needs to be done over time and through multiple iterations. The continuous cycles of receiving information, incorporating change, collecting information, analyzing it, and planning for the next iteration is critical to creating cultural shifts. Understanding the student center community through the experiences of students falls within qualitative analysis but making changes to those experiences and analyzing them is action research. "Action research seeks to develop and maintain social and personal interactions that are non-exploitative and enhance the social and emotional lives of all people who participate" (Stringer, 2013, p. 23). Stringer discusses relationships, communication, participation, and inclusion as the principles that researchers should use to formulate their action research methodology.

CYCLE 1 RESULTS

The data shows the experiences of students engaged in the student center are different depending on the student center department they are engaged in. Table 7.1 shows each participant's experience with the student center. These experiences are represented through the themes that emerged during the data analysis process. Sense of community was the centralized

TABLE 7.1	Themes Compared With Interview Answers									
Participant	Main Involvement	Staff Engagement	Staff Communication	Reason for Engagement	Support	Identity Represented	Sense of Responsibility	Celebration of Community	Student Center Community
1	Multicultural Advising	−	−	Events	Peer	+	+	−	−
2	Governing Board	+	+	People	Staff and Peer	+	+	−	+
3	Governing Board	−	+	People and Facilities	Peer	+	+	−	+
4	Student Activities	+	−	People	Staff	+	+	−	+
5	Student Activities	+	+	People	Staff	+	+	−	+
6	Governing Board	+	+	People	Peer	+	+	+	+
7	Student Activities	+	−	Facilities and Events	Staff	+	+	−	−
8	Student Activities	+	+	People	Staff and Peer	+	−	−	−
9	Multicultural Advising/Wellness	+	−	Events	Staff and Peer	+	−	−	−

Note: +Indicates a positive response; − Indicates a negative response.

theme that was the result of the combined experiences. The themes of staff community engagement, peer networks, identity represented, and sense of responsibility contribute to the participants' sense of community in the student center.

Sense of community represents the times when the participants spoke of being members of the student center community and times when the participants spoke of the lack of or being an outsider to the community. Some participants spoke of the community as a single entity, all the separate pieces working together, while others felt that there was not a singular community, and that the separate pieces were their own individual communities. "There isn't one standard [student center] community, and I think it would be a mistake to call it that... I think that there are distinct subcultures inside of [the student center] and distinct ways that someone would identify their involvement" (Participant 7, personal communication, 2019). This is not necessarily a bad thing as individual parts can provide an entry point into the community.

Staff are frequently members of the community longer than the students are, sometimes being the first connection students have to the overall community and playing a part in creating social norms.

> Yes, we need the closet for physical storage things, but we also need our staff advisor and complain in his office and take naps on his couch to grow that community to make us function better as an organization, and I think he would see similar things throughout basically every group that uses (the student center) as a space. (Participant 7, personal communication, 2019)

Staff community engagement emerged having three subthemes: inconsistent staff engagement with students regarding community, interdepartmental communication among staff members in the student center, and staff being a support system for the students. These three parts are important because they show how the participants perceive the staff members' level of engagement with the community.

Peer Networks shows how participants interact with their peers regarding the student center community. Peer networks are important to a student's sense of community, engagement, and sense of belonging. This theme demonstrates how the participants view their interactions and their perception of support from their fellow students.

All participants could see their own work reflected, or at the very least associate part of their identity in the programs and events that happen at the student center. Almost all participants spoke of experiences that touched upon identity in broad strokes, but one differed slightly in their experience when it comes to representation, speaking about the issue in providing opportunities for the majority populations.

I think some of the criticisms that I've heard from my friends is that it's too broad. It feels kind of fake because it's like, just because you're a woman and I'm a woman doesn't make me connect with you. Right? Or just because you're like...Asia is huge. Just because you are Asian and I'm Asian means nothing to me. Stuff like that. (Participant 9, personal communication, 2019)

While all participants could see part of their identity represented, it doesn't necessarily mean it is representative of campus or encompassing their full identity. A lack of engagement could mean certain identities, or groups within those identities, are not being represented.

Most of the participants felt a sense of responsibility to the student center. Sense of responsibility is not a cause for engagement but serves as an indicator for potential engagement, indicating a person's willingness to engage with the community. It can be easy for students to continually take from the resources provided by the student center, so there must be opportunities to capitalize on those with a sense of responsibility to give back to the community.

Each of these themes are opportunities to increase engagement, and over time, strengthen the students' sense of community within the student center. While cultural shifts take time to develop, a combination of these themes was used to develop the action step as part of Cycle 2.

INTRODUCTION TO CYCLE 2

The action step focused on three things: student engagement, sense of community in the student center, and sense of belonging on campus. The participants took part in a student engagement project that created an introduction to the student center for new students, designed to increase engagement with the student center, while also increasing their knowledge of the student center, to better understand how it contributes to a student's sense of community and belonging within the student center and on campus. The action step consisted of four 1-hour meetings that took place over the course of a few weeks.

The action step was planned to align with orientation planning at the research site, but due to the COVID-19 pandemic, the plans for fall term and orientation were not finalized in time for the action step to take place at that time. The action step was delayed until after the fall term had occurred.

For the Cycle 2 data collection process, participants were asked to complete a survey and participate in an interview after the action step was completed. The survey was administered to evaluate the effectiveness of the individual activities that took place during the four meetings. The interviews were designed to better understand the experience participants had during the overall process of creating an introduction to the student center.

CYCLE 2 RESULTS

As the data was consolidated, five themes emerged: perception of the student center community, sense of belonging on campus, and increased engagement. Several subthemes emerged contributing to these themes: student center identity, building relationships, inclusivity and representation, reflective of student experience, staff investment in the community, resources, and programs.

Perception of the Student Center Community

Community emerged in many of the answers across the interviews, but in the survey, it was mentioned that experiences where students from all areas of the student center were involved, were rare.

For many participants, the action step created a shift in the understanding of the student center community, who is part of the community, and their ability to work with them. Perception of the student center community is built upon the identity of the student center, the relationships that develop over time, and how the various experiences are represented.

Sense of Belonging on Campus

When asked about the connection between the student center community and their sense of belonging on campus, multiple participants discussed the student center's connection to their identity.

The sense of belonging being tied to the student center community is two-fold, first being that it is shaped by the student experience. There are no requirements or limitations that prevent a person from utilizing the space, and while the institution owns the physical building, it is adaptable to the needs of the student population. It is a central hub of student life on campus, and a place where all members of the community, not just students, can come together to take part in the student experience.

The second piece is the institutional connection that the student center has in relation to the staff members being invested in the success of the community. Staff members work for the institution, and their investment in the student center community is symbolic of the institution's investment in the students. Sense of belonging emerged from the subthemes that the student center is reflective of the student experience and the investment staff members have in the community.

Increased Engagement

Engagement with the student center community was the goal of the research study and the foundation for the research question. The participants discussed their own engagement with the student center community, but also considered their peers who are not engaged. Increased engagement is built on areas that contribute to or hinder engagement with the student center community.

Most participants described their engagement with the student center as attending or hosting events or needing resources not available elsewhere. The action step provided that opportunity. An increase in engagement from the participants led to ideas for how to increase engagement with their own programs, participants becoming interested in each other's engagement opportunities, and making their resources more accessible for their peers.

DISCUSSION

Findings

This study demonstrated that this student center is a series of networks that has not reached its full potential. Peer to peer and student–staff networks form the heart of the system. Creating the environment for these networks to be established requires helping students create new networks with peers or staff in other areas. Systems theory can be used as a model for increasing networks among community members, leading to increased information seeking and sharing.

In their study on communities of practice, Alexander Ardichvili and colleagues (2003) investigated why people share or don't share information, and why they seek or don't seek information. In their study, participants who shared information felt the information belonged to their organization, rather than to themselves. Believing that information belongs to the organization can only happen if the participants believe they themselves are a part of the overall organization, like the students and the student center.

As shown in the building relationships theme in Cycle 2, information is being shared through the already established networks within the sub-organizations. This confirms Ardichvili et al.'s (2003) other finding that many of their participants went to their already developed community for answers when seeking information. The Cycle 2 subthemes of resources and collaboration also confirm the findings of Borgatti and Cross (2003) noting that social interactions help increase accessibility in a person's decision to seek help or ask for information. The social interactions during the Cycle 2 action step increased the accessibility and validity of information since it came from students closely associated with the department. The purposes of their resources also became more accessible, extending the findings of Borgatti and Cross (2003).

There is a desire for engagement, but engagement must be accessible. The Cycle 2 subtheme of staff investment in the community confirmed the findings of Kuh (1995), and the impact staff have on student engagement. Kuh used his research to create the NSSE and used engagement indicators to help colleges better understand what they are doing well or missing in terms of student engagement. The theme of staff investment in the community from Cycle 2 of this study confirms the NSSE engagement indicator called quality of interactions which contributes to the NSSE theme of campus environment (NSSE, 2015). "Colleges cannot force students to participate in organized campus activities or perform leadership roles. However, they can and should be accountable for creating the conditions that promote such behavior" (Kuh, 1995, p. 150).

Staff having a connection to the student center community is linked to engagement from the students they interact with, leading to increased or lower levels of engagement. "It is also important to discover the qualities of an institution's culture that are perceived as affirming as well as those that are perceived as alienating by students from historically underrepresented groups" (Kuh, 1995, p, 149). The theme of staff investment in the community from Cycle 2 confirms the work of Kuh (1995, 2003) about student engagement in educational opportunities outside of the classroom, "What is clear is that student-faculty interaction matters most to learning when it encourages students to devote greater effort to other educationally purposeful activities during college" (Kuh, 2003, p. 29). Engagement is needed, and how students are introduced or encouraged to participate can shift their college experience.

The participants expressed a desire to collaborate with their peers in different areas of the student center, as shown in the Cycle 2 subtheme of collaboration. The action step of creating an introduction to the student center community did not require a new skill or additional work, just a shift in who they were working with. It was an invitation for collaboration, providing the environment for students with differing experiences to come together, as shown in the Cycle 2 subtheme of collaboration, confirming the findings of the NSSE (2015) indicator of learning with peers. There is a need for additional opportunities where students of differing experiences can work together on a single project.

Cycle 2 data showed it is possible to shift a student's perception of the student center community, which the participants confirmed is tied to their sense of belonging on campus. The sense of community within the student center is different for each student and is in large part because each student is approaching the student center from a different lens and organization.

The participants identified that being open does not just mean that the doors to the physical space are open, but that different experiences are welcomed and valued, confirming Boyer's (1990) principle that an open community lays the foundation for the ideal college community. This study demonstrated that when students are invited to engage in a community-based program, that invitation confirms their membership in the community. For the participants in Cycle 2, the community became not limited to the sub-organizations, but encompassed the entire student center complex. The student center is a place for all students, but it is especially for students who have not found support or a community elsewhere.

The Cycle 2 theme of sense of belonging confirms the work of Tinto (2012) and Cheng (2004). Cheng (2004) found that students finding a community within a subsection of the larger community is not enough for students to feel a sense of belonging at the institution, with Tinto (2012) stating, "The fact is, students are not integrated. They interact with people and situations on campus, both academic and social, and they derive meaning from those interactions in ways that may lead them to feel at home and/or a member of a place or community" (p. 253). All participants from Cycle 2 expressed a sense of a student center community, that they were part of that community, and 8 out of 9 participants stated that their sense of community within the student center was connected to their sense of belonging on campus. "Mattering is 'the feeling that others depend on us, are interested in us, are concerned with our fate'" (Rosenberg & McCollough, 1981, p. 165; Quaye & Harper, 2015, p. 294). The student center is the place where the institutional administration and the student experience come together, as shown in the subthemes of being reflective of student experience and staff investment in the community, aligning with the community being a just one (Boyer, 1990).

The student center is an institutional building filled with resources to support student success and experiences, but is also an institutional facility, making it a connection to the institution for many students. This extends the findings of Tinto (2012) and Cheng (2004) in the Cycle 2 subthemes of reflective of student experience and staff investment in the community. As the Cycle 2 theme of sense of belonging shows, students are looking for a connection to the larger institutional community and the student center is that connection for those who are engaged with the community.

Implications for the Organization

Establishing the student center as its own organization allowed all the parts to contribute to the overall system, the student center community. The interaction of parts serves as a connection of networks. The functionality of the student center at the research site is as a community space, with each area functioning as its own organization in the same space. Information is shared through limited networks created by already established personal interactions. Based on Marcelo Castilho and Carlos Quandt's (2017) study of workspaces, a coworking space is a better design for an organization with a goal of functioning as a system as it allows people working on different projects to be in the same general area, with the goal of those working to create networks and share information. If done correctly, the student center as a coworking space contributes to two of Ernest Boyer's (1990) six principles of community, an open and academically purposeful community, and aligns with the collaborative learning, discussions with diverse others, student–faculty (or staff) interactions, and supportive environment engagement indicators from the NSSE (2015).

Castilho and Quandt (2017) found that there are two types of coworking spaces, convenience and community. Convenience coworking leads to information gathering or sharing information so an individual can do better work, while community coworking leads to individuals sharing their information for a collaborative goal. In the interviews, the participants expressed a desire to collaborate on future projects with other areas of the student center, but for many of the participants, this was the first time they had this type of opportunity. There are a few established networks that have led to collaborations among student organizations, but the student center at the research site is not yet a community coworking space. It is a convenient coworking space, where departments and sub-organizations share the same buildings, but information sharing is often limited to information collection rather than collaboration. At the research site, the physical environment for a community coworking space is already established, but the community part is still needed.

There are several ways to achieve increased student networks, through already established means and creating new opportunities. This can be achieved by reimagining the student center as its own organization with each department serving as a sub-organization, valued members that contribute to the student center community. If a student needs to gather information but does not have a direct connection with a student in a different area, they usually go to a staff member they have a connection with who talks to another staff member. Creating the environment for new networks to develop is the work of the student center staff and requires stepping back and letting the students create these networks, aligning the information seeking of a student with the findings of Kuh (1995) and the student–faculty interactions and quality of interactions engagement indicators of NSSE (2015).

The action step was an opportunity for each sub-organization to show their value to current and new members, while also learning about opportunities and resources in other areas. Fostering networks leads to increasing engagement opportunities through the various parts of the student center. The student center governing board is the group to lead the student side, connecting the various student organizations, establishing student networks, and increasing the accessibility for information sharing and collaborative opportunities.

On the staff side, the student center operations staff should create opportunities for shared knowledge and resources. Regular communication between similar functioning positions would contribute to establishing communities of practice.

Access and accessibility are different in this situation and can lead to different outcomes in terms of engagement. Creating low commitment engagement opportunities would provide greater accessibility for engaging. Low commitment requiring little work on the participant's part or no future involvement. This can come in the form of programs that students can engage with on their own time and at their own pace.

As Tinto (2012) has shown in his research on student engagement, the meaning that students attach to their experience in the space is what gives them a sense of community and belonging. Creating celebratory community moments also creates moments of engagement for the student population, either through planning of the moments or participating in them.

There are many moments of celebration that already occur that may not need to be exclusive to individual communities. Individual community celebrations could become student center community celebrations, but that requires students to see themselves and the community to see them as valued members of the overall student center community.

Another moment the student center community should come together is when the student community needs extra support. This would be when the student population or a population of the student community is working through a tragedy, crisis, or any difficult moment. These are times when the staff within the student center can provide support for anyone impacted in that moment, not limiting it to students within their own department or organization.

FUTURE RESEARCH

As established in the findings, fostering networks increases community, engagement, and belonging within the student center community and on campus. The impact of race, gender, sexual identity, and other demographics on the strength of the networks should be explored, specifically in the areas of student-staff networks and staff engagement with the community. This could provide further answers as to creating cultural shifts within the student center community. Further investigation is needed to understand what role staff play in levels of engagement with the student center community. A longitudinal study following action research methodology would be ideal to measure the shifts over a longer timeframe. As many colleges, including the research site, are making commitments towards diversity, equity, and inclusion, this research has the potential to evaluate the impact a more diverse staff population has on student community engagement and sense of belonging.

REFERENCES

Ackoff, R. L. (1971). Towards a system of systems concepts. *Management Science, 17*(11), 661–671. https://doi.org/10.1287/mnsc.17.11.661

Ardichvili, A., Page, V., & Wentling, T. (2003). Motivation and barriers to participation in virtual knowledge-sharing communities of practice. *Journal of Knowledge Management, 7*(1), 64–77. https://doi.org/10.1108/13673270310463626

Borgatti, S. P., & Cross, R. (2003). A relational view of information seeking and learning in social networks. *Management Science, 49*(4), 432–445. https://doi.org/10.1287/mnsc.49.4.432.14428

Boyer, E. L. (1990). *Campus life: In search of community.* Carnegie Foundation for the Advancement of Teaching.

Castilho, M., & Quandt, C. (2017). Collaborative capability in coworking spaces: Convenience sharing or community building? *Technology Innovation Management Review, 7*(12), 32–42. https://doi.org/10.22215/timreview/1126

Cheng, D. X. (2004). Students' sense of campus community: What it means, and what to do about it. *NASPA Journal, 41*(2), 216–234. https://doi.org/10.2202/0027-6014.1331

Elkins, D. J., Forrester, S. A., & Noël-Elkins, A. V. (2011). Students' perceived sense of campus community: The influence of out-of-class experiences. *College Student Journal, 45*(1), 105–121. https://eric.ed.gov/?id=EJ996353

Harper, S. R. (2008). *Creating inclusive campus environments for cross-cultural learning and student engagement.* NASPA. https://www.naspa.org/book/creating-inclusive-campus-environments-for-cross-cultural-learning-and-student-engagement

Kuh, G. D. (1995). The other curriculum: Out-of-class experiences associated with student learning and personal development. *Journal of Higher Education, 66,* 123–155).

Kuh, G. D. (2003). What we're learning about student engagement from NSSE: Benchmarks for effective educational practices. *Change, 35*(2), 24–32. https://doi.org/10.1080/00091380309604090

National Survey of Student Engagement. (2015). *Engagement annual results 2015—scholarworks.iu.edu.* Engagement insights: Survey findings on the quality of undergraduate education. https://scholarworks.iu.edu/dspace/bitstream/handle/2022/23404/NSSE_2015_Annual_Results.pdf?sequence=1

National Survey of Student Engagement. (2019). *Engagement indicators and high-impact practices.* https://scholarworks.iu.edu/dspace/bitstream/handle/2022/23404/NSSE_2015_Annual_Results.pdf?sequence=1&isAllowed=y

Quaye, S. J., & Harper, S. R. (2015). *Student engagement in higher education: Theoretical perspectives and practical approaches for diverse populations* (2nd ed.). Routledge.

Smyth, C. J. (2016). *Where all may meet on common ground: Elements of college unions evident in campus community* [Unpublished doctoral dissertation]. University of Minnesota. https://conservancy.umn.edu/bitstream/handle/11299/182206/Smyth_umn_0130E%20_17218.pdf?sequence=1&isAllowed=y

Stringer, E. (2013). *Action research* (4th ed.). SAGE Publishing.

Tinto, V. (2012). Moving from theory to action: A model of institutional action for student success. In A. Seidman (Ed.), *College student retention* (2nd ed., pp. 251–266). Rowman & Littlefield Publishers.

CHAPTER 8

UNDERSTANDING AND RESPONDING TO CAREER COUNSELING NEEDS OF CHINESE INTERNATIONAL GRADUATE STUDENTS

Lindsey Plewa

The financial impact that international students have on U.S. colleges cannot be ignored. In 2018 international students contributed $45 billion to the U.S. economy (Institute of International Education, 2020). Students from China represent the largest group of international students studying in the United States, contributing $14.9 billion to the economy in 2018 (Institute of International Education, 2019). Chinese international students significantly contribute to the U.S. economy, but studies show that once these students are on campus they struggle with acculturative stress which impacts their ability to search for employment (Liu, 2009; Mesidor & Sly, 2016; Park et al., 2016; Wang, 2016).

Taking Action, pages 119–133
Copyright © 2024 by Information Age Publishing
www.infoagepub.com
All rights of reproduction in any form reserved.

In the last few years the unstable environment surrounding immigration regulations has impacted their potential to obtain U.S.-based employment after graduation (Briggs & Ammigan, 2017; Harmening, 2018; Lopez, 2018; Mitchell, 2018). Acculturative stress and an unstable regulatory environment put Chinese international students in a vulnerable position to navigate the already muddy job-search waters. Career services offices must understand their unique challenges and provide additional support (Bertram et al., 2014; Carr et al., 2003; Crockett & Hays, 2011; Liu, 2009; Nadermann & Eissenstat, 2018; Wang, 2016; Yao, 2018). Therefore, this research is aimed at increasing an understanding of how career services can support Chinese international graduate students in their quest to find work in the United States.

BACKGROUND AND CONTEXT

Many studies demonstrate the acculturative stress international students experience when studying in a foreign country for the first time (Berry, 1997; Liu, 2009; Mesidor & Sly, 2016; Park et al., 2016; Wang, 2016; Yao, 2018; Zhang-Wu, 2018). More recently, the changes to the regulatory environment surrounding immigration policies and executive orders by the U.S. government during the Trump presidency undoubtedly added to the stress and uncertainty felt by international students (Allen & Ye, 2021; Bartram, 2018; Briggs & Ammigan, 2017; Harmening, 2018; Laws & Ammigan, 2020; Rose-Redwood & Rose-Redwood, 2017). Additionally, perceived discrimination from American peers has added to that feeling of "other" experienced by Chinese international students (Jiang & Kim, 2019; Lee & Rice, 2007; Yao, 2018; Zhang-Wu, 2018). On top of those stressors, some studies point to the additional challenges that cultural values have in helping Chinese international students acclimate to U.S. culture (Wang, 2016). Given this combination of stressors impacting the experience of Chinese international students, tailored culturally sensitive career services support is recommended (Arthur & Popadiuk, 2010; Lee, 2012; Loo, 2016).

METHODS

This study takes place at a large 4-year public institution in a major metropolis in the Northeast. The college being studied is one of ten senior colleges within a large public urban university in the Northeast. The college offers undergraduate, master's, and PhD programs across three colleges separated by study areas. The college enrolls more than 18,000 students annually who speak more than 110 languages and come from more than

160 countries. In the Spring semester of 2021, 20% of graduate students identified as international, and 35% of the international graduate students were from China.

Participants

Participants for Cycle 1 and Cycle 2 were selected based on the following criteria for inclusion: (a) candidates in the Master of Science program, (b) from China studying on an F-1 student visa, (c) between the ages of 20 and 30, and (d) did not complete an undergraduate degree in the United States. Potential subjects were identified through the career center's database that the researcher regularly uses, and the researcher was also granted permission to use the database for this project by the study site's IRB.

The researcher sent emails through her Northeastern student email account to students that fit the inclusion criteria. The researcher followed up with non-responders one time, to ensure that they had an opportunity to respond. In addition to email outreach, the researcher also marketed the project to two colleagues in other student-facing roles who helped identify potential participants. The student researcher followed up with potential participants via telephone to discuss the consent procedures. Once participants confirmed, the researcher utilized snowball sampling to locate additional participants. Based on the inclusion criteria and students' interest in the project, six students participated in cycle one interviews and seven students participated in Cycle 2 interviews.

Data Collection

Cycle 1 consisted of individual semi-structured interviews. Each face-to-face interview ranged from 30 to 60 minutes. Open-ended questions helped participants explore their feelings and describe their own experience around searching for a job in the United States as an international student. The participants were informed that the interview would be recorded and signed a consent form. In addition to the audio recording (through Temi software), handwritten notes were taken during the interview.

In Cycle 2 an action step was implemented based on the findings from Cycle 1. The action step was a semester-long career services program specifically for Chinese international graduate students. Seven students participated in the program. At the conclusion of the program, semi-structured interviews were conducted with all seven participants. The interviews were on Zoom (an alternative to the originally scheduled in-person format given the COVID-19 pandemic) and each interview was 30 to 60 minutes. The protocol for the interviews consisted of questions that would enable the researcher to understand if the program was effective at meeting their unique job search needs.

Data Analysis

Data analysis was conducted throughout the study. In vivo coding, the practice of assigning a label (or code) to a section of data, was used to honor the participants' voice (Miles et al., 2014; Stringer, 2014). A codebook was then assembled with the goal being to retrieve the most meaningful material that addressed the research question and to begin assembling chunks of data (Miles et al., 2014). The researcher then reviewed analytical memos written immediately after each interview alongside interview transcripts to begin grouping the codes according to similarity and to develop themes. Once themes were established, member checking was employed to ensure the validity of the conclusions (Miles et al., 2014). Through the NVivo software, a data display was created to highlight the most predominant and least predominant themes. Lastly, the visual display was shared with a participant ahead of time via email, and a phone call was scheduled where the participant was asked to comment on the data display.

CYCLE 1 RESULTS

Cycle 1 Themes

Three themes emerged from Cycle 1: responding to language barriers, changing regulatory environment, and addressing cultural differences between China and the United States.

Responding to Language Barriers

When describing their experience searching for a job in the United States, participants identified the language barrier as one major element that affects this process. Sentiments were shared around the difficulty conversing casually with other students, professors, administrators, potential employers, and professional colleagues. The ability to converse casually with others and the difficulty that comes along with being able to do so as an ESL (English as a second language) student, was referenced 29 times amongst five participants. On this topic, one participant shared, "I mean sometimes you can talk a lot about topics, like very diverse topics, but in China, it's like sometimes you cannot just talk about whatever [*sic*]." This student was referencing the ease in which Americans talk about political interests or affiliations as a common topic of conversation which is very different from their experience in China.

Changing Regulatory Environment

The second theme that emerged was the impact of the changing regulatory environment by the American government and its effect on international students. Concerns about securing employment with an H-1B visa were cited 28 times across all six interviews. All participants were on an F-1 visa. The U.S. Citizenship and Immigration Services (2020) defines an F-1 student as one who enters the United States and enrolls as a full-time student at an accredited college or university. To legally stay in the United States after graduation, international students on an F-1 visa need an employment offer that includes H-1B sponsorship. One participant said, "Um, sometimes I, this is really hard for international students because in the beginning we don't even get an opportunity. Like I uploaded like tons of jobs and I don't get any opportunities. I thought I was not good enough [*sic*]." Many expressed the process of applying online to many jobs and not hearing back, then feeling defeated. While this experience can be true for domestic applicants too, the lack of employer response was brought up in relation to the lack of companies being willing to sponsor candidates for an H-1B visa.

Addressing Cultural Differences

Cultural differences between China and the United States is the final most referenced theme, cited 101 times across all six interviews. One cultural difference that was cited among two of the participants was the relationship with authority figures such as professors and supervisors at work. One participant shared,

> We think twice when we want to raise our hands to answer the questions because we don't want to bother other people . . . we would rather just like listen and learn from them. I think that's the way we have classes in China, like we just listen to the teacher . . . it's more like teacher centered, but here it's like student centered so it's totally different [*sic*]."

Whereas American students are taught to raise their hand in class and speak up to show they're engaged, participants noted that Chinese students are taught that staying quiet in the classroom is a sign of respect.

Establishing trust was another difficulty participants shared related to cultural differences. The process of approaching someone new and establishing trust can be very intimidating as talking to strangers is not encouraged back home. For example, one participant shared,

> Let's just say for example you go on the street, and you say, "Oh I like your outfit," people wouldn't feel weird. But in China, if you say that they will judge you like, "Oh what is wrong with you, why would you say that to me?" Expressing yourself you can talk about whatever you think, and the people will respect your views . . . but back home they judge you. (personal communication, October 18, 2019)

These differences can be connected to *guanxi*, a Chinese term meaning "networks" or "connections" and refers to trust that is built out of a long-term relationship. In Chinese culture a willingness to pursue long-term relationships with trust is a worthwhile pursuit of *guanxi*, while a fleeting interaction with a stranger is not worthwhile (Chang, 2011).

Another cultural difference shared by the participants was how they struggled with the American concept of networking. One participant stated, "I think it's really important to have a lesson about how to communicate . . . my friends from back home, they think networking is embarrassing." Referring to networking as "embarrassing" may also be connected to *guanxi* and the notion that connections should be built with trust over a longer period. Approaching a stranger purely with a goal to advance one's professional pursuits negates *guanxi* and is therefore difficult for Chinese international students to initially understand.

Lastly, expected demeanor, or desired personality traits in China as compared to the United States, was cited 42 times across five participant interviews. One concept that was shared which describes highly esteemed personality traits is *mianzi*, which translates to "lose face." "Mianzi, the so-called face, which denotes an individual's social position, as well as the roles that are expected of him or her by others" (Wang, 2016, p. 624). Mianzi is connected to self-management and independence (Liu, 2009). A participant stated, "I think the losing face thing it occurs in our life like on a daily basis. You know, we care about our behaviors, we care about the things that we say and, most importantly is that I think we really care about what other people think of us [*sic*]." Being hyper-aware and critical of the words one chooses is connected to mianzi. Searching for a job is tough enough; when compounded with ESL difficulties and cultural expectations such as mianzi, it makes the process even more difficult.

INTRODUCTION TO CYCLE 2

The goal of Cycle 1 was to understand, "How do graduate international students from China experience searching for a job in the United States?" Through participant interviews, three main themes emerged, and an analysis of the data revealed that these themes are not weighted equally. The theme of "cultural differences" was referenced the most. Given this finding from the participant interviews, the next cycle of this research focused on a program that supports Chinese international students navigating these cultural differences. In Cycle 2, the action step taken was to host a program for graduate international Chinese students that created space for them to share challenges they faced with understanding cultural differences between China and the United States. The program also sought to provide information around learning how to navigate those cultural differences when searching for employment or working in the United States for the first time.

The program, "Culture and Career: A Six-Session Program for International Chinese Graduate Students," consisted of six 1-hour sessions that ran throughout the fall semester. The program was delivered through Zoom, a video conferencing platform. The program was hosted by the researcher (a full-time career counselor) and supported by one part-time career counselor. For every session, a guest speaker, or speakers, were also present to add additional expertise about the topic. To facilitate group conversation and enable honest, open dialogue, the program was not recorded and was limited to a small group. Seven students attended the program.

CYCLE 2 RESULTS

The results of Cycle 2 analysis provided rich feedback related to the content of the program. The most effective content cited was the workshop with an immigration attorney that focused on the H-1B visa. At the request of the immigration attorney, the session was held less than a month after the U.S. presidential election. The reason behind this schedule request was so that the attorney could speak to how the presidential election outcome could have implications on the future of the H-1B visa. For example, just a week before the workshop, a judge ruled in favor of plaintiffs suing the U.S. Department of Homeland Security about a policy that affected the future of the H-1B (Anderson, 2020). The immigration attorney clearly explained the lawsuit and the implications of the judge's ruling on the filing of H-1B visas moving forward.

Commenting on the most effective part of the program, one participant shared:

> I think the most recent one on visas because I have those concerns. Like, what is the timeline and when should I start preparing for it . . . and when I asked this question to the international student office, they said, don't worry, we'll have this workshop later [*sic*]. (personal communication, December 10, 2020)

For this participant, understanding the timeline of the H-1B visa process was especially a concern, since after successfully finishing an internship, they had accepted a full-time offer with H-1B sponsorship. Acquiring information both for themself and for the company was the logical next step, yet workshops about the H-1B visa were at the time of the interview, were only offered once a semester by the college's Office of International Student Services.

Cycle 2 interviews also revealed content improvement ideas. Participants were asked, "What, if anything, would have improved the program?" In response to this question, four out of seven participants mentioned that they would have liked more information about networking and specifically: (a) the networking process and its importance, (b) sustaining networking relationships, and (c) how to obtain a referral from networking. Related to networking remaining a difficult part of the job search process, another participant commented:

> I really wanted to know something about networking and how you'll always have to actively find people literally working in the company and build a relationship. Sometimes I think it's time consuming... I think networking is maybe also a cultural difference and is also very important to get your first job, especially in America. It's important and we don't know how to do it effectively [sic].

The student acknowledged that networking is "important... especially in America" but even though it's important, they still "don't know how to do it effectively." At the time of the Cycle 2 interview, the participant was interning at an investment bank, an opportunity that they secured by applying online, not through networking. It is interesting to note that even though their current employment opportunity came from efforts that didn't include networking, they still recognized that networking is "very important" and may be necessary to help secure their next employment opportunity.

During the second session of the program, two Master of Science alumni (both previously on an F-1 student visa from China), shared the basics of networking including how to start a conversation and how to maintain a relationship after that first networking encounter. While networking was the focus of the second session, the process of how to secure a referral was not the focal point. The participant's feedback demonstrates that the referral process is also a component of networking where they need more clarity. The feedback from the participant interviews reveal that more information is needed on this important job search topic. As one participant noted, "You really could do a whole six session program just on networking."

DISCUSSION

The findings from this research contribute to the literature surrounding the job search experience of Chinese international graduate students.

First, this research supports the finding that H-1B sponsored employment remains a challenge. Second, the research supports and adds to the limited literature that points to challenges related to cultural differences as a dominant concern in the students' search for U.S. employment.

Difficulties Securing H-1B Sponsored Employment

The first finding answers to the first and second research question that guided this project: "How do Chinese international students experience the job search process and what difficulties do they face?" Clearly, the H-1B visa, an employer-sponsored work visa that legally allows an international student to perform a specialty occupation related to their degree after graduation, is one such difficulty (U.S. Citizenship and Immigration Services, 2021a). While searching for a job can be difficult for any student, searching for a full-time job as an international student is even more challenging because they need to find an employer that will sponsor their H-1B visa to legally remain in the US after graduation. This finding came up in Cycle 1 interviews, Cycle 2 interviews, and supports the literature.

The 2016 Election of Donald Trump and the H-1B Visa
In the years following the 2016 U.S. presidential election, executive orders related to immigration policy caused concern for international students as noted in the literature (Allen & Ye, 2021; Bartram, 2018; Briggs & Ammigan, 2017; Laws & Ammigan, 2020; Rose-Redwood & Rose-Redwood, 2017). Specifically, international student concerns related to securing an H-1B visa were heightened following Trump's 2017 "Buy American and Hire American" executive order which aimed "to help reduce illegal immigration and preserve jobs for U.S. workers" (U.S. Citizenship and Immigration Services, 2021b, para. 5). Before signing that executive order, Trump remarked, "Widespread abuse in our immigration system is allowing American workers of all backgrounds to be replaced by workers brought in from other countries ... Right now, H-1B visas are awarded in a totally random lottery—and that's wrong" (Smith, 2017, paras. 5, 6). By taking aim at the H-1B lottery, Trump instilled a feeling of instability for international students who had otherwise looked to that path as a primary way to secure legal work opportunities after graduation (Smith, 2017).

Trump's messaging about the "Buy American, Hire American" executive order not only led to feeling unwelcome for international students, but it also led to a decline in opportunities as the rate of H-1B approvals declined (National Foundation for American Policy, 2021). From the third to the fourth quarter of the fiscal year 2017, denials of H-1B increased by 41% (rising from 15.9% in the third quarter to 22.4% in the fourth quarter;

National Foundation for American Policy, 2021). The lack of opportunities with employers willing to sponsor the H-1B was present in the findings from cycle two participant interviews and points to the reality that many international students seeking employment are facing; being qualified for a job but repeatedly being turned away since the employer is not able to sponsor candidates for the H-1B visa.

Tension Between Chinese Cultural Values and American Job Search Norms

The second finding also answers the first and second research question, as another difficulty faced by Chinese international students is their ability to navigate the tension between their upbringing and the American norms of job search. This finding was initially revealed in Cycle 1 interviews where cultural differences related to authority figures, establishing trust with others, networking, and valued personality traits were shared by the participants. Two areas that support the findings from the literature are the impact of Chinese valued personality traits associated with mianzi and differences in how one leverages connections to find employment opportunities.

In Chinese culture, mianzi, or the so-called "face," refers to an individual's position in society, the projection of a self-image, and the roles expected by others (Wang, 2016). The connection that mianzi has to Chinese international students' ability to speak confidently with classmates, with coworkers, or when speaking with a prospective employee was revealed in Cycle 1 and two interviews. This finding supports the literature which notes how traditional Chinese culture values such as having concern for others and placing concern for the group over concern for the self, is in direct contrast with American culture, which is characterized by independence and self-reliance (Carr et al., 2003; Wang, 2016).

In addition to mianzi's influence on why Chinese international students may not seek the help of others, is another cultural difference related to leveraging connections to find employment. Participant interviews from Cycle 1 revealed difficulty approaching strangers and a reluctance to network with professionals to help find employment. In China students relied on their familial connections to help them secure interviews, whereas in the United States it is expected that students seek out professionals in their field of interest who likely do not have a connection to a family member. Therefore, seeking a job in the United States for the first time can be quite jarring, as the process of networking with those outside of one's family members is a completely new concept. At the conclusion of the "Culture and Career" program, participants shared that they could have used more support around networking.

This theme from the interviews supports the literature about this fundamental difference in job search approach. Betram et al. (2014) studied the effects of social support on acculturation amongst Chinese international studies. The study concluded that the most common stressors were feeling disconnected from others and confronting different cultural/values systems (Bertram et al., 2014). For example, due to cultural misinterpretations, international students may abstain from networking all together (Nadermann & Eisenstat, 2018). Although several participants expanded their social circle to include Americans, it was revealed that those connections lacked depth and they did not consider those connections primary sources of social support (Bertram et al., 2014).

IMPLICATIONS FOR PRACTICE

The participant interviews revealed the culturally based barriers to employment faced by Chinese international students. Some of those barriers include a clash in cultural values when pressed against American norms of job search, such as leveraging connections to secure employment, and a hesitancy to seek external support (which could include faculty, mental health counseling, or career counseling) due to cultural values connected to mianzi. There are samples from the literature that support a culturally sensitive approach to career counseling international students given these culturally based barriers to employment (Ammigan & Laws, 2018; Arthur & Popadiuk, 2010; Barton & Ryan, 2020; Roberts, 2012).

In addition to culturally sensitive individual career counseling, the interviews, supported by the literature, suggests a need for a new higher education model that supports international students whereby offices such as career services, admissions and international student services work collaboratively to best serve the students (Ammigan & Laws, 2018; Laws & Ammigan, 2020). An extensive research study from Loo (2016) for World Education Services compiled 175 survey responses from U.S.-based international student services officers and career services staff who work with international students to gauge what services have proved most effective. The study found that when institutions' career services efforts adhered to the following, they were most effective: an understanding of international students' unique needs and tailoring programs accordingly, support of helping students develop culturally competent soft skills related to job search and working collaboratively across offices to provide a high level of service (Loo, 2016). Working collaboratively across the institution to provide effective support for international students through intentional programming can help to connect students to the college community and increase support they may not otherwise seek on their own (Ammigan & Laws, 2018).

CONCLUSION

Connecting findings from participant interviews with literature helps to provide context around sentiments shared by the students. The first finding which recognizes the difficulties Chinese international students encounter when searching for employment with H-1B sponsorship supports the literature around the impact of the 2016 U.S. presidential election. The second finding, how cultural values impact Chinese international students' search for employment, also supports the literature. Specifically, the impact of esteemed personality traits such as mianzi, and the impact that cultural values have on one's desire to participate in the Americanized quest for finding employment through networking outside the family. Given these findings, tailored career services through interculturally sensitive career counseling and through collaborative intentional programming across the institution is recommended.

LIMITATIONS AND FUTURE RESEARCH

The participants all studied at a single public college in the Northeast and the program was designed to fit the needs of participants of this study in this context. Therefore, one limitation of this study is that the experience of the participants may not be generalized to students at other colleges and universities. Another limitation is the small sample size of participants at a specific moment in time. Although the participants shared a range of experiences, they may not constitute a representative sample. Follow-up research might explore a longitudinal study with a larger sample size. Studying students over a longer period may provide insight into how a longer residency may affect their job search experience. It should also be noted that data was primarily collected through participant interviews conducted in English which was not the primary language of the participants. However, the researcher provided clarification on interview questions when prompted and practiced reflexivity when reviewing the interview transcripts.

Lastly, given that Chinese international students are a heterogeneous group, further research could compare the experiences of Chinese international students from different regions (i.e., Mainland China, Taiwan, and Hong Kong). This could add to the research around the nuanced job search challenges related to differences in cultural practices. Despite these limitations, the results contribute to the limited research regarding Chinese international graduate student challenges in finding U.S.-based employment.

REFERENCES

Allen, R. M., & Ye, Y. (2021). Why deteriorating relations, xenophobia, and safety concerns will deter Chinese international student mobility to the United States. *Journal of International Students*, 11(2), i–vii. https://doi.org/10.32674/jis.v11i2.3731

Ammigan, R., & Laws, K. N. (2018). Communications preferences among international students: Strategies for creating optimal engagement in programs and services. *Journal of International Students*, 8(3), 1293–1315. https://doi.org/10.32674/jis.v8i3.54

Anderson, S. (2020, October 22). Economic research exposes significant flaws in DOL H-1B visa rule. *Forbes*. https://www.forbes.com/sites/stuartanderson/2020/10/22/economic-research-exposes-significant-flaws-in-dol-h-1b-visa-rule/?sh=71c911a96146

Arthur, N., & Popadiuk, N. (2010). A cultural formulation approach to career counseling with international students. *Journal of Career Development*, 37(1), 423–440. https://doi.org/10.1177/0894845309345845

Barton, G., & Ryan, M. (2020). What does reflection look and feel like for international students?: An exploration of reflective thinking, reflexivity and employability. *Journal of International Students*, 10(S2), 1–16. https://doi.org/10.32674/jis.v10iS2.2848

Bartram, B. (2018). International students in the era of Trump and Brexit: Implications, constructions and trends. *Journal of International Students*, 8(4), 1479–1482. https://doi.org/10.32674/jis.v8i4.210

Berry, J. W. (1997). Immigration, acculturation, and adaptation. *Applied Psychology: An International Review, 46*, 5–34.

Bertram, D. M., Poulakis, M., Elsasser, B. S., & Kumar, E. (2014). Social support and acculturation in Chinese international students. *Journal of Multicultural Counseling and Development*, 42(2), 107–124. https://doi.org/10.1002/j.2161-1912.2014.00048.x

Briggs, P., & Ammigan, R. (2017). A collaborative programming and outreach model for international student support offices. *Journal of International Students*, 7(4), 1080–1095. https://doi.org/10.32674/jis.v7i4.193

Carr, J. L., Miki Koyama, M., & Thiagarajan, M. (2003). A women's support group for Asian international students. *Journal of American College Health*, 52(3), 131–134. https://doi.org/10.1080/07448480309595735

Chang, C. L. (2011). The effect of an information ethics course on the information ethics values of students—A Chinese Guanxi culture perspective. *Computers in Human Behavior*, 27(5), 2028–2038. https://doi.org/10.1016/j.chb.2011.05.010

Crockett, S. A., & Hays, D. G. (2011). Understanding and responding to the career counseling needs of international college students on U.S. campuses. *Journal of College Counseling*, 14(1), 65–79. https://doi.org/10.1002/j.2161-1882.2011.tb00064.x

Harmening, D. S. (2018). [Review of the book *Wellness Issues for Higher Education: A Guide for Student Affairs and Higher Education Professionals* ed. by David S. Anderson]. *The Review of Higher Education, 41*(3), 479–484.

Institute of International Education. (2019). *Open Doors*. https://www.iie.org/research-initiatives/open-doors/economic-impact-of-international-students/

Institute of International Education. (2020). *Open Doors*. https://www.iie.org/research-initiatives/open-doors/economic-impact-of-international-students/

Jiang, X., & Kim, D. (2019). The price of being international. *Journal of International Students, 9*(3), 732–757. https://doi.org/10.32674/jis.v9i3.700

Laws, K., & Ammigan, R. (2020). International students in the Trump era. *Journal of International Students, 10*(3), xviii–xxii. https://doi.org/10.32674/jis.v10i3.2001

Lee, C. C. (2012). A conceptual framework for culturally competent career counseling practice. *The Career Planning and Adult Development Journal, 28*(1), 7–14.

Lee, J. J., & Rice, C. (2007). Welcome to America? *Higher Education, 53*(3), 381–409. https://doi.org/10.1007/s10734-005-4508-3

Liu, M. (2009) Addressing the mental health problems of Chinese international college students in the United States. *Advances in Social Work, 10*(1), *69–86*. https://doi.org/10.18060/164

Loo, B. (2016). *Career services for international students: Fulfilling high expectations.* World Education Services.

Lopez, I. (2018). Universities sue DHS, immigration services over Trump administration re-entry policy. *New York Law Journal.*

Mesidor, J. K., & Sly, K. F. (2016). Factors that contribute to the adjustment of international students. *Journal of International Students, 6*(1), 262–282. https://doi.org/10.32674/jis.v6i1.569

Miles, M. B., Huberman, A. M., & Saldana, J. (2014). *Qualitative data analysis: A methods sourcebook* (3rd ed.). SAGE Publishing.

Mitchell, T. (2018). *Statement by ACE President Ted Mitchell on the U.S. Supreme Court's travel ruling.* American Council on Education. https://www.acenet.edu/News-Room/Pages/Statement-by-ACE-President-Ted-Mitchell-on-the-US-Supreme-Court-Travel-Ban-Ruling.aspx

Nadermann, K., & Eissenstat, S. J. (2018c). Career decision making for Korean international college students: Acculturation and networking. *The Career Development Quarterly, 66*(1), 49–63. https://doi.org/10.1002/cdq.12121

National Foundation for American Policy. (2021). *H1-B denial rates through second quarter of FY 2021.* https://nfap.com/wp-content/uploads/2021/08/H-1B-Denial-Rates-Analysis-Through-Second-Quarter-FY-2021.NFAP-Policy-Brief.August-2021.pdf

Park, H., Lee, M. J., Choi, G. Y., & Zepernick, J. S. (2016). Challenges and coping strategies of East Asian graduate students in the United States. *International Social Work*, 1–17.

Roberts, D. L. (2012). International graduate student mobility in the US: What more can we be doing? *Journal of College and Character, 13*(1). https://doi.org/10.1515/jcc-2012-1868

Rose-Redwood, C., & Rose-Redwood, R. (2017). Rethinking the politics of the international student experience in the age of trump. *Journal of International Students, 7*(3), i–ix. https://doi.org/10.32674/jis.v7i3.201

Smith, B. (2017). *H-1B visa review needed but "Hire American" is the wrong approach.* Retrieved from https://thepienews.com/news/h1b-visa-review-needed-but -hire-american-is-the-wrong-approach-say-educators/

Stringer, E. T. (2014). *Action research: A handbook for practitioners* (4th ed.). SAGE.

U.S. Citizenship and Immigration Services. (2020). *Students and employment.* https:// www.uscis.gov/laws-and-policy/other-resources/unlawful-presence-and -inadmissibility

U.S. Citizenship and Immigration Services. (2021a). *Options for noncitizen STEM professionals to work in the United States.* https://www.uscis.gov/working-in-the -united-states/options-for-noncitizen-stem-professionals-to-work-in-the-unit- ed-states

U.S. Citizenship and Immigration Services. (2021b). *Buy American and hire American: Putting American workers first.* Retrieved from https://www.uscis.gov/archive/ buy-american-and-hire-american-putting-american-workers-first

Wang, M. (2016). The impact of cultural values on Chinese students in American higher education. *The Qualitative Report, 21*(4), 611–628. https://doi.org/ 10.46743/2160-3715/2016.2225

Yao, C. W. (2018). "They don't care about you": First-year Chinese international students' experiences with neo-racism and othering on a U.S. campus. *Journal of the First-Year Experience & Students in Transition, 30*(1), 87–101. https://digital commons.unl.edu/cehsedadfacpub/84/?utm_source=digitalcommons.unl .edu%2Fcehsedadfacpub%2F84&utm_medium=PDF&utm_campaign= PDFCoverPages

Zhang-Wu, Q. (2018). Chinese international students' experiences in American higher education institutes: A critical review of the literature. *Journal of International Students, 8*(2), 1173–1197. https://doi.org/10.32674/jis.v8i2.139

CHAPTER 9

A STUDY OF COMMUNITY COLLEGE DROPOUTS

Action Research on How a Peer Mentorship Program Through Phi Theta Kappa (PTK) Honor Society Can Improve Students' Performance

Chunfu Jeff Cheng

The purpose of this research was to understand the student dropout issue and to examine the reasons behind the issue at community colleges where the researcher currently works. The knowledge and findings obtained through this research study provides practical insights into developing a mentorship model to support community colleges in retaining students and improving graduation rates.

This chapter begins with an introduction related to the issues of student dropouts at community colleges to provide context and background of the study. The second section of this chapter provides a brief explanation of

Taking Action, pages 135–152
Copyright © 2024 by Information Age Publishing
www.infoagepub.com
All rights of reproduction in any form reserved.

the action research approach and the rationale for why this methodology was used in the research. The third section describes the research results.

The fourth section contextualizes the research study by situating the findings from Cycle 2 in the extant literature. Implications of the study are described including future research directions, specific examples of how findings can be used in the practice setting, and suggestions for areas of future investigations.

BACKGROUND AND CONTEXT

Since the 2008 financial crisis, states' budgets for higher education have been decreasing drastically almost all over the United States (Mitchell, 2017). Public-funded higher education through community colleges is critical for American college students. Many nontraditional college students benefit from the opportunities of public community colleges education because of their open admission policies, low tuition, and convenient geographic locations. Unfortunately, public colleges and universities which heavily rely on public funding continuously increase tuition to operate, making college education for many students less affordable, forcing many of them into student loan debt (Mitchell, 2017). Many students come from low-income families and rely on financial aid at community colleges. The rising costs and financial pressure from higher education have a significant impact on the college dropout situation. Fifty-one percent of students dropped out of colleges or universities due to costs (Scipioni, 2018). Thirteen percent of community college students graduate in 2 years; 22% in 3 years; 28% in 4 years (Chen, 2022). About 33% of students who enroll in college never earn a degree (Leonhardt & Chinoy, 2019). Strauss (2019) reported by interviewing college experts that the dropout rate is the highest at the community college level, and fewer than 40% of them graduate or transfer in 6 years (three times the norm). Strauss (2019) also indicated that 50% of students at public universities drop out, and the graduation rate for minority students and those Pell grants recipients is even 10 to 20% lower than that. Therefore, American higher education faces a dropout problem.

As an educator in a community college, the researcher has also observed that every semester students drop out for various reasons. Furthermore, studies show that community college students tend to have very low graduation and retention rates. Kantrowitz (2021) determined that the average 3-year graduation rate at community colleges in the United States is about 20%. Many students have to drop out of college because it is stressful to deal with financial struggles and to balance between school and work (Scott-Clayton, 2012). Yet, community colleges play a significant role in higher education. According to a report from the National Student Clearinghouse

(NSC), 46% of all students who completed a degree at a 4-year institution in 2013–2014 had enrolled at a community college in the previous 10 years (Ma & Baum, 2016). In Fall 2014, the National Center for Education Statistics (NCES) showed 42% of all undergraduate students and 25% of all full-time undergraduate students were enrolled in community colleges (Ma & Baum, 2016). Unfortunately, the retention and graduation rates in community colleges are far from satisfying. Such low graduation rates imply a very high dropout rate. Considering the discussed problems above, it is imperative to examine student dropout at community colleges and to develop practical and feasible solutions to prevent them from dropping out.

Purpose of the Research

The purpose of this research was to understand and explore the student dropout issue and the reasons behind the issue at community colleges, particularly at the institution where the researcher currently works. For the purpose of the study, the term "dropout" refers to any student who leaves college or university for practical reasons without either graduation or completion of a program of studies or transferring to another institution (Bonneau, 2015). The audience for the work included faculty, professional staff, academic staff, college administrators, and the board of regents at community colleges. The goal was to bring awareness about the issue and to propose action steps for community colleges to consider implementing.

Research Question(s)

The following broad and overarching research questions were advanced:

1. What are the characteristics of the students who study at community colleges?
2. What are the fundamental reasons that cause students to drop out from community colleges?
3. What feasible measures can community colleges take using participatory action research to improve graduation rates and retention rates?

The study took place at a rural community college in Oklahoma, which is the place of the researcher's current employment. This college was established in 1931 and has a student body of approximately 1,600. It is a comprehensive public community college, serving a nearby five-county services area. This college is a member of Oklahoma State System of Higher

Education which serves as the state' legal structure to provide public education. There are approximately 40 full-time faculty members and 150 full-time employees on campus. The researcher has worked here since 2014, and he has built very strong relationships with his colleagues and stakeholders. As an insider at the research site, he already gained the access and site permission to conduct the research.

METHODS

The research question that informed the study was, "How can the research site prevent students from dropping out?" The following broad and overarching research questions were advanced to guide this study:

1. What are the characteristics of the students who study at community colleges?
2. What are the fundamental reasons that cause students to drop out from community colleges?
3. What feasible measures can community colleges take using participatory action research to improve graduation rates and retention rates?

Research Approach

Some work on community college student dropouts has been done using traditional research methodology (Posa, 2011; Bound et al., 2012; Casanova et al., 2018). However, it is significant and urgent to seek feasible and practical solutions for these issues by using action research. The key characteristics of action research include elements such as seeking full collaboration and active participation, enabling people to find effective solutions, and bringing action and reflection to impact social changes. As an insider in higher education, the researcher's intention was to bring awareness about the issue and propose action steps for community colleges to consider implementing by identifying problems, engaging participants, and bringing about changes in the setting of higher education. Action research has enjoyed widespread success in the field of education by helping an individual with professional development and leading collaborative effort to professional and institutional change (Herr & Anderson, 2005). In summary, action research is a methodology for change because it requires active interaction and participation with the group who are in the middle of issues. Its unique reflective process requires researchers to constantly review and reflect the plan or strategy that had been adopted. Therefore, action research represents the best vehicle to explore the problem of practice.

Action research is one type of qualitative research methodology that integrates the methods of "observing, documenting, analyzing, and interpreting characteristics, attributes, and meanings of human phenomena" (Gillis & Jackson, 2002, p. 34).

Participants

The main participants were students. To better understand and investigate the research problem wholly, the student participants were intentionally categorized into two different groups: traditional students and nontraditional students. All the participants in different cycles of the action research study can be found in Table A2. The roles of the collaborators and stakeholders vary depending on their positions at the college and their proximity to the students.

In Cycle 0/Baseline, 6 participants were interviewed. They are staff and administrators. The roles of staff are participants and stakeholders who provide insight on students' daily lives and their observations on students outside of the classroom through their daily experiences of advising students. The director of financial aid provided the knowledge, expertise, and understandings on the finance side of students. The roles of administrators are participants and stakeholders provided information, knowledge, and expertise on the issue from a macro-level institutional perspective. They were also involved in the inquiry, the application of findings and administrative support in the form of providing resources such as time, technical and material assistance necessary to the research project. In Cycle 1, there were 5 student participants. The roles of students are participants, stakeholders, co-researcher who shared their experience of being college students at the research site, provided insight of their struggles, shared their understandings of which factors cause them to drop out, and informed their needs. In Cycle 2, there were 21 participants. The roles of staff from federal grants-sponsored programs are participants and stakeholders who provided knowledge and shared experience of how their peer mentoring programs were developed, and how they functioned on campus and what challenges they faced in their programs. The roles of PTK regional coordinator are collaborator and outsider who shared information of whether other community colleges in the region implement peer mentoring programs in concert with PTK, who also shared knowledge, experience, and advice of how community colleges should implement peer mentoring programs through PTK. The roles of student mentors are participants and stakeholders who are main characters in this program, shared their experience of being mentors, shared their insight of how to improve this program. The roles of student mentees are participants and stakeholders who are main characters in this program, shared their experience of being mentees, shared their experience of how this program benefits them.

The researcher engaged with faculty, staff members, and administrators in informal and formal discussions related to student dropouts prior to developing the interview protocol. After several discussions with various members within the institutions, the interview protocol was established, and IRB authorization was obtained. Student participants were identified and recruited for Cycle 1 data collection.

Data Collection

The primary methods used in the research for data collection were through face-to-face, semi-structured interviews, and site observations. Semi-structured in-depth interview methods have been widely used in qualitative (Dicicco-Blooom & Crabtree, 2006). Face-to-face interviews allow researchers to understand other people's life stories and reveal personal biography, therefore exploring social issues and personal matters of the interviewees (Atkinson, 1998; Birren, 1996). Each session of interviews lasted no more than 45 minutes. With the permissions of participants, follow-up interviews were conducted to clarify their responses. All the interviews were recorded with the permission of each participant.

Data Analysis

Data analysis contains concurrent flows and steps of activity: data condensation, data display, and conclusion drawing/verification (Miles et al., 2019). Manual coding and Nvivo software were utilized to condense the data. Themes were established and placed into categories.

CYCLE 1 RESULTS

The themes served as findings from Cycle 1:

- Finding 1: College financial issues are an obstacle as participants do not find enough financial aid on campus to help them with their education.
- Finding 2: Personal financial constraints means that participants have limited financial resources to pay their daily expenses while going to college.

- Finding 3: Time management is an obstacle representing a lack of ability and skills to plan and manage on-campus with off-campus tasks.
- Finding 4: Health-related issues are obstacles that participants have with themselves or family members that cause them to miss classes or drop out of college entirely.

The findings showed that there are many obstacles and stumbling blocks for college students, no matter whether they are traditional or non-traditional, to prevent them from succeeding. This is consistent with several studies reported in the literature review (Araque et al., 2009; Choi, 2018; Oriol et al., 2017; Rosário et al., 2014). The findings and analysis from Cycle 1 indicated that there is a strong need for quality student services at the institution. Quality student services should include teaching students time management skills, providing peer mentors to encourage and assist mentees, and educating students about financial aid. These findings are also aligned with the literature (Castleman & Page, 2016; Colling et al., 2016; Millea et al., 2018). Thus, the researcher decided to focus on one main objective in this action research project, which is to establish a peer mentoring program at the college. The next section describes the detailed action step plan and the evaluation plan to assess its effectiveness of implementation. This allowed the researcher to strive for continuous improvements on this project as it moves forward.

The student focus group and stakeholders group enriched the collected data. This section of Cycle 1 results/findings are based on analysis of the informative data. The literature review supports and strengthens the results and findings in this research (Araque et al., 2009; Castleman & Page, 2016; Pantages & Creedon, 1978). The findings in this research were consistent across different participants and stakeholders. The primary findings through this round of interviews with participants and data collection reveal that there are many stumbling blocks for community college students that cause them to drop out of college. These stumbling blocks include, but not limited to, the following factors: lack of motivation/mentors, college unpreparedness/readiness, time management skills, health-related issues, communication skills, growth mindset, personal/family issues, work issues, transportation issues, college financial aid, personal financial constraints, and technological skills (Davis-Kean, 2005; Pantages & Creedon, 1978; Mabel et al., 2017; Martinez et al., 2013).

Key findings of stumbling blocks for community college students which can be categorized into two attributions: endogenous variables and exogenous variables. In the study, endogenous variables are the factors that are internal to participants themselves, which essentially impact their college performance whereas, exogenous variables are the factors that are external to participants lives over which they may have little control which make an impact on their college performance.

The findings from the qualitative data provided the researcher with answers to the research questions and deeper understandings of the problem of practice. The findings within the literature suggest that a peer mentoring program should be established, in which higher-level students can provide mentorship, accompaniment, and encouragement. The researcher believes this could be a feasible solution to increase retention rates and persistence rates, to improve graduation rates, and ultimately to change the current situation of college dropout at the institution.

INTRODUCTION TO CYCLE 2

This section provides an overview of the action steps informed by Cycle 1 data analysis and literature review. The action step for Cycle 2 was to establish a peer mentoring program in concert with Phi Theta Kappa (PTK) International Honor Society members at the research site. The literature review and data analysis from Cycle 1 supported that there is a strong need for developing this program. Currently, there are two peer mentoring programs on campus that are funded by federal grants. However, these programs exist for groups of students, such as at-risk students, Native American group students, and first-generation college students, which means a larger group of students have been overlooked and do not have access to the service.

Therefore, actions are warranted to fill the gap. This project involves stakeholders throughout the process of developing this program as well as involving participants in implementing the program. The ultimate objective for this project was to establish a peer mentoring program in concert with current PTK International Honor Society members at the research site. PTK members on campus are those who have over 3.5 cumulative GPAs. This project allows PTK members to have opportunities to be mentors for their peers and fulfill their oath when they swore in to be members and to aid others during the formal induction ceremony. In addition, it provides opportunities for students who struggle in their studies to seek help. It benefits both mentors and mentees. Even though there are a few peer mentors' programs on campus, some students cannot get the help and advice they need. Therefore, this project filled the gap for some students who cannot receive assistance from campus student services.

The goals and objective of the Cycle 2 action steps and activities were to prevent college dropout at the college and to increase retention rates and graduation rates by establishing a peer mentoring program in concert with the PTK honor society on campus. The activities included investigating the current campus peer mentoring programs by interviewing the programs leaders. The researcher worked closely with PTK co-sponsor and PTK officers to develop the peer mentoring program, such as interviewing collaborators and participants, providing training sessions for mentors, and designing mentoring sign-in forms. The researcher received nearly 50 submissions from mentors which indicated they performed nearly 50 peer mentoring sessions with the mentees. The past few months of implementing this peer mentoring program was an eye-opening experience. It not only improved the researcher's understanding of the operations of the institution, but also helped the researcher to understand more about the peer mentoring program.

CYCLE 2 RESULTS

This section discusses the results/findings of Cycle 2. After the implementation and evaluation of the project, the study revealed that students feel connected, encouraged, and motivated after signing up and participating in the project. However, many students lack clear understandings of federal grant sponsored programs on campus and there were many challenges to implementing a peer mentoring program at the research site. In the end of this section, the study discusses how the researcher and research site benefited from implementing this project. The findings and results from the Cycle 2 data collection support the literature review, which aligns with the need for establishing this peer-mentoring program at the college.

The findings answer research questions in this study and support study purposes. The feedback collected from stakeholders, collaborators, and participants via Zoom interviews were incorporated into the improvement of this action research project. Improvements were made throughout the process of implementation. The worth, effectiveness, and outcomes of those activities within the program were judged collectively by the feedback from stakeholders, academic performance of mentees (GPAs, classroom and campus engagement, enrollment and retention, etc.), evaluation plans, and improvement plans later as the program moves forward and beyond. The project performance, worthiness, and effectiveness informed the audience of this project by displaying the report in PowerPoint slides and to solicit their support.

This project was very successful from different institutional perspectives. First, it gained support from collaborators, stakeholders, and participants. Some mentees even would like to advocate this project to their peers as they found it beneficial to themselves. Second, it was the first peer mentoring program established through PTK at the research site since PTK was founded a few decades ago. Third, it has a good start with four mentors signing up with nearly 50 sessions between mentors and mentees so far.

Finally, this project fills the need for certain groups of students who do not meet the requirements of the other programs and are not able to access the student services due to the restrictions of the federal grants. NASNTI does offer student services to all students. However, most students do not seek help from them because they think the program is only for native American students. Therefore, the lack of similar student services to other groups of students makes this peer mentoring project through PTK more meaningful. It is needed on campus for many students who do not have full access to the wonderful student services that the federal grants provide and fills the gap of meeting every student's need of mentoring and coaching. Both mentees have rated the highest score in the survey and expressed, "I would recommend the peer mentoring program to others."

Since the researcher started the implementation process of developing a peer mentoring program through PTK International Honor Society, he gained a deeper understanding of how similar programs were developed on campus and outside of campus by interviewing different participants, including the NASNTI engagement specialist, the NASNTI director, the SSS/STEM SSS director, and the PTK OK/AR regional coordinator. Implementing this project not only assists the researcher to better understand the operation of the institution, but the research also helps him understand more depth about the peer mentoring program and better designing of the program.

DISCUSSION OF CYCLE 2 FINDINGS

Contextualization

This section discusses the findings of Cycle 2 in relation to the literature, implications of the study for the college, and the researcher's professional practice.

In the first finding, the study found that this project serves as a platform for students to connect with each other, to encourage each other, and to support each other, particularly during this era of the COVID-19 pandemic. Many extant studies acknowledged that peer mentoring programs benefits mentees in practical, emotional, and social perspectives (Crisp & Cruz, 2009; Christie, 2014; Colvin & Ashman, 2010; Geesa et al., 2018). The study found this project was beneficial to mentors, since it assisted mentors to learn new things (Bunting et al., 2012), to cultivate their leadership skills, to improve their social network, and to increase their sense of fulfillment (Castleman & Page, 2014; Power et al., 2011; Thorngren et al., 2013).

Second, students lack a clear understanding of student support services on campus, do not know how to access them, how to seek help properly, or fear seeking assistance. Many studies tried to investigate the causes and discovered various reasons, such as breakdown in communication (Cummings, 2014), lack of information (Cummings, 2014), and lack of emotional connection (Thoman et al., 2013; Winograd & Rust, 2014). Furthermore, the study also found that some students have a bias towards federal grants-sponsored programs due to their special qualifications of signing up, which moves beyond the findings of existing literature.

The third finding addressed the challenges of implementing a peer mentoring program on campus. Due to the demographics of the researcher's site, the researcher identified two specific challenges for the mentees: They did not have time for mentees and there were no good matches for mentees. Once the program was established, the researcher found it difficult for mentees to sign up for the program, which confirms previous literature suggesting that students do not want to seek academic help (Pellegrino, 2012; Pillai, 2010; Winograd & Rust, 2014). The findings also support reasons identified by previous research, such as lack of motivation (Fowler & Boylan, 2010), self-regulation (Perry et al., 2005), and learning-goal orientation (Pillai, 2010; Thoman et al., 2013). Some students may not want to change, while some expressed concerns about confidentiality (Pillai, 2010). Similar to Ciscell et al. (2016) who found barriers of preventing students from seeking help, this study also found it hard to recruit mentors due to their busy schedule or low confidence, while some literature recommended using financial compensation and additional forms of motivation (Esplin et al., 2012).

Overall, the findings in this action research are consistent with the extant literature. A few pieces of the findings move beyond the findings of extant literature. The existing studies also helped to explain and support the researcher's study. The researcher found no contradictions between the study and the current literature. Next, as a scholar-practitioner, the researcher hopes to provide recommendations of practice for his organization based on the knowledge generated in this study, the implications and conclusion drawn from this study, and research implications for the organization.

Implications for Practice

The findings and the new knowledge generated in this doctoral study underscore the importance of contributing social justice within the organization. As an insider, researchers should act as a scholar-practitioner in their field of higher education for systemic change. Bell (2007) stated that "social justice is a process and goal," which aims to distribute resources equitably in order to meet the physical and psychological needs of all the groups (p. 1).

First, the institution administrators should acknowledge the importance of such campus projects, therefore continue to invest more financial resources and provide support to such projects and services on campus which focus on student success. In Cycle 1 research, it studied the issue of dropouts and discovered the obstacles that cause community college students to drop out. The findings in Cycle 1 indicate an action research project is needed, which is to implement a peer mentoring program in concert with PTK International Honor Society at the study site. Practice is always shaped by theory because theory enables us to think about our intentions and it also provides a framework for questioning and challenging our practices (Bell, 2007). This action research project utilized peer mentors to point directions and assist the institution to distribute the resources equitably, in order to meet the needs of student mentees, particularly at-risk students.

Second, the implication for the institution is to provide more resources by educating students about the available resources on campus and encouraging them to utilize the services. There are many services available on campus for students to access. However, this study found that many students are not aware of the services, do not know how to utilize the services, or do not want to seek help. In the study, the researcher found that the two main student services (NANSTI & TRIO) on campus are sponsored by federal grants, which means that there are constraints and requirements for students to be qualified. Even though NANSTI is accessible to every student who wants to utilize its service, the study discovered many students have a wrong perception of the service as only serving "Native American" student groups due to its unique name of the program. The research site is a very diverse college with a diverse student body. Meanwhile, the institution needs not to neglect the rest of the study groups who do not belong to any certain groups and provide free quality resources and services to all the students on campus. This action research project fills the gap and provides a platform and opportunity for those underserved students to develop and progress.

Lastly, it is recommended that institutions in higher education need to be innovative by working and partnering with civil organizations to tackle the problems that students face in their daily lives. Knowing that transportation is an issue preventing some students from coming to class, the researcher took the initiative to talk with stakeholders on campus and found there are free local available transit services for students. Thereafter, the NASNTI director compiled a list of local community resources from Central Oklahoma Community Action Agency (COCAA) and emailed to all faculty and staff groups on campus, so they can share these resources with the college students. Bell (2007) argued that oppression is not discrimination, bias, or prejudice because it emphasizes the synthesis of institutional and systemic discrimination, personal bias, and social prejudice in a complex society that shapes every aspect of life. Bell (2007) also pointed out that oppression indicates structural and material constraints that restrict a person's life chances, self-development, and self-determination, which leads to the discussion of fighting for social justice.

FUTURE WORK AND RESEARCH

Eacott (2016) argued that the current systems for achieving social justice through the Doctor of Education (EdD) program in educational leadership have yet to actually alter the status quo as they have only relied on credentialing to influence educational labor. The Doctor of Education program needs to cultivate new methods of understanding educational leadership, management, and administration in order to serve as an incubator for social justice (Eacott, 2016). Lumby and Coleman (2007) stated educators are potential leaders by influencing those in their organizations. This research study also changed his perceptions of community colleges and helped him better understand the root causes of many issues in higher education. In Cycle 1 of the study, it found that there are many stumbling blocks for community college students, such as financial burdens, time management skills, and lack of guidance and mentorship. Many students come from low-income families and need financial aid. Some of them have to drop out of college because they cannot afford it. Some have to drop out of college because it is too stressful to deal with financial struggles and to balance between school and work. In the research, he learned that some students assumed they are not eligible for financial aid because of lack of knowledge or applying for financial aid late. The researcher plans to work with financial aid staff in the future and invite them to his peer mentoring training, so they can train peer mentors and let them be the bridge to inform their mentees with financial aid literacy.

This study inspires the researcher to be a change agent and an advocate for the underrepresented students who deserve more financial support from the government for their education. Blackmore (2013) emphasized that the core of social justice theory is the significance of agency that moves beyond the limitations of equal access and participation. Social justice in education elucidates different forms of inequality arising out of different forms of oppression. As a change agent, researchers should employ education to improve one's condition. Many students at community colleges are nontraditional adult students who have dropped out before due to various reasons and decided to come back to school to better their lives. The study found that students have many other responsibilities in their lives, particularly nontraditional students. He found that non-traditional students get behind because of missing tests or assignments when they have to miss classes to take care of their children. Therefore, the researcher plans to work with the staff of the current two federal grants sponsored programs and investigates the possibilities of establishing the daycare center in the college.

As for future research, the researcher will continue the research on how to improve the peer mentoring program, how peer mentoring programs help with the institutional objectives: graduation rates and retention rates, and how to develop quality student services on campus. As an educator, he plans to continue to investigate this issue and be an advocate for students to receive the best possible opportunities.

CONCLUSION

As an educator in higher education, the researcher learned that teaching should not be just a job, but he should use his leadership skills to make a difference in students' lives. Fullan (1993) expressed that beyond better pedagogy, it is important for educators to improve conditions that surround the classroom to enhance students' learning in the classroom. The author gave many guidelines including redefining educators' role to extend beyond the classroom, engaging as a vital part of the university, and articulating your inner voice. Lunenburg (2010) said that every organizational change, whether large or small, requires multiple leaders. As an educator and a scholar-practitioner, the researcher has been working with stakeholders and colleagues on campus for the past 3 years using action research to provide practical solutions for students to graduate and for colleges to increase graduation rate and retention rate, which is his passion and action to promote social justice in education. This program potentially contributes to institutional objectives which are to increase retention rate and graduation rate, to improve students' academic performance by increasing student engagement in the classroom and their involvement on campus. The student participants who signed up for the project got empowered and motivated, which inspired them to actively participate in other student organizations and get involved with community services. This project brings potential contributions to other community colleges in the United States. Many community colleges in the United States have PTK honor society. The successful model of this project can be duplicated and implemented to other community college settings in the United States. This research brought awareness for more support from society because education does make a big difference in people's lives and the society.

REFERENCES

Araque, F., Roldán, C., & Salguero, A. (2009). Factors influencing university drop out rates. *Computers & Education, 53*(3), 563–574. https://doi.org/10.1016/j.compedu.2009.03.013

Atkinson, R. (1998). *The life story interview.* SAGE Publications.

Bell, L. A. (2007). Theoretical foundations for social justice education. In M. Adams, L. A. Bell, & P. Griffin (Eds.), *Teaching for diversity and social justice* (pp. 1–14). Routledge.

Birren, J. E., & Birren, B. A. (1996). Autobiography: Exploring the self and encouraging development. In J. E. Birren, G. M. Kenyon, J. E. Ruth, J. J. F. Schroots, & T. Svensson (Eds.), *Aging and biography: Explorations in adult development* (pp. 283–299). Springer Publishing.

Blackmore, J. (2013). A feminist critical perspective on educational leadership. *International Journal of Leadership in Education, 16*(2), 139–154. https://doi.org/10.1080/13603124.2012.754057

Bonneau, K. (2015, July). *Brief 3: What is a dropout?* North Carolina Education Research Data Center, Center for Child and Family Policy. https://www.purdue.edu/hhs/hdfs/fii/wp-content/uploads/2015/07/s_ncfis04c03.pdf

Bound, J., Lovenheim, M. F., & Turner, S. (2012). Increasing time to baccalaureate degree in the United States (NBER working paper 15892). *Education Finance and Policy, 7*(4), 375–424. https://www.nber.org/system/files/working_papers/w15892/w15892.pdf

Bunting, B., Dye, B., Pinnegar, S., & Robinson, K. (2012). Understanding the dynamics of peer mentor learning: A narrative study. *Journal of the First-Year Experience & Students in Transition, 24*(1), 61–78. http://www.ingentaconnect.com/content/fyesit/fyesit/2012/00000024/00000001/art00004?crawler=true

Casanova, J. R., Cervero, A., Núñez, J. C., Almeida, L. S., & Bernardo, A. (2018). Factors that determine the persistence and dropout of university students. *Psicothema, 30*(4), 408–414. https://doi.org/10.7334/psicothema2018.155

Castleman, B. L., & Page, L. C. (2014). Summer nudging: Can personalized text messages and peer mentor outreach increase college going among low-income high school graduates? *Journal of Economic Behavior and Organization, 115*, 144–160. https://doi.org/10.1016/j.jebo.2014.12.008

Castleman, B. L., & Page, L. C. (2016). Freshman year financial aid nudges: An experiment to increase FAFSA renewal and college persistence. *Journal of Human Resources, 51*(2), 389–415. https://doi.org/10.3368/jhr.51.2.0614-6458R

Chen, G. (2022, May 30). The catch-22 of community college graduation rates. *Community College Review.* https://www.communitycollegereview.com/blog/the-catch-22-of-community-college-graduation-rates

Choi, Y. (2018). Student employment and persistence: Evidence of effect heterogeneity of student employment on college dropout. *Research in Higher Education, 59*(1), 88–107. https://doi.org/10.1007/s11162-017-9458-y

Christie, H. (2014). Peer mentoring in higher education: Issues of power and control. *Teaching in Higher Education, 19*(8), 955–965. https://doi.org/10.1080/13562517.2014.934355

Ciscell, G., Foley, L., Luther, K., Howe, R., & Gjsedal, T. (2016). Barriers to accessing tutoring services among students who received a mid-semester warning. *The Learning Assistance Review, 21*(2), 39–54. https://eric.ed.gov/?id=EJ1114513

Collings, R., Swanson, V., & Watkins, R. (2016). Peer mentoring during the transition to university: Assessing the usage of a formal scheme within the UK. *Studies in Higher Education, 41*(11), 1995–2010. https://doi.org/10.1080/03075079.2015.1007939

Colvin, J. W., & Ashman, M. (2010). Roles, risks, and benefits of peer mentoring relationships in higher education. *Mentoring & Tutoring: Partnership in Learning, 18*(2), 121–134. https://doi.org/10.1080/13611261003678879

Crisp, G., & Cruz, I. (2009). Mentoring college students: A critical review of literature between 1990 and 2007. *Research in Higher Education, 50*(6), 525–545. https://doi.org/10.1007/s11162-009-9130-2

Cummings, A. M. (2014). *The impact of student support services on academic success at a select historically Black college and university* (Publication No. 532) [Doctoral dissertation, University of North Florida]. UNF Graduate Theses and Dissertations. https://digitalcommons.unf.edu/etd/532

Davis-Kean, P. E. (2005). The influence of parent education and family income on child achievement: The indirect role of parental expectations and the home environment. *Journal of Family Psychology, 19*(2), 294–304. https://doi.org/10.1037/0893-3200.19.2.294

DiCicco-Bloom, B., & Crabtree, B. F. (2006). The qualitative research interview. *Medical Education, 40*(4), 314–321. https://doi.org/10.1111/j.1365-2929.2006.02418.x

Eacott, S. (2016). Disruptions in production. In A. L. Ellis (Ed.), *Ed.D. Programs as incubators for social justice leadership* (pp. 1–13). Sense Publishers.

Esplin, P., Seabold, J., & Pinnegar, F. (2012). The architecture of a high-impact and sustainable peer leader program: A blueprint for success. *New Directions for Higher Education, 2012*(157), 85–100. https://doi.org/10.1002/he.20008

Fowler, P. R., & Boylan, H. R. (2010). Increasing student success and retention: A multidimensional approach. *Journal of Developmental Education, 34*(2), 2–10. https://files.eric.ed.gov/fulltext/EJ986268.pdf

Fullan, M. G. (1993). Why teachers must become change agents. *Educational Leadership, 50*(6), 12–17. https://eric.ed.gov/?id=EJ459419

Geesa, R., Lowery, K., & McConnell, K. (2018). Mentee perspectives of a first-year peer mentoring program for education doctoral (EdD) students. *International Journal of Doctoral Studies, 13*, 471–495. https://doi.org/10.28945/4148

Gillis, A., &. Jackson, W. (2002). *Research methods for nurses: Methods and interpretation*. F.A. Davis.

Herr, K., & Anderson, G. L. (2005). *The action research dissertation: A guide for students and faculty*. SAGE Publications.

Kantrowitz, M. (2021, November 19). Shocking statistics about college graduation rates. *Forbes.* https://www.forbes.com/sites/markkantrowitz/2021/11/18/shocking-statistics-about-college-graduation-rates/?sh=16e68bb82b69

Leonhardt, D., & Chinoy, S. (2019, May 23). Opinion: The college dropout crisis. *The New York Times.* https://www.nytimes.com/interactive/2019/05/23/opinion/sunday/college-graduation-rates-ranking.html

Lumby, J., & Coleman, M. (2007). *Leadership and diversity: Challenging theory and practice in education.* SAGE Publications.

Lunenburg, F. C. (2010). Managing change: The role of the change agent. *International Journal of Management Business, and Administration, 13,* 1–6. https://scirp.org/reference/referencespapers.aspx?referenceid=2647311

Ma, J., & Baum, S. (2016). Trends in community colleges: Enrollment, prices, student debt, and completion. *College Board Research Brief, 4,* 1–23. https://research.collegeboard.org/media/pdf/trends-community-colleges-research-brief.pdf

Mabel, Z., Castleman, B. L., Bettinger, E. P. (2017). *Finishing the last lap: Experimental evidence on strategies to increase college completion for students at risk of late departure.* https://scholar.harvard.edu/files/zmabel/files/n2fl_pilot_year_working_paper_draft_9-6-17.pdf

Martinez, E., Ordu, C., Della Sala, M. R., & McFarlane, A. (2013). Striving to obtain a school–work–life balance: The full-time doctoral student. *International Journal of Doctoral Studies, 8,* 39–59. http://ijds.org/Volume8/IJDSv8p039-059Martinez0375.pdf

Millea, M., Wills, R., Elder, A., & Molina, D. (2018). What matters in college student success? Determinants of college retention and graduation rates. *Education, 138*(4), 309–322. https://eric.ed.gov/?id=EJ1180297

Miles, M. B., Huberman, A. M., & Saldaäna, J. (2019). *Qualitative data analysis: A methods sourcebook* (3rd ed.). SAGE Publications.

Mitchell, M. (2017, August 24). *Higher ed funding down in nearly every state over past decade.* Center on Budget and Policy Priorities. https://www.cbpp.org/blog/higher-ed-funding-down-in-nearly-every-state-over-past-decade

Oriol, X., Mendonza, M., Covarrubias, C. G., & Molina, V. M. (2017). Positive emotions, autonomy support and academic performance of university students: The mediating role of academic engagement and self-efficacy. *Revista de Psicodidáctica, 22*(1), 45–53. https://doi.org/10.1387/RevPsicodidact.14280

Pantages, T. J., & Creedon, C. F. (1978). Studies of college attrition: 1950–1975. *Review of Educational Research, 48*(1), 49–101. https://doi.org/10.2307/1169909

Pellegrino, J. W. (2012). Assessment of science learning: Living in interesting times. *Journal of Research in Science Teaching, 49*(6), 831–841. https://doi.org/10.1002/tea.21032

Perry, R., Hladkyi, S., Pekrun, R., Clifton, R., & Chipperfield, J. (2005). Perceived academic control and failure in college students: A three-year study of scholastic attainment. *Research in Higher Education, 46*(5), 535–596. https://doi.org/10.1007/s11162-005-3364-4

Pillai, M. (2010). Locating learning development in a university library: Promoting effective academic help seeking. *New Review of Academic Librarianship, 16*(2), 121–144. https://doi.org/10.1080/13614531003791717

Posa, K. L. (2011). *A study of satisfaction and perceived learning and development of peer mentors in higher education* (Publication No. ED535800) [Doctoral dissertation, West Virginia University]. ProQuest Dissertations and Theses Global.

Power, R. K., Miles, B. B., Peruzzi, A., & Voerman, A. (2011). Building bridges: A practical guide to developing and implementing a subject-specific peer-to-peer academic mentoring program for first-year higher education students. *Asian Social Science, 7*(11). 75–80. https://doi.org/10.5539/ass.v7n11p75

Rosário, P., Pereira, A., Núñez, J. C., Cunha, J., Fuentes, S., Polydoro, S., & Fernández, E. (2014). An explanatory model of the intention to continue studying among non- traditional university students. *Psicothema, 26*(1), 84–90. https://doi.org/10.7334/psicothema2013.176

Scipioni, J. (2018). *51% of college students dropped out of school due to costs, study finds.* FOX Business. https://www.foxbusiness.com/features/51-of-college-students-dropped-out-of-school-due-to-costs-study-finds

Scott-Clayton, J. (2012). What explains trends in labor supply among U.S. undergraduates, 1970–2009? *National Tax Journal, 65*(1), 181–210. https://doi.org/10.17310/ntj.2012.1.07

Strauss, V. (2019, September 10). 'A dereliction duty': College dropout scandal—And how to fix it. *The Washington Post.* https://www.washingtonpost.com/education/2019/09/10/a-dereliction-duty-college-dropout-scandal-how-fix-it/

Thoman, D. B., Smith, J. L., Brown, E. R., Chase, J., & Lee, J. Y. K. (2013). Beyond performance: A motivational experiences model of stereotype threat. *Educational Psychology Review, 25*(2), 211–243. https://doi.org/10.1007/s10648-013-9219-1

Thorngren, J. M., Nelson, M. D., Baker, L. J., Zuck, B., & Koltz, R. L. (2013). On track: A university retention model utilizing school counseling program interns. *Journal of School Counseling, 11*(16), 1–18. https://eric.ed.gov/?id=EJ1034739

Winograd, G., & Rust, J. P. (2014). Stigma, awareness of support services, and academic help-seeking among historically underrepresented first-year college students. *The Learning Assistance Review, 19*(2), 19–44. https://nclca.wildapricot.org/resources/Documents/Publications/TLAR/Issues/19_2.pdf

CHAPTER 10

IMPROVING RETENTION OF HIGH-ACHIEVING, GENERATION Z STUDENTS AT A PRIVATE, LIBERAL ARTS UNIVERSITY

Lars Farabee

The focus of this action research study was the retention of high achieving, Generation Z students at a private, liberal arts institution. The research site was an institution in central North Carolina, which has suffered from less than desirable retention numbers from freshman to sophomore year, with additional deficiencies in retention from sophomore to junior and junior to senior years. While retention at the institution has hovered around the 80%–85% mark, which nationally is a respectable level, the administration has sought to improve this rate and to increase the number of students that continue through their academic program. The university relies on many of these high-achieving student groups persisting through a 4-year program, and as such, the institution has looked towards new initiatives

Taking Action, pages 153–166
Copyright © 2024 by Information Age Publishing
www.infoagepub.com
All rights of reproduction in any form reserved.

that could help engage and retain these higher achieving students more effectively.

While retention overall is an issue that many colleges and universities throughout the country face, much of the research focuses on improving retention for "at-risk" students while not as much attention has been paid to why high-achieving students leave after their freshman year (Echternacht, 2016; Gray, 2013; Griffith University et al., 2015). This action research study sought to understand the experience of the high-achieving students to attract and retain more effectively this group. It also explored to what extent a sense of community was important to these high achieving, Generation Z students, and what they believe are the components of a strong community.

BACKGROUND

The project sought to help to improve the quality and meaningfulness of the educational program for high-achieving Generation Z students and beyond, with the idea that this would eventually lead to an uptick in retention. The students participating in the educational program in question have been defined as those having high GPAs, high optional test scores, and a willingness to participate in a fellows program designed to offer specific content and opportunities related to their area of academic interest. After initial conversations and a review of the extant literature, it was believed that these students required a sense of community, which is often not found in many of the traditional honors programs found at colleges and universities today (Bowman & Culver, 2018).

METHODOLOGY

The researcher used a qualitative, action research approach for the design and implementation of this study and its subsequent recommended action plan. A variety of data collection methods were used, including semi-structured interviews, surveys, and direct classroom observations. Cycle-1 data collection focused on the sense of community, or lack thereof, within each of the fellow's programs and across the host research site. In the tradition of action research, the goal of the initial data collection cycles was to create an action plan to help solve the problem or problems posed by the research questions.

The Cycle-2 action plan centered around the creation of a Communication Fellows competition. The goal of this program was to encourage students to work with their peers from different departments to create a collaborative educational product. The idea of "bubble bursting" was central to the action plan, as this was a chief complaint and concern among students within Cycle-1; students felt as if their experience at the host research site was "living in a bubble within a bubble."

The first phase of data collection consisted of surveys distributed via email to different groups on campus. Groups consisted of sophomores, juniors, and seniors in the fellows programs; as well as juniors and seniors that had the same "academic index" (an admissions score comprised of GPA and SAT/GRE scores) as students that enrolled in a fellow's program but who had not enrolled in one of the programs; and a group of sophomores with the same academic index as their peers in the fellow's programs who for some reason or another had not choose to enroll in a fellow's program. These last two groups helped to form a baseline of comparison between the traditional program and the newly enhanced fellow's programs.

The second phase of data collection consisted of individual interviews with members of each of the three survey groups. An additional, more observational method of gathering data included attending meetings and events conducted by students in the fellow's programs, as well as attendance at a co-curricular committee meeting in which the fellow's programs were discussed at length. This type of mixed methods approach seeks to create what Stringer (2014) calls "triangulation." By having multiple sources of data, the hope is that more reliable information could be gathered throughout the study.

The process of collecting and analyzing data was inspired by a variety of different resources. A key feature was informed by Carl and Ravitch's work on "member checking," which is the "set of processes in which researchers 'check in' with participants in a qualitative study" (Carl & Ravitch, 2018). This can be a formal re-evaluation or an informal meeting, and in an effort to not want to take up more of the participant's time, the "member-check" was comprised of a short discussion a couple of weeks after the initial interview. The gap in time allowed both the participant and the interviewer to think through responses that may have come out raw or in the moment. This gave the interviewer a much better perspective on what the participant was trying to get across in the interview.

Identifying and tracking these high-achieving students was aided by a group of stakeholders that were cultivated at the early stages of the research study. What concerned upper levels of the administration most was that the largest drop in retention had been in the most academically qualified groups of students.

Each group of participants and stakeholders came to this project with their own agendas and interests in the research (Stringer, 2014), and it was important for the process that the researcher worked towards each of these goals over the course of the project. Each goal, from the faculty wanting to have better students in their programs to the administration wanting those students to stay at the research site for longer to the students themselves wanting to have a better, more connected experience, ultimately flavored the research project over time. That kind of collaboration between researcher and stakeholder is a hallmark of action research (Herr & Anderson, 2014), and could be seen throughout the process as the researcher sought a means to help create lasting change at the research site.

CYCLE 1 FINDINGS & DISCUSSION

A lack of connection within the fellow's program and across campus was represented in a number of survey responses, as well as in the individual interviews and the co-curricular meetings. Participants stated that even though the community was strong within the fellow's program, "I still wish I knew more of the members." Discussions of cliques came up multiple times. One participant described how "the media fellows have separated into different cliques based off of majors and personalities." Another stated, "The fellows are a pretty tight knit group, but I don't think the university as a whole has a strong community." The literature points to this as a main concern for students, regardless of their academic ability (Bott-Knutson et al., 2020; Scager et al., 2016). These authors describe methods in which this kind of connection can be built out through, for instance, collaborative learning spaces or shared educational products.

One key factor that was expressed throughout the data gathering process was that community building was extremely important to these students, which is reflective in literature concerning these high-achieving students (Bott-Knutson et al., 2020; Hébert & McBee, 2007; Kezar & Kitchen, 2020). The researcher used this data, in addition to a review of the extant literature and discussions with university stakeholders, to create the Communication Fellows competition. This completion sought to bring students together from various academic majors with the Communication Fellows program and have them work together to work on a shared academic project. These projects would then be judged by a panel of faculty and staff members at the host research site. Participants in the competition would all receive some kind of prize, with the winning group getting sponsorship to a regional or national conference or festival. Participants stated that even though the community was strong within the fellow's program, "I still wish I knew more of the members." The Communication Fellows competition aimed to connect more members with each other.

Communication Fellows Competition

The action step was implemented during the Fall 2020 semester. Four groups ended up submitting work for the competition. Two of these groups were independent, and two of them worked together as a part of a class assigned project. Each of the four groups reported a greater sense of belonging and a strong sense of community during the process. More importantly, they attributed their desire to do well in the project not to the need to increase their GPA through a higher grade, but instead increase their knowledge base through obtaining a skill they could use later on in their career. This is mirrored through the ideas posed by the achievement-goal theory (Scager et al., 2016; Senko et al., 2011).

CYCLE 2 FINDINGS AND DISCUSSION

It was during Cycle 2 that an action step was initiated. This step was the creation of a collaborative educational product across majors within the Communication Fellows. This collaboration brought students together from different grade levels and from different backgrounds in a way that they might not have been able to in their regular curriculum. Through this action step, the following findings came to light: collaboration leads to community, students did not compete for a grade, and students competed to gain a skill. These findings are framed by the existing literature regarding community, student retention, and the goals and characteristics of high-achieving, Generation Z students.

Learning Communities

The common thread between all these students was that they were all interested in some form of communication and had been drawn to the Communication Fellows program because of that interest. Bonet and Waters (2013) found similar success with learning communities at a community college in New York. This shared learning experience aided in both the understanding and retention of the knowledge being taught in the classrooms, as well as in the retention of these groups of students. Similar studies also found that working in communities with shared educational experiences benefited these high-achieving students (Hébert & McBee, 2007; Hébert, 2018; Kezar & Kitchen, 2020).

A Sense of Belonging

In a study conducted by Bott-Knutson et al. (2020), first year fellowship programs were investigated as a method to connect honors students together and to build a strong community. They found that these types of programs, which not only highlight the academic features of an honors program, but also promote fellowship and collaboration amongst members, show positive outcomes. They highlight a sense of community and heighten a sense of belonging felt by participating students (Bott-Knutson et al., 2020). This need to belong is also highlighted in work by Scager et al. (2016) and Silver Wolf et al. (2017), studies show a positive connection between the sense of belonging to that community as a key factor for student success and satisfaction.

Not for a Grade

For the independent projects, those completed outside of a class requirement, grades obviously did not play a factor in the motivation to participate in the Communication Fellows competition. What was surprising, however, was that for those that did have a grade attached to their participation, the grade itself was not the motivating factor for wanting to do well on the particular project that they worked on. The researcher had believed that because these students were high-achieving and had been placed into the Communication Fellows program based on an additional application, the desire to get the highest grade possible would be paramount in their minds. This is reflected by the perfectionist nature in many parents of this type of student (Giancola & Kahlenberg, 2016; Miller et al., 2012; Miller & Spiers Neumeister, 2017; Spiers Neumister, Fletcher, & Burney, 2015), a nature that is often passed along to their Generation Z children.

A Disconnect Between Points A and B

The lack of concern for grades felt by some participants in the Communication Fellows competition may be attributed to several factors, the largest of which is that the colloquium classes that were the focal point of this action step are typically one-credit courses that showcase a special topic in the Communication Fellows curriculum. Students' responses in regards to these courses highlight a disconnect between "A to B," the idea that a student's educational experience has to lead them to somewhere meaningful. These high achieving, Generation Z students demand a higher value for their experience than from generations that came before them (Johnson &

Sveen, 2020). They want a clear path from what they are learning to the career that they will apply those skills to in the future (Rinn & Plucker, 2019). The Communication Fellows competition showed that for some students, that path is not always clear.

Gaining a Skill

Students that participated in the Communication Fellows competition did so for a variety of reasons. One that came up time and again was the opportunity to gain a specific skill that they had otherwise not been exposed to during their time in the Communication Fellows program, or the chance to practice a skill that they thought would be beneficial to them in their future careers. Mega et al. (2014) found that self-regulated learning and strong intrinsic motivations directly impacted the overall success of students in an educational environment. Students that participated in the Communication Fellows competition shared similar traits and characteristics in learning styles. They enjoyed the autonomy of creating their own projects, and the student leadership board appreciated the freedom of coming up with the theme of the competition. Despite this, students also responded that they liked having some guidance at the beginning of the process, including help with learning the game engine and having a topic given to them instead of having to come up with one on their own. "We had a starting point to jump off from" was how one participant described it, which leads the researcher to believe that while these successful students are laser-focused on their goal (Stelnicki et al., 2015), they still need the support and guidance of engaging faculty.

Mastery of a Skill

Instead of the prospect of a good grade pushing students to do well and to participate in the competition, it was the mastery of a certain skill that was ultimately the strongest motivator. For some who worked on the independent documentary, *Empty Sanctuary*, the chance to pilot a drone to collect aerial footage was a significant piece of his experience in the competition. For one student who worked on the documentary, *Masked Heroes*, the competition exposed him to RED HD cameras, which he did not know that the university had access to. "I didn't know we could just check these things out and use them," he said later in an interview, "That was something I wouldn't have known about unless I'd worked on this project."

Students that worked on the video game arguably learned the most over the course of the completion. The professor leading that course was impressed by the amount of work that they were able to accomplish in such a short amount of time, particularly because they were all learning a new game engine while they were trying to complete the project for the competition.

In an interview conducted with one of the students who worked on it, the student said that the potential to learn this skill was why he signed up to take the colloquium in the first place.

This skill mastery fits with the "achievement-goal theory," which describes the motivations of high-achieving students as a function of reaching a specific goal or task (Senko et al., 2011; Wolters, 2004). Rather than simply wanting to learn a skill that they will later forget, achievement-goal theory advances the idea towards mastery of a knowledge base as a method of increased engagement for students in each field of study (Wolters, 2004).

The Communication Fellows competition is still in its infancy and will require many more iterations for it to be a truly successful program. However, even after its first cycle, the competition has yielded a variety of success stories. One of the independent group projects was submitted into several film festivals around the country, with plans to screen the other projects at national festivals and conferences. Students who participated in the competition showed excitement for the process and an enthusiasm to work together towards a common goal. They made important connections with their peers across academic grade levels (Rinn & Plucker, 2019; Turner & Thompson, 2014), which should ultimately lead to greater rates of retention for these high-achieving, Generation Z students (Bowman & Culver, 2018). They surprisingly sought knowledge, not a letter grade to boost their GPAs. The competition engaged them in their work by exposing them to a set of skills that they could readily connect to their desired career paths (Scager et al., 2016; Senko et al., 2011). Further study is needed, but the future looks bright for these participants and for the future of the Communication Fellows competition.

IMPLICATIONS FOR PRACTICE

There is evidence that the type of collaborative learning that took place during the Communication Fellows competition could take hold at the host research site quickly and with the support of university stakeholders. Practices such as interprofessional education (IPE) are already being implemented within the curricula for the PharmD, DPT, MSAT, and MPAS programs at the graduate level. This kind of collaborative approach to learning could take place at the undergraduate level as well, with the fellow's programs acting as the vanguard of this kind of effort.

Throughout the study, students discussed wanting to know what other students in other programs were doing. The university is already gated off from the rest of the surrounding community, giving some students the feeling of disconnection from the outside world. Within the walls of campus, students are curious to learn more about what their peers are interested in and what people from different academic disciplines are engaged in during their time at the university. What were they researching? What were they learning? What were they creating? A competition where students from a variety of academic disciplines and backgrounds could easily meet the needs of these high-achieving, Generation Z students. This is the real opportunity for continued change, where student groups who have been segmented out based on academic interests can be brought back together to create a larger sense of campus community and inclusion. The initial theme, "building bridges" was chosen as a less "controversial" option by the student leadership board of the Communication Fellows program. Despite this desire to avoid confrontation, issues of social justice came to light within that broader theme, due in large part to the COVID-19 pandemic.

The colloquium group that worked on the documentary film chose to highlight a group of women who began making masks for local hospitals, clinics, and elder care facilities that did not have enough access to adequate PPE (personal protective equipment). The documentary was an inspiring look at a group of women who did what they could to help their community in a time of need. It also underscored the disparity of access to health care resources among communities in our area, a topic that many of the students participating in the competition had not been exposed to.

Similarly, the independent group who worked on a documentary called *Empty Sanctuary*, about a local church's struggles to maintain services and connect with the community in a remote area, were exposed to issues of inequity. By documenting the church's challenges, students highlighted the fact that many in their community did not have easy access to high-speed internet or adequate training to use it.

This kind of tangential exposure to issues of social justice was what the researcher hoped for from the outset of this action research study. While not the primary focus of the research of the main problem being addressed, the ability of educators to expose students of means to issues of inequity has the potential to lead to change. At the very least, it offers the chance for students to begin to question their own viewpoints, to challenge where they see themselves in the world. It forces them to consider a life experience beyond their own, pushing them to think critically in a way that could lead them to becoming change agents themselves.

This kind of exposure shows gaps within the community at large. Killinger et al. (2019) discussed how identifying these kinds of gaps can be important work for honors students, which are similar to the research site's fellow's programs in many respects. By linking these gaps to the work that the students complete in class, they not only create a richer experience for those involved, but also provide an opportunity to bring in issues of social justice and equity into the program and have them match up seamlessly with the rest of the curriculum.

FUTURE RESEARCH

There were several areas that could be seen as jumping off points for future research that resulted from this action research study. While the researcher was primarily focused on student engagement and community building as a tool to improve retention of high-achieving, Generation Z students, these additional topics could add to the body of literature regarding this group of highly sought-after students.

Hesitancy for Controversy

Students in the study seemed hesitant to take on issues of social justice, or those that they deemed to be controversial. This leads back to the classroom observation that the researcher took part in early in the data collection process. In that setting, students were making empathetic leaps in understanding an experience that was outside their own. When it came time to select the theme for the Communication Fellows competition, however, students did not want to select a topic that would meet some of the issues facing the world today "head-on" and instead went with something broader.

The researcher is interested in learning more about the roots of this hesitancy, which seems to go against movements like March for Our Lives or other social protests that took place during the 2020–2021 academic year.

Scholarship: Financial Aid

The scholarship component of the fellow's programs was mentioned in every survey and interview conducted during this action research study. However, the responses tended to mirror the findings of Jalal and Khaksari (2019), where short-term merit-based aid programs had little impact on lasting increases in retention or success in 4-year programs.

Participants in the Communication Fellows competition, and in the wider fellow's program population, regularly cited other reasons more readily than the scholarship as to why they remained in the program. The scholarship might have been a strong recruitment tool, but it was not one that greatly impacted retention. Further research specifically focused on the scholarship component of the fellow's program students would be beneficial to the institution moving forward to aid in their awarding strategies, as it is often the college environment, and not the aid amount, that has a more lasting impact on performance and retention (Cohodes & Goodman, 2014; Cornwell et al., 2006).

COVID-19

The COVID-19 pandemic cannot be overlooked when researching these groups of high-achieving, Generation Z students. The pandemic affected nearly every aspect of their lives, and it will assuredly have a lasting impact for years to come.

The research site was more fortunate than many colleges and universities throughout the country, as remote coursework only took place from March to May 2020. Classes were held in person (with few exceptions) for the 2020–2021 academic year, which aided in the completion of projects during the Communication Fellows competition. With that said, students did have to do a large part of their group work after class over virtual meeting platforms, group text chains, and phone calls. Studying the sense of community built without having to resort to these measures could help strengthen the in-class experience for the fellow's programs.

On the other hand, studying the successes and failures of using virtual spaces could lead to a richer experience for students looking for an online experience. The research site is just now working its way into the online arena, with graduate programs being its first foray into online options. Studying how this group of students in the Communication Fellow's program used these virtual tools to create impressive, high-quality educational products could better inform the host site on its plans for online program expansion.

CONCLUSION

These programs were created to address an issue many college universities face today: "How can we keep better students on our campuses for longer periods of time?" The sense of community that educators and administrators have attempted to foster is there for some students. For others, the connection has yet to have been made. Additional data will have to be gathered to gain a greater understanding of why that polarization is occurring, and what can be done to create a more unified, positive response.

There are signs, however, that the tide is shifting slowly in the right direction. The limited scope of the action step in Cycle 2 allows for the ability to scale the project up and out beyond the Communication Fellows. The researcher has already contacted the new head of the Communication

Fellows program to ensure that this type of competition is something that can be integrated into the program moving forward. In addition to this, the researcher will be scheduling meetings with the heads of the remaining fellow's programs currently in place (business, education, leadership, and natural science). It is the hope of the researcher that these programs may be able to incorporate some type of competition which focuses on collaborative group work into their structure.

Because of the increase in both retention and recruitment that have come from the implementation of these fellow's programs, the administration has elected to expand the programs into different areas. The researcher is committed to continuing to work with the co-curricular committee that was formed to evaluate these programs in real time. Trends do point to a positive increase in both retention and recruitment for these highly sought-after students, with early retention numbers showing an 11-point increase of students enrolled in the fellow's programs returning from year to year. In addition to this, more than 40% of all incoming freshmen are enrolled in one of the fellow's programs offered at the host site for the 2021–2022 academic year. These positive trends reinforce the need for these programs, and the success of the action step implemented in this study could potentially lead to the creation of even more programming for students.

REFERENCES

Bott-Knutson, R. C., Duque, C., Mook, N., & Grassel, M. (2020). First-year fellowship: Fostering an inclusive community within honors. *Journal of College Student Development, 61*(1), 121–125. https://eric.ed.gov/?id=EJ1242011

Bowman, N. A., & Culver, K. C. (2018). When do honors programs make the grade? Conditional effects on college satisfaction, achievement, retention, and graduation. *Research in Higher Education, 59*(3), 249–272. https://doi.org/10.1007/s11162-017-9466-y

Carl, N., & Ravitch, S. (2018). Member check. In B. Frey (Ed.), *The SAGE encyclopedia of educational research, measurement, and evaluation* (Vols. 1–4; p. 1050). SAGE Publications.

Cohodes, S., & Goodman, J. (2014). Merit aid, college quality, and college completion: Massachusetts' Adams Scholarship as an in-kind subsidy. *American Economic Journal: Applied Economics, 6*(4), 251–285. https://doi.org/10.1257/app.6.4.251

Cornwell, C., Mustard, D. B., & Sridhar, D. J. (2006). The enrollment effects of merit-based financial aid: Evidence from Georgia's HOPE program. *Journal of Labor Economics, 24*(4), 761–786. https://doi.org/10.1086/506485

Cronin, J., & Horton, H. (2009, May 22). Will higher education be the next bubble to burst? *The Chronicle of Higher Education, 55*(37), A56. https://www.chronicle.com/article/will-higher-education-be-the-next-bubble-to-burst/

Echternacht, J. (2016). Check & connect: A model for engaging and retaining students with intellectual disabilities in higher education. *Journal of Intellectual Disability Research, 60*(7–8), 660. https://doi.org/10.1111/jir.12305

Giancola, J., & Kahlenberg, R. (2016). *True merit: Ensuring our brightest students have access to our best colleges and universities.* Jack Kent Cooke Foundation.

Gray, S. (2013). Framing "at risk" students: Struggles at the boundaries of access to higher education. *Children and Youth Services Review, 35*(8), 1245–1251. https://doi.org/10.1016/j.childyouth.2013.04.011

Griffith University, & Professor Keithia Wilson. (2015). Engaging, supporting and retaining academic at-risk students in a Bachelor of Nursing: Setting risk markers, interventions and outcomes. *The International Journal of the First Year in Higher Education, 6*(1), 121–134. https://doi.org/10.5204/intjfyhe.v6i1.251

Hébert, T. P. (2018). An examination of high-achieving first-generation college students from low-income backgrounds. *Gifted Child Quarterly, 62*(1), 96–110. https://doi.org/10.1177/0016986217738051

Hébert, T., & McBee, M. (2007). The impact of an undergraduate honors program on gifted university students. *Gifted Child Quarterly, 51*(2), 136–151. https://doi.org/10.1177/0016986207299471

Herr, K., & Anderson, G. L (2014). *The action research dissertation: A guide for students and faculty.* SAGE Publications.

Jalal, A., & Khaksari, S. (2019). Effects of tuition discounting on university's financial performance. *Review of Quantitative Finance and Accounting, 52*(2), 439–466. https://doi.org/10.1007/s11156-018-0715-8

Johnson, D., & Sveen, L. (2020). Three key values of Generation Z: Equitably serving the next generation of students. *College and University, 95*(1), 37–40. https://eric.ed.gov/?id=EJ1246052

Kezar, A., & Kitchen, J. A., (2020). Supporting first-generation, low-income, and underrepresented students' transitions to college through comprehensive and integrated programs. *American Behavioral Scientist, 64*(3), 223–229. https://doi.org/10.1177/0002764219869413

Killinger, M., Jackson, M., & Saucier, S. (2019). Honors work: Seeing gaps, combining gifts, focusing on wider human needs. *Honors in Practice—Online Archive, 290.* http://digitalcommons.unl.edu/nchchip/290

Mega, C., Ronconi, L., De Beni, R., & Graesser, A. C. (2014). What makes a good student? How emotions, self-regulated learning, and motivation contribute to academic achievement. *Journal of Educational Psychology, 106*(1), 121–131. https://doi.org/10.1037/a0033546

Miller, A. L., Lambert, A. D., & Speirs Neumeister, K. L. (2012). Parenting style, perfectionism, and creativity in high-ability and high-achieving young adults. *Journal for the Education of the Gifted, 35,* 344–365. https://doi.org/10.1177/0162353212459257

Miller, A. L., & Speirs Neumeister, K. L. (2017). The influence of personality, parenting styles, and perfectionism on performance goal orientation in high ability students. *Journal of Advanced Academics, 28,* 313–344

Rinn, A. N., & Plucker, J. A. (2019). High-ability college students and undergraduate honors programs: A systematic review. *Journal for the Education of the Gifted, 42*(3), 187–215. https://doi.org/10.1177/0162353219855678

Scager, K., Boonstra, J., Peeters, T., Vulperhorst, J., & Wiegant, F. (2016). Collaborative learning in higher education: Evoking positive interdependence. *CBE–Life Sciences Education, 15*(4), 9. https://doi.org/10.1187/cbe.16-07-0219

Senko, C., Harackiewicz, J., & Hulleman, C. (2011). Achievement goal theory at the crossroads: Old controversies, current challenges, and new directions. *Educational Psychologist, 46*(1), 26–47. https://doi.org/10.1080/00461520.2011.53 8646

Silver Wolf (Adelv unegv Waya), D. A. P., Perkins, J., Butler-Barnes, S. T., & Walker, T. A., Jr. (2017). Social belonging and college retention: Results from a quasi-experimental pilot study. *Journal of College Student Development 58*(5), 777–782. https://doi.org/10.1353/csd.2017.0060.

Speirs Neumeister, K. L., Fletcher, K. L., & Burney, V. H. (2015). Perfectionism and achievement motivation in high-ability students: an examination of the 2×2 model of perfectionism. *Journal for the Education of the Gifted, 38*(3), 215–232. https://doi.org/10.1177/0162353215592502

Stelnicki, A. M., Nordstokke, D. W., & Saklofske, D. H. (2015). Who is the successful university student? An analysis of personal resources. *Canadian Journal of Higher Education, 45*(2), 214–228. https://doi.org/10.47678/cjhe.v45i2.184491

Stringer, E. (2014). *Action research* (4th ed.). SAGE Publications.

Turner, P., & Thompson, E. (2014). College retention initiatives meeting the needs of millennial freshman students. *College Student Journal, 48*(1), 94–104. https://eric.ed.gov/?id=EJ1034162

Wolters, C. A. (2004). Advancing achievement goal theory: Using goal structures and goal orientations to predict students' motivation, cognition, and achievement. *Journal of Educational Psychology, 96*(2), 236–250. https://doi.org/10.1037/0022-0663.96.2.236

CHAPTER 11

SEEING THE UNSEEN

An Action Research Study of First-Generation College Student Persistence at a Mid-Size Private Institution in the Northeast

Michael A. Urmeneta

Only 60% of students who enroll at 4-year colleges in the United States complete a bachelor's degree within 6 years (National Center for Educational Statistics, 2021). First-generation college students are even less likely to earn a degree than their peers. In their research, Cataldi et al. (2018) determined that 33% of first-generation college students dropped out after 3 years, compared to only 14% for their continuing-generation peers. Furthermore, researchers indicate that a blanket approach to student services may be a disadvantage to first-generation student populations (Stephens et al., 2012; Stuber, 2011). Institutions can fail to notice and address equity gaps as they attempt to treat all students equally.

This study aims to investigate and improve the persistence of first-generation college students at a mid-size, private school in the Northeast. This project arose from a convergence of three different issues at the research site. The first was concern over graduation rates. At the time of the study, the site's overall graduation rate was 6.5% below the national average of all institutions, 13.9% below the national average of private institutions, and 19.4% below the average of private institutions with similar characteristics.

The second issue was that first-generation students were rendered essentially invisible. Historically, the host institution did not code or track first-generation college students. Therefore, outcome data beyond the aggregate was unknown. The only things available were anecdotal reports from concerned staff and faculty reporting that first-generation students (a) felt disconnected, (b) had difficulty with institutional services, and (c) were leaving the university without returning.

The last issue stemmed from the previous. A consequence of not tracking this population was the blanket treatment of all student populations, potentially disadvantageous to the first-generation student population.

BACKGROUND

For this study, a first-generation college student was defined as one whose parents did not attend college (Billson & Terry, 1982; Choy, 2001; Nunez, 1998). In addition, persistence was defined as the "desire and action of a student to stay within the system of higher education from the beginning year through degree completion" (Berger & Lyon, 2005, p. 7). Although there were several definitions for first-generation college students (Peralta & Klonowski, 2017; Toutkoushian et al., 2018), the one used was chosen so it could contrast to the definition of a continuing-generation student—someone with at least one parent who attended college (Mehta et al., 2011; Raque-Bogdan & Lucas, 2016).

A review of existing literature can be organized around three central themes. The first investigates the background and struggles of first-generation college students. The second examines how successful first-generation college students take personal agency as they navigate their educational development and critical relationships. Lastly, the third summarizes the landscape of institutional responses to first-generation needs by the level of investment and involvement.

First-Generation Background and Barriers

According to a report from the National Center for Educational Statistics, one-third of all undergraduate students in the United States indicated that high school was their parents' highest level of education (Cataldi et al., 2018). However, most of the research is focused on the experiences of first-generation college students at community colleges or institutions in the South. This focus was understandable as historically, these institutions and regions had higher concentrations of students who were the first in their families to attend college. However, first-generation students are not limited to these schools and areas and attend many different institutions all over the country. Thus, a study of private institutions in the Northeast bore further exploration.

First-generation college students encounter several biographical, personal, and environmental barriers to their success. Their biographical challenges ranged from indifference to hostility. Compared to their continuing-generation peers, some first-generation students reported no family support (Gibbons & Borders, 2010; Horn & Nunez, 2000), while others reported growing up in adversity (Hébert, 2018; Stieha, 2010). Additionally, these students faced personal challenges including feeling disconnected from home (Azmitia et al., 2018), while others struggled with imposter phenomenon (Clance, 1985). These students also faced environmental challenges that ranged from benign to hostile. Students reported lacking sufficient background information at one end of the spectrum (Longwell-Grice et al., 2016; Pascarella et al., 2004) while feeling alienated (Bergerson, 2007) or marginalized (Longwell-Grice et al., 2016) on the other.

Success Strategies Employed by First-Generation College Students

Previous research identified successful strategies employed by first-generation college students; it examined how successful first-generation students engaged with their coursework, environment, and available opportunities. These students advanced in their degrees by (a) being conscious actors in their personal development, (b) maintaining connections to a supportive community at home, (c) actively engaging in their coursework, and (d) taking advantage of institutional opportunities (Demetriou et al., 2017; Hébert, 2018; Longwell-Grice et al., 2016; Means & Pyne, 2017; Mitchall & Jaeger, 2018; Raque-Bogdan & Lucas, 2016; Rood, 2009; Whitehead & Wright, 2017).

In addition to taking active agency in their own lives, these students consciously sought out and cultivated relationships with faculty, staff, employers, and peers; and these relationships have contributed to the students' success (Astin, 1997; Cruce et al., 2006; Demetriou et al., 2017; Dennis et al., 2005; Garriott et al., 2015; Hébert, 2018; Longwell-Grice et al., 2016; Terenzini et al., 1996; Terenzini & Pascarella, 1980).

Finally, much of the prevailing student success literature regarding first-generation college students used a deficit-focused approach that focused on needs and addressed weaknesses (Atherton, 2014; Green, 2006; Herrmann & Varnum, 2018; Mitchall & Jaeger, 2018; Rood, 2009).

Institutional Interventions Developed for First-Generation College Students

An overview of predominant first-generation interventions through the lenses of involvement and investment was beneficial for this research. Strategies employed can be characterized by the resources and time needed to implement. Interventions could be placed on a continuum, ranging from minimally invasive to more intrusive. From this perspective, the programs in the literature can be grouped into two distinct categories: short-term and long-term interventions. These views allow one to grasp a range of options in context.

Some researchers have made the case that minimally invasive, "light touch" interventions can improve student outcomes (Broda et al., 2018; Yeager & Walton, 2011). These can take the form of one-time assessments or training sessions. Conversely, other researchers have made the case that effective interventions should be intrusive (Barry et al., 2009; Habley & McClanahan, 2004; Herrmann & Varnum, 2018; Longwell-Grice et al., 2016; Varney, 2007). Interventions can take the form of early assessment, advising, and outreach (Ishitani, 2006; Swecker et al., 2013; Varney, 2007), expanded social support services (Padgett et al., 2012), multi-week summer enrichment programs (Clauss-Ehlers & Wibrowski, 2007), and job shadowing programs (Raque-Bogdan & Lucas, 2016).

An effective intervention must consider the distinct characteristics of the school and students to which it is introduced (Barry et al., 2009; Habley & McClanahan, 2004; Longwell-Grice et al., 2016). Appropriate interventions will depend on the time, energy, resources, and personnel available (Clauss-Ehlers & Wibrowski, 2007). Flexibility in implementation will be particularly helpful in institutional environments, such as the researcher's study site, where resources are constrained by time, money, personnel, and circumstance.

METHODS

This study used a qualitative dominant, action research approach. Jencik (2011) asserted that qualitative research aimed to understand social issues from multiple perspectives to gain a better understanding of a particular group. Furthermore, the use of action research was ideal because its flexible, participative, and iterative nature was well-suited to the evolving environment of the host site (Stringer, 2014). As Herr and Anderson (2015) noted, the adaptability of action research is why it is successful in dynamic settings like education. It was beneficial during the COVID-19 pandemic as interactions with the host site shifted from in-person to virtual.

Action research attempts to close the gap between theory and practice (Kemmis, 2009). The emphasis on collaboration and real-world application makes it useful for the scholar-practitioner (Brydon-Miller et al., 2003; Costello et al., 2015). It is invaluable for educational change agents seeking to implement interventions since it includes developing concrete activities as part of the research process (Lewin, 1946).

The site selected for this study was a mid-sized, 4-year, private, nonprofit institution based in the Northeast. The institution enrolls over 10,000 students, offering undergraduate, graduate, and professional degrees at campuses in New York City, Long Island, Arkansas, Vancouver, Abu Dhabi, and China. This research focused on the 3,720 undergraduate students who attend the New York City and Long Island locations. Of these students, 886 (23.8%) were first-generation students (Urmeneta, 2019).

The research was conducted over multiple cycles of data collection and analysis. Cycle 0 (baseline) data collection and analysis focused on semi-structured interviews with first-generation staff and faculty members. These interviews supported the assessment of the current first-generation student environment and informed selection criteria of participants and co-collaborators for subsequent cycles. Cycle 1 data collection and analysis focused on semi-structured interviews with first-generation students on track to graduate. These interviews helped identify first-generation college students' experiences, characteristics, and strategies to help create targeted interventions to improve persistence. Cycle 2 focused on implementing and evaluating the action step: a year-long event series, a resource website, and a communications campaign. Data collection and analysis involved event collaborators and student attendees. An assessment of Cycle 2 identified key findings, which offered potential solutions to the problem of persistence.

Participants

Cycle 1 participants were first-generation students who were on track to graduate at the host site. Interviews with staff and faculty members were used to inform the Cycle 1 selection criteria of first-generation students who earned 90 credits or more and maintained a 2.7 or higher grade-point average (GPA). Stakeholders suggested that these students were likely to persist to graduation.

A report was generated, showing that 180 of 886 first-generation college students enrolled in the New York campuses for Fall 2019 fit the above criteria (Urmeneta, 2019). The 180 students in this report formed the basis of the initial contact list. Recruitment of participants continued until the desired target sample size was met. This number was based on Creswell and Poth's (2016) suggestion of three to ten subjects and Guest et al.'s (2006) suggestion of sampling until no new insights emerge.

Recruitment consisted of multiple phases and involved a combination of (a) purposive sampling based on recommendations from front-facing student services offices (Stringer, 2014, p. 79), (b) snowball sampling to obtain recommended new participants from current ones, and (c) direct email contact with potential participants. Collaborators from the offices of Student Affairs, Career Services, Experiential Education, Veterans Affairs, Academic Advising, and the Higher Education opportunity program (HEOP) assisted in identifying potential students and scheduling interviews. Recruitment resulted in 11 semi-structured interviews (Harrell & Bradley, 2009) conducted in person at the two New York campuses of the host institution.

Cycle 2 participants were first-generation students who took part in any of the First Generation Initiative's activities by (a) attending events, (b) using the resource website, or (c) responding to the communications campaign. Additional participants included co-collaborators and stakeholders who helped create, support, and implement the initiative. Student participants were recommended and introduced by co-collaborators. Other meetings were organized with co-collaborators and stakeholders.

Data Collection

Cycle 1 data collection and analysis focused on semi-structured interviews with first-generation students on track to graduate. These interviews helped identify first-generation college students' experiences, characteristics, and strategies to help create targeted interventions to improve persistence.

Cycle 1 recruitment resulted in 11 semi-structured interviews. After the seventh interview, saturation appeared to have been achieved as no new insights emerged. The recorded interviews resulted in 7 hours and 41 minutes of audio, translating to 202 pages of written transcripts. A layered, iterative approach identified 486 quotes and 137 initial codes from these transcripts. From these codes, themes were established.

Cycle 2 focused on implementing and evaluating the action step: a year-long event series, a resource website, and a communications campaign. Data collection and analysis involved event collaborators and student attendees.

An assessment of Cycle 2 identified key findings, which offered potential solutions to the problem of persistence.

Cycle 2 included data collection methods with participants, collaborators, and stakeholders. These methods included field observations, field notes, analytic memos, attendance records, external stakeholder reports, questionnaires, and member checks.

The First Generation Initiative resulted in six hosted events, one resource website, and one communications campaign. It was implemented by nine interdepartmental task force members and two dedicated student workers. It involved 24 co-collaborator meetings, two primary stakeholder meetings, and 13 secondary stakeholder meetings. The three main components of the initiative were evaluated separately and in concert.

The following data were collected to evaluate the events. First, a count of attendees was used as a gauge of interest. Second, feedback from attendees was solicited by questionnaire after every event. Third, the researcher recorded field notes on behaviors, activities, and observations from events. Fourth, transcripts from recorded events were used to gain further insight. Fifth, field notes and analytics memos were generated from follow-up meetings with co-collaborators discussing general feedback, participant comments, and future considerations. Sixth, feedback from first-generation panelists and participants was elicited to capture event impressions and assess effectiveness. Seventh, external stakeholders and Cycle 1 participants' impressions of the event series were obtained.

To evaluate the communications campaign, data was collected from the following sources. First, an external report from the director of digital strategy was used to measure email engagement. Second, Instagram followers and interaction counts measured social media interest. Third, field notes and analytic memos were generated from meetings with co-collaborators discussing general feedback, participant comments, and future considerations. Fourth, feedback from external stakeholders and Cycle 1 participants was elicited to assess the communications campaign effectiveness.

Lastly, the following data were collected to evaluate the resource website. First, an external report from the director of digital strategy was used to measure website engagement. Second, field notes and analytic memos were generated from meetings with co-collaborators discussing general feedback, participant comments, and future considerations. Third, input from external stakeholders and Cycle 1 participants was elicited to assess website effectiveness. Fourth, feedback from external stakeholders and Cycle 1 participants was elicited to evaluate website effectiveness.

The program also included member checks with collaborators, stakeholders, and participants to gauge progress and clarify the analysis. The process was integrated into everyday interactions with collaborators and stakeholders. Feedback was solicited on events and activities from bi-weekly meetings with co-collaborators, regular meetings with stakeholders, and email communications with both.

Data Analysis

The overall aim of the First Generation Initiative was to increase persistence by strengthening a sense of belonging. Thus, a sense of belonging needed to be measured both directly and indirectly from the hosted events, resource website, and communications campaign of the initiative.

Field observations, field notes, transcripts, analytic memos, attendance records, external stakeholder reports, questionnaires, and member checks were analyzed using Atlas.ti. In these analyses, the researcher looked explicitly for evidence pointing to an increased sense of belonging and persistence from any three initiative components.

Additionally, other emergent themes from initiative activities were cataloged. The researcher used a layered analysis process similar to the one used in Cycle 1. An initial pass focused on tone. Subsequent passes focused on codes and themes. Redundancy was eliminated by condensing findings, and a mind map was created using MindManager to help with organization and condensing.

Member checking was built into the activities of the initiative. The 24 co-collaborator meetings, two primary stakeholder meetings, and 13 secondary stakeholder meetings provided several opportunities to verify findings.

Two assessment activities were planned but not implemented due to students dealing with Zoom, email, and survey fatigue from the COVID-19 pandemic. A survey instrument was developed to assess sense of belonging, intention to persist, and effectiveness of initiative elements. In addition, Zoom interviews with panelists and participants were planned but proved challenging to secure. The researcher recommends that these elements be included in future research cycles.

Ultimately, Cycle 2 revealed that establishing a series of targeted activities and events increased first-generation college students' sense of belonging. Future data can be collected to assess whether the action step increased persistence for participants.

TRUSTWORTHINESS AND QUALITY ASSURANCE

The trustworthiness of this research project's findings was ensured using criteria suggested by Lincoln and Guba (1986) and strategies offered by Shenton (2004).

Credibility was demonstrated in the following ways. First, the researcher had familiarity with the culture under observation before data collection took place. Having worked at the institution for 16 years in different roles, he understood the participants in depth. Procedures were also used to help ensure participant honesty. The interview protocol included many opportunities for participants to withdraw from the study before, during, and after each session. Semi-structured interviews also included iterative questioning; they were intentionally designed to be repetitive to confirm insights. Finally, member checking was incorporated into the research (Carl & Ravitch, 2018). An immediate member check was conducted within 24–48 hours of the initial interview. Subsequent member checks with summary insights were also used.

To establish transferability, robust descriptive and contextual information on collaborators, participants, and data collection methods were recorded to allow others to make research comparisons and distinctions.

To establish dependability, the processes used in the study were recorded in detail to enable future researchers to repeat the work. These descriptions included information about (a) research design and implementation, (b) data gathering details through field notes, and (c) reflective memos about the research process after every cycle.

Finally, to establish confirmability, an audit trail was created to allow anyone to trace the course of the research in a stepwise fashion through the decisions made and procedures described. Visual representations of the action research project and mind maps of research cycle insights helped communicate the audit trail.

FINDINGS

This study revealed that establishing a series of targeted activities and events could increase first-generation college students' sense of belonging. Cycle 1 research revealed that first-generation students were disconnected and dissatisfied with the host institution, showing low engagement and a weak sense of belonging. The First Generation Initiative sought to strengthen these students' sense of belonging by addressing Cycle 1 struggles, supports, and success strategies through an event series, resource website, and communications campaign. In evaluating the First Generation Initiative, findings for Cycle 2 were identified for each of the initiative's three components, as well as for the program overall. Feedback for improvement of these elements is also included. These findings are discussed below.

The First-Generation Event Series Strengthened Sense of Belonging

A review of evidence pointed to a strengthened sense of belonging due to the event series. The series aimed to increase the students' sense of belonging by addressing the struggles, bolstering the supports, and leveraging the success strategies employed by first-generation participants in the first cycle of research. All the events were designed to target three of the six focus areas of Cycle 1: (a) offering targeted and sustained support, (b) improving relationships with institutional representatives, and (c) encouraging a vision for a better life (Table 11.1). In addition, specific events were designed to target the other three focus areas: (a) navigating the social and cultural gap, (b) gaining support from family, and (c) participating in extracurricular activities (Table 11.1). Five of the six events performed better than expected, with one leaving room for improvement. Overall, the event series performed better than expected in engaging students. In addition, using information from Cycle 1 helped keep the events focused on issues of importance to participants.

The First Generation Initiative Website Fostered Positive Engagement

Evidence indicated an increase of positive engagement with the website. The website was First Generation Initiative's central information hub. It aimed to increase sense of belonging by targeting all six key focus areas identified by participants in Cycle 1 (Table 11.1). A digital strategy report showed that the website had 461 unique visitors since its inception. According to the director of digital strategy, the site was averaging 100 visitors per month and appeared to be on an upward trend. The director further reported that engagement appeared to be organic, meaning visitors were not just stumbling upon the page but consciously seeking the website out using the university's search function.

Additionally, a web analytics report showed that site visitors went on to view academic and financial aid pages after visiting the main site. Previous research findings and the literature have suggested that these subjects are essential to first-generation students. This search behavior suggested that first-generation students intentionally sought out the resource site to resolve these issues. Finally, member checking Cycle 1 participants indicated approval for the site. One participant stated, "I think the website looks like a great resource for first-gen students."

TABLE 11.1 How First-Generation Initiative Elements Addressed Cycle 1 Target Areas

Initiative Element		Cycle 1 Target Area					
		Struggles			Supports	Success Strategies	
		Offering Targeted and Sustained Support	Helping to Navigate the Social and Cultural Gap	Improving Relationships With Institutional Representatives	Helping Students Gain Support From Family	Promoting Participation in Extracurricular Activities	Developing a Vision for a Better Life
Event Series	Event 1: Sharing First-Generation Experiences	X	X	X	X	X	X
	Event 2: Pitching Your Story as a First-Generation Student	X	X	X		X	X
	Events 3 & 4: Paying for College	X		X	X		X
	Event 5: Finding the Right Academic Resources to Maintain Your GPA	X		X			X
	Event 6: Making the Most of Your College Experience	X	X	X		X	X
Resource Website		X	X	X	X	X	X
Communications Campaign		X	X	X	X	X	X

The First-Generation Communications Campaign Supported Increased Involvement

Although it was difficult to directly measure the communications strategy's impact on sense of belonging, the researcher could indirectly find evidence of increased involvement. The communications campaign aimed to increase sense of belonging by targeting all six focus areas identified by participants in Cycle 1 (Table 11.1). At the task force's direction, the office of Institutional Research generated a contact list of 683 potential first-generation participants for the 2020–2021 school year. These students were included in bi-weekly communications from the associate provost. The bulk of email communications tended to be directed outward to inform about the Initiative's events, Instagram channel, and website. Several emails did offer a feedback mechanism but garnered little response. A planning survey administered on December 4, 2020, at the end of the fall semester, received only ten responses from the list of 683.

Additionally, surveys that went out after events only had two respondents. Several external stakeholders offered a possible reason for the low response rates, reporting that students, faculty, and staff were experiencing email, Zoom, and survey fatigue. Before the planning survey was administered, the institution went from hybrid instruction to fully remote on November 25, 2020. Feedback surveys were administered several days after events and were optional.

Despite this, email effectiveness could be inferred from the number of participants attending the events. Outreach was communicated through email and social media. The six events attracted an average of 22 participants each. The attendance level suggests that outgoing messages were at least being read. Further evidence of email effectiveness comes from the university webmaster, who indicated that 10% of the resource website visitors came from emails.

Social media outreach provided further evidence of increased involvement. The invitation to follow the First Generation Instagram channel came from emails and information cross-posted to other university Instagram accounts. At the close of the event series, the Instagram channel had 109 followers. Several student panelists asked whether clips of the sessions would be available because they were excited to post and share. Additionally, member checking with Cycle 1 participants garnered positive reactions to the Instagram page. One participant stated, "The Instagram page looks really well coordinated." Another offered, "If you have anything that ends up being a feature: spotlight, face pick, name, let me know so I can repost it on my Insta! I followed the page."

Overall Program

Although some of the initiative components were difficult to assess individually, the program as a whole appears to have been successful in increasing engagement and sense of belonging. The events of the initiative were well attended, except for one; traffic to the website appeared to be focused and on the rise; the communications campaign appeared to be yielding desired attendance results.

DISCUSSION

The results of the First Generation Initiative were favorable. Cycle 2 findings indicated that the event series strengthened sense of belonging, the resource website fostered positive engagement, and the communications campaign supported increased involvement.

The Event Series Strengthened Sense of Belonging

A key finding of this research was that the event series strengthened first-generation students' sense of belonging. Existing literature and results from prior research cycles suggested that interventions that were consistent, relevant, and accommodating impacted a sense of belonging.

Events Were Consistent
Events provided consistency. Means and Pyne (2017) noted that one's sense of belonging is not fixed and can change over time. Consistent and ongoing attention was thus needed. Additionally, participants in Cycle 1 specifically requested more consistency. The literature confirmed the effectiveness of a consistent approach. Although some researchers proposed that "light touch" interventions can improve student outcomes (Broda et al., 2018; Yeager & Walton, 2011), many scholars stated that interventions needed to be proactive and intrusive (Barry et al., 2009; Habley & Mc-Clanahan, 2004; Herrmann & Varnum, 2018; Longwell-Grice et al., 2016; Varney, 2007). In resource-constrained environments, institutions may not have the capacity to develop proactive interventions like research internships or mentoring programs. However, this research showed that a collaborative event series could provide consistent support without overtaxing institutional stakeholders.

Events Were Relevant
In addition, the events offered relevant content. Topic selection had much to do with program success. The series aimed to strengthen a sense of belonging by targeting six focus areas identified from Cycle 1 research (Table 11.1). Although each event had specific objectives, collectively, they worked to address all six focus areas.

Additionally, the researcher worked with students and collaborators to develop topics of interest rooted in the literature. The five topics for the six events in the series were (a) sharing first-generation experiences, (b) pitching your story as a first-generation student, (c) paying for college, (d) finding the right academic resources to maintain your GPA, and (e) making the most of your college experience (Alvarado et al., 2017; Azmitia et al., 2018; Bourdieu, 1986; Bronfenbrenner & Morris, 2007; Demetriou et al., 2017; Guiffrida, 2006; Lee & Mueller, 2014; Longwell-Grice et al., 2016; Pascarella et al., 2004; Portes, 1998; Rood, 2009; Sirin, 2005; Stanton-Salazar, 2011; Stephens et al., 2014; Stieha, 2010; Tierney & Venegas, 2006; Tinto, 1993).

Based on attendance records and participant feedback, each topic interested first-generation students. Overall, the event series appeared to have provided valuable and relevant content.

Events Were Accommodating

Strategic timing was necessary for program success. Scholars indicated that first-generation students are more likely to work longer hours than their continuing-generation peers (Pascarella et al., 2004). Additionally, several Cycle 2 participants shared that they had little privacy at home. This situation aligned with the literature that maintained that first-generation college students held significant family responsibilities (Terenzini et al., 1996). This information was critical to the event-planning process. Every effort was made to offer events at different times on different days throughout the year to accommodate first-generation students.

The event series was supported by a resource website and communications campaign. A discussion of the website's effectiveness follows.

The Website Fostered Positive Engagement

Another key finding of this research was that the resource website could foster positive engagement. It did so by being accessible, empowering, and inclusive. The following discusses each of these in turn.

The Website Was Accessible

A website provides information consistently without being bound by traditional office hours. Access was important for first-generation students who were likely to spend more time at home than their peers (Horn & Nunez, 2000). This living situation was true for Cycle 2 participants who indicated a lack of privacy and a need to time-share internet access throughout the day. In addition, the 2020 global pandemic only magnified the need for information and resources available to first-generation students at any time.

Therefore, a website was ideal for providing 24/7 resources for students, parents, and stakeholders alike.

The Website Was Empowering

Students during the pandemic reported that they were suffering from mental fatigue. Knowing this, the institution developed a website with self-service options that would enable students to access resources on their terms, in their own time. Students took advantage of this resource, and the website averaged 100 visits a month over several months. Furthermore, visitors continued to access academic and financial resource pages from the primary site, indicating an active level of engagement.

Several scholars found that first-generation students were reluctant to take advantage of university resources (Housel & Harvey, 2009; Johnson et al., 2011; Ostrove & Long, 2007). However, this assertion ran counter to the experience of several Cycle 2 participants who actively sought resources online.

The Website Was Inclusive

The website engaged critical first-generation support systems. Cycle 1 findings and Cycle 2 event feedback indicated that parental support was crucial to participants. In addition, the literature affirmed the importance of first-generation parental support (Mitchall & Jaeger, 2018). Hébert (2018) even suggested that the emotional support provided by parents was more important than a parent's knowledge (or lack thereof) about college. The website was thus developed as much for the parents as it was for the students. Creating the website for both helped reinforce this existing support network.

The event series and resource website were supported and accompanied by a targeted communications campaign. The following section discusses the campaign's effectiveness.

The Communications Campaign Supported Increased Involvement

One last finding from this research project was that a targeted communications campaign supported increased involvement. Events were advertised over email and social media. As a result, 109 people subscribed to the initiative's Instagram channel, and 129 students participated in the initiative's six events. Therefore, the campaign increased involvement by being trustworthy, proactive, and inclusive. The following discusses each of these elements.

Communications Were Trustworthy

Every effort was made to ensure that trusted community members performed outreach and extended invitations. Research conducted by Garriott et al. (2015) showed that first-generation college students who developed relationships with staff members reported greater satisfaction and academic progress. At the same time, Barry et al. (2009) found that first-generation college students were less likely to approach or disclose information to staff in their study. Thus, it was important for the institution to take a proactive approach to outreach. All communications started with emails from the assistant provost. Detailed follow-up emails were then sent from the offices that developed specific events. Taskforce members then conducted personal outreach. Each level of communication was meant to assure students that administration members were looking out for their best interests.

Communications Were Proactive

In this intervention, forging better student–administration relationships required a proactive approach. It thus required a steady and consistent level of communication. This approach aligned with research showing that effective interventions should be more intrusive (Barry et al., 2009; Habley & McClanahan, 2004; Herrmann & Varnum, 2018; Longwell-Grice et al., 2016; Varney, 2007). The assistant provost maintained a contact list of first-generation students and scheduled regular communications with them. Students were contacted as soon as new events were added or new web resources became available. Thus, a cascade of communications followed, providing a steady level of contact from multiple sources throughout the year.

Communications Were Inclusive

Students were involved in the design and operation of the initiative's social media from the outset. These student workers designed announcements and managed the initiative's social media accounts. Including students in these activities ensured that the initiative's events and activities were communicated and broadcast in accessible ways. In addition, participants tended to respond better to social media than to emails, suggesting they were willing to share and repost content. Engaging student workers also strengthened the bond between student employees and the administration. According to Garriott et al. (2015), a solid student-administrator relationship led to greater satisfaction and academic progress.

LIMITATIONS

As with any research study, the research had limitations. First, the participants' experiences may have been unique to this institution alone. The study was conducted at one institution—a mid-sized, private school in New York. Thus, findings may only apply to institutions of similar makeup with students of similar backgrounds, and transferability to other institutions will require further study.

Secondly, the institution had two locations—one in New York City and the other in Long Island. The experiences of students attending college in urban and suburban areas may differ. Further research will need to be conducted to assess the differences experienced in these different settings.

Next, interactions that were heavily in person at the outset became completely virtual toward the end. Upon finishing Cycle 1 data collection, the researcher left the host site's employ. A month later, New York State enacted quarantine and social distancing protocols in response to the COVID-19 pandemic. As a result, all in-person interventions had to be conducted virtually. The worldwide pandemic added an unplanned layer of complexity to the implementation and evaluation process that may have limited the number of participants.

Finally, the research might benefit from lengthening the timeframe of the study. The interventions in this study occurred over two semesters. The ultimate goal of the study was to increase first-generation college student persistence at the host site. Yet, typical institutional metrics—like retention and graduation rate—are measured over 1-year and 6-year periods, respectively. Long-term impact analysis can be conducted if the research site continues the intervention over time.

IMPLICATIONS

For the Organization

This research study has led to positive and systemic change at the host institution. Before this project, first-generation students were essentially invisible; no information about them could be found on the university website. They were not flagged in any university systems, and no reports were generated. Only a handful of administrators were even aware of them or that they experienced potential issues. Thus, they were a group recognized in concept by specific individuals but not in practice by the institution.

Several notable changes had occurred at the host site by the conclusion of the action research project. First, a robust first-generation program now exists, offering sustained support with focused events and activities. These activities are supported by a centralized website that offers targeted resources to first-generation students and a process to communicate proactively and responsively to this group to keep them regularly engaged.

In addition, the management of the program is now a permanent part of campus operations. The task force has grown to include student and faculty stakeholders and has expanded to cover more of the student life cycle.

Collaborators and stakeholders have taken full ownership of the process, scheduling meetings, building infrastructure, promoting services, developing communications, and hosting events. The initiative has a life of its own beyond the research project.

Lastly, first-generation students have become an officially recognized population at the institution. A prominent place on the university website now exists to recognize, serve, empower, and celebrate this group. Practices were implemented to identify and flag first-generation students in official record systems. Administrators are now able to track progress and measure outcomes. The result is that first-generation students now have real visibility both in theory and in practice.

For the Profession and Practice

In terms of impact on the profession and practice, this research showed that targeted interventions—in this case, an event series, a resource website, and a communications campaign—could indeed impact a sense of belonging, positive engagement, and increased involvement among first-generation students. Furthermore, it showed that robust programming could occur even in resource-constrained environments, despite the challenges of a global pandemic.

Furthermore, this study sought to address a gap in the literature regarding first-generation students at private schools in the Northeast. According to the National Center for Education Statistics, 1.9 million students attend the 490 private institutions in New England and the Mid-East regions of the United States. If the percentage of first-generation students at these institutions mirrors the research site's 24%, this equates to 475,000 students. Expanding this research to similar institutions in the Northeast region could have a significant impact. Furthermore, if the findings are applicable beyond private schools or the Northeast, the implications for students across the country could be substantial.

CONCLUSION

The results of the First Generation Initiative were favorable. Cycle 2 findings indicated that the event series strengthened sense of belonging, the resource website fostered positive engagement, and the communications campaign cultivated increased involvement. Although the three components of the initiative tackled first-generation issues in different ways, a common thread was a focus on increasing supports, removing obstacles, and leveraging student strengths to support student persistence. Though typical metrics for persistence are measured over 1-year and 6-year time-frames, the results of this study present a promising early indicator.

REFERENCES

Alvarado, A., Spatariu, A., & Woodbury, C. (2017). Resilience & emotional intelligence between first generation college students and non-first generation college students. *FOCUS on Colleges, Universities & Schools, 11*(1), 1–11. http://www.nationalforum.com/Electronic%20Journal%20Volumes/Alvardo%20Andreeina,Resilience%20and%20Emotional%20Intelligence%20FOCUS%20V11%20N1%202017.pdf

Astin, A. W. (1997). *What matters in college? Four critical years revisited.* Jossey-Bass.

Atherton, M. C. (2014). Academic preparedness of first-generation college students: Different perspectives. *Journal of College Student Development, 55*(8), 824–829. https://eric.ed.gov/?id=EJ1046416

Azmitia, M., Sumabat-Estrada, G., Cheong, Y., & Covarrubias, R. (2018). "Dropping out is not an option": How educationally resilient first-generation students see the future. *New Directions for Child and Adolescent Development, 160*, 89–100. https://doi.org/10.1002/cad.20240

Barry, L. M., Hudley, C., Kelly, M., & Cho, S. (2009). Differences in self-reported disclosure of college experiences by first-generation college student status. *Adolescence, 44*(173), 55–68. https://pubmed.ncbi.nlm.nih.gov/19435167/

Berger, J. B., & Lyon, S. C. (2005). *Past to present. A historical look at retention.* In T. A. Seidman (Ed.), *College student retention: Formulas for student success* (pp. 1–30). Greenwood Press.

Bergerson, A. A. (2007). Exploring the impact of social class on adjustment to college: Anna's story. *International Journal of Qualitative Studies in Education, 20*(1), 99–119. https://doi.org/10.1080/09518390600923610

Billson, J. M., & Terry, M. B. (1982). *In search of the silken purse: Factors in attrition among first-generation students (Revised)* [Paper presentation]. Annual Meeting of the Association of American Colleges, Denver, CO. https://eric.ed.gov/?id=ED214431

Bourdieu, P. (1986). The forms of capital. In J. Richardson (Ed.), *Handbook of theory and research for the sociology of education* (pp. 241–258). Greenwood.

Broda, M., Yun, J., Schneider, B., Yeager, D. S., Walton, G. M., & Diemer, M. (2018). Reducing inequality in academic success for incoming college students: A randomized trial of growth mindset and belonging interventions. *Journal of Research on Educational Effectiveness, 11*(3), 317–338. https://doi.org/10.1080/19345747.2018.1429037

Bronfenbrenner, U., & Morris, P. A. (2007). The bioecological model of human development. In R. M. Lerner (Ed.), *Theoretical models of human development* (pp. 793–828). Wiley.

Brydon-Miller, M., Greenwood, D., & Maguire, P. (2003). Why action research? *Action Research, 1*(1), 9–28. https://doi.org/10.1177/14767503030011002

Carl, N. M., & Ravitch, S. M. (2018). Member check. In B. B. Frey (Ed.), *The SAGE encyclopedia of educational research, measurement, and evaluation* (pp. 1050–1050). SAGE Publications, Inc. https://doi.org/10.4135/9781506326139.n426

Cataldi, E. F., Bennett, C. T., & Chen, X. (2018). *First-generation students: College access, persistence, and postbachelor's outcomes.* NCES. https://nces.ed.gov/surveys/B&B/

Choy, S. P. (2001). *Students whose parents did not go to college: Postsecondary access, persistence, and attainment.* National Center for Education Statistics, U.S. Department of Education.

Clance, P. R. (1985). Clance IP scale. In *The impostor phenomenon: When success makes you feel like a fake* (pp. 20–22). Bantam.

Clauss-Ehlers, C. S., & Wibrowski, C. R. (2007). Building educational resilience and social support: The effects of the educational opportunity fund program among first- and second-generation college students. *Journal of College Student Development, 48*(5), 574–584. https://doi.org/10.1353/csd.2007.0051

Costello, G. J., Conboy, K., & Donnellan, B. (2015). Reflections on 'reflection' in action research. *Action Research, June,* 1–32. https://core.ac.uk/download/pdf/297031607.pdf

Creswell, J. W., & Poth, C. N. (2016). *Qualitative inquiry and research design: Choosing among five approaches* (4th ed.). SAGE Publications.

Cruce, T. M., Wolniak, G. C., Seifert, T. A., & Pascarella, E. T. (2006). Impacts of good practices on cognitive development, learning orientations, and graduate degree plans during the first year of college. *Journal of College Student Development, 47*(4), 365–383. https://doi.org/10.1353/csd.2006.0042

Demetriou, C., Meece, J., Eaker-Rich, D., & Powell, C. (2017). The activities, roles, and relationships of successful first-generation college students. *Journal of College Student Development, 58*(1), 19–36. https://doi.org/10.1353/csd.2017.0001

Dennis, J. M., Phinney, J. S., & Chuateco, L. I. (2005). The role of motivation, parental support, and peer support in the academic success of ethnic minority first-generation college students. *Journal of College Student Development, 46*(3), 223–236. https://doi.org/10.1353/csd.2005.0023

Garriott, P. O., Hudyma, A., Keene, C., & Santiago, D. (2015). Social cognitive predictors of first- and non-first-generation college students' academic and life satisfaction. *Journal of Counseling Psychology, 62*(2), 253–263. https://doi.org/10.1037/cou0000066

Gibbons, M. M., & Borders, L. D. (2010). Prospective first-generation college students: A social-cognitive perspective. *The Career Development Quarterly, 58*(3), 194–208. https://doi.org/10.1002/j.2161-0045.2010.tb00186.x

Green, D. (2006). Historically underserved students: What we know, what we still need to know. *New Directions for Community Colleges, 2006*(135), 21–28. https://eric.ed.gov/?id=EJ761076

Guest, G., Bunce, A., & Johnson, L. (2006). How many interviews are enough?: An experiment with data saturation and variability. *Field Methods, 18*(1), 59–82. https://doi.org/10.1177/1525822X05279903

Guiffrida, D. A. (2006). Toward a cultural advancement of Tinto's theory. *The Review of Higher Education, 29*(4), 451–472. https://doi.org/10.1353/rhe.2006.0031

Habley, W. R., & McClanahan, R. (2004). *What works in student retention? Four-year public colleges*. ACT. https://eric.ed.gov/?id=ED515398

Harrell, M. C., & Bradley, M. A. (2009). *Data collection methods: Semi-structured interviews and focus groups*. RAND National Defense Research Institute.

Hébert, T. P. (2018). An examination of high-achieving first-generation college students from low-income backgrounds. *Gifted Child Quarterly, 62*(1), 96–110. https://doi.org/10.1177/0016986217738051

Herr, K., & Anderson, G. L. (2015). *The action research dissertation: A guide for students and faculty* (2nd ed.). SAGE Publications.

Herrmann, S. D., & Varnum, M. E. W. (2018). Utilizing social class bicultural identity integration to improve outcomes for first-generation college students. *Translational Issues in Psychological Science, 4*(2), 165–175. https://doi.org/10.1037/tps0000159

Horn, L., & Nunez, A. (2000). Mapping the road to college: First-generation students' math track, planning strategies, and context of support. *Education Statistics Quarterly, 2*(1), 81–86. https://nces.ed.gov/pubs2000/2000153.pdf

Housel, T. H., & Harvey, V. L. (2009). *The invisibility factor: Administrators and faculty reach out to first-generation college students*. Universal-Publishers.

Ishitani, T. T. (2006). Studying attrition and degree completion behavior among first-generation college students in the United States. *The Journal of Higher Education, 77*(5), 861–885. https://doi.org/10.1080/00221546.2006.11778947

Jencik, A. (2011). Qualitative versus quantitative research. In J. T. Ishiyama & M. Breuning (Eds.), *21st century political science: A reference handbook* (pp. 506–514). SAGE Publications, Inc. https://doi.org/10.4135/9781412979351

Johnson, S. E., Richeson, J. A., & Finkel, E. J. (2011). Middle class and marginal? Socioeconomic status, stigma, and self-regulation at an elite university. *Journal of Personality and Social Psychology, 100*(5), 838–852. https://doi.org/10.1037/a0021956

Kemmis, S. (2009). Action research as a practice-based practice. *Educational Action Research, 17*(3), 463–474. https://doi.org/10.1080/09650790903093284

Lee, J., & Mueller, J. A. (2014). Student loan debt literacy: A comparison of first-generation and continuing-generation college students. *Journal of College Student Development, 55*(7), 714–719. https://doi.org/10.1353/csd.2014.0074

Lewin, K. (1946). Action research and minority problems. *Journal of Social Issues, 2*(4), 34–46. https://doi.org/10.1111/j.1540-4560.1946.tb02295.x

Lincoln, Y. S., & Guba, E. G. (1986). But is it rigorous? Trustworthiness and authenticity in naturalistic evaluation. *New Directions for Program Evaluation, 1986*(30), 73–84. https://doi.org/10.1002/ev.1427

Longwell-Grice, R., Adsitt, N. Z., Mullins, K., & Serrata, W. (2016). The first ones: Three studies on first-generation college students. *NACADA Journal, 36*(2), 34–46. https://doi.org/10.12930/NACADA-13-028

Means, D. R., & Pyne, K. B. (2017). Finding my way: Perceptions of institutional support and belonging in low-income, first-generation, first-year college students. *Journal of College Student Development, 58*(6), 907–924. https://eric.ed.gov/?id=EJ1155237

Mehta, S. S., Newbold, J. J., & O'Rourke, M. A. (2011). Why do first-generation students fail? *College Student Journal, 45*(1), 20–36. https://eric.ed.gov/?id =EJ996345

Mitchall, A. M., & Jaeger, A. J. (2018). Parental influences on low-income, first-generation students' motivation on the path to college. *The Journal of Higher Education, 89*(4), 582–609. https://doi.org/10.1080/00221546.2018.1437664

National Center for Educational Statistics. (2021). *Trend generator: Graduation rate within 150% of normal time at 4-year postsecondary institutions for the 2013 cohort year.* https://nces.ed.gov/ipeds/TrendGenerator/app/answer/7/19

Nunez, A.-M. (1998). *First-generation students: Undergraduates whose parents never enrolled in postsecondary education.* Diane Publishing.

Ostrove, J. M., & Long, S. M. (2007). Social class and belonging: Implications for college adjustment. *The Review of Higher Education, 30*(4), 363–389. https://doi.org/10.1353/rhe.2007.0028

Padgett, R. D., Johnson, M. P., & Pascarella, E. T. (2012). First-generation undergraduate students and the impacts of the first year of college: Additional evidence. *Journal of College Student Development, 53*(2), 243–266. https://doi.org/10.1353/csd.2012.0032

Pascarella, E. T., Pierson, C. T., Wolniak, G. C., & Terenzini, P. T. (2004). First-generation college students: Additional evidence on college experiences and outcomes. *The Journal of Higher Education, 75*(3), 249–284. https://doi.org/10.1080/00221546.2004.11772256

Peralta, K. J., & Klonowski, M. (2017). Examining conceptual and operational definitions of "first-generation college student" in research on retention. *Journal of College Student Development, 58*(4), 630–636. https://doi.org/10.1353/csd.2017.0048

Portes, A. (1998). Social capital: Its origins and applications in modern sociology. *Annual Review of Sociology, 24*(1), 1–24. https://www.jstor.org/stable/223472

Raque-Bogdan, T. L., & Lucas, M. S. (2016). Career aspirations and the first generation student: Unraveling the layers with social cognitive career theory. *Journal of College Student Development, 57*(3), 248–262. https://doi.org/10.1353/csd.2016.0026

Rood, R. E. (2009). Driven to achieve: First-generation students' narrated experience at a private christian college. *Christian Higher Education, 8*(3), 225–254. https://doi.org/10.1080/15363750802708494

Shenton, A. K. (2004). Strategies for ensuring trustworthiness in qualitative research projects. *Education for Information, 22*, 63–75. https://doi.org/10.3233/EFI-2004-22201

Sirin, S. R. (2005). Socioeconomic status and academic achievement: A meta-analytic review of research. *Review of Educational Research, 75*(3), 417–453. https://doi.org/10.3102/00346543075003417

Stanton-Salazar, R. D. (2011). A social capital framework for the study of institutional agents and their role in the empowerment of low-status students and youth. *Youth & Society, 43*(3), 1066–1109. https://doi.org/10.1177/0044118X10382877

Stephens, N. M., Fryberg, S. A., Markus, H. R., Johnson, C. S., & Covarrubias, R. (2012). Unseen disadvantage: How American universities' focus on independence undermines the academic performance of first-generation college students. *Journal of Personality and Social Psychology, 102*(6), 1178–1197. https://doi.org/10.1016/j.comptc.2014.02.035

Stephens, N. M., Hamedani, M. Y. G., & Destin, M. (2014). Closing the social-class achievement gap: A difference-education intervention improves first-generation students' academic performance and all students' college transition. *Psychological Science, 25*(4), 943–953. https://doi.org/10.1177/0956797613518349

Stieha, V. (2010). Expectations and experiences: The voice of a first-generation first-year college student and the question of student persistence. *International Journal of Qualitative Studies in Education, 23*(2), 237–249. https://doi.org/10.1080/09518390903362342

Stringer, E. T. (2014). *Action research* (4th ed.). SAGE Publications.

Stuber, J. M. (2011). Integrated, marginal, and resilient: Race, class, and the diverse experiences of white first-generation college students. *International Journal of Qualitative Studies in Education, 24*(1), 117–136. https://doi.org/10.1080/09518391003641916

Swecker, H. K., Fifolt, M., & Searby, L. (2013). Academic advising and first-generation college students: A quantitative study on student retention. *NACADA Journal, 33*(1), 46–53. https://doi.org/10.12930/NACADA-13-192

Terenzini, P. T., & Pascarella, E. T. (1980). Toward the validation of Tinto's model of college student attrition : A review of recent studies. *Research in Higher Education, 12*(3), 271–282. https://www.jstor.org/stable/40195370

Terenzini, P. T., Springer, L., Yaeger, P. M., Pascarella, E. T., & Nora, A. (1996). First-generation college students: Characteristics, experiences, and cognitive development. *Research in Higher Education, 37*(1), 1–22.

Tierney, W. G., & Venegas, K. M. (2006). Fictive kin and social capital: The role of peer groups in applying and paying for college. *American Behavioral Scientist, 49*(12), 1687–1702. https://doi.org/10.1177/0002764206289145

Tinto, V. (1993). *Leaving college: Rethinking the causes and cures of student attrition.* The University of Chicago Press.

Toutkoushian, R. K., Stollberg, R. A., & Slaton, K. A. (2018). Talking 'bout my generation: Defining "first-generation college students" in higher education research. *Teachers College Record, 120*(4). https://doi.org/10.1177/016146811812000407

Urmeneta, M. (2019). *First-generation data analysis report* [Unpublished internal report]. New York Institute of Technology.

Varney, J. (2007, September 1). *Intrusive advising.* Academic Advising Today. https://nacada.ksu.edu/Resources/Academic-Advising-Today.aspx

Whitehead, P. M., & Wright, R. (2017). Becoming a college student: An empirical phenomenological analysis of first generation college students. *Community College Journal of Research and Practice, 41*(10), 639–651. https://doi.org/10.1080/10668926.2016.1216474

Yeager, D. S., & Walton, G. M. (2011). Social-psychological interventions in education: They're not magic. *Review of Educational Research, 81*(2), 267–301. https://doi.org/10.3102/0034654311405999

HERSTORY

Giving a Voice to the College Experiences of Black Female Students in the New England Area

Nicole Johnson

While growing up, I was constantly told by my parents that I had to go to college and get an education to succeed in life. When looking at what institution to attend, I was forced to select the one that offered me the most financial resources and support to help me be successful while trying to obtain a degree. Through a unique college program, I was afforded multiple grants and scholarships to assist with paying for college, a faculty, and staff mentor who I met with on a monthly basis, as well as tutoring services. This program provided me with individualized resources and support that were readily available to me and took into consideration my needs as a Black female student. Without these resources, my college experience would have been much different. My transition from high school to college would have been more difficult, and I would have graduated with far much more debt. While I was grateful to be a part of this program, it made me think about

Taking Action, pages 191–214
191

what resources and support are offered to other students who were not in this program and identified as a Black female.

Gaining an education is key to success. The level of education an individual obtains is directly related to earnings and socioeconomic status. As such, the claim can be made that earning a college degree is essential. Despite this, there are many barriers that affect a person's ability to enroll in college and earn a college degree. Barriers such as finances and college readiness play a role in an individual's success at college. When looking at minority groups, such as Black female students, they are faced with additional challenges, such as racial disparities, to overcome as they seek a college degree. It is important for institutions of higher education to look at the factors negatively impacting students, especially Black female students, as they work towards graduating with a college degree, to assist with increasing the graduation rates of students. African American women are continuing to enroll in colleges and universities at higher rates every year. Despite these figures, African American women are still not graduating at the same rates of women of other races (Bartman, 2015). There are interpersonal factors and external elements that institutions of higher education must consider when offering resources for Black female students. Such factors as slavery and discrimination have had a negative impact on minority groups, and have created barriers to educational opportunities (Arao, 2016). As a result of these interpersonal and external factors, African American women bring a distinctive set of needs that universities and colleges are not fulfilling. Tangible and intangible identities must be considered as these identities help shape a student's experience at college. Universities not only need to consider what resources they offer to this group of students, but also how they advertise on-campus support to demystify the stigma around seeking help. It is important to resolve this problem of lower graduation rates of Black female students, as education is directly correlated to socioeconomic status. This issue is of significance because of the lasting negative impact not having a college degree can have.

The purpose of this action research study was to investigate and understand the experiences of Black female students during their time at college, with the intent to improve the graduation rates of Black female students from predominantly White colleges and universities in the New England area.

BACKGROUND AND CONTEXT

Today, it is extremely important to obtain a college degree. Statistics show that education is directly related to socioeconomic status (Creusere et al., 2019). Each year, more and more Black female students submit applications to colleges and universities and increase their rates of enrollments. Despite this, Black female students are still graduating at low rates each year (Bartman, 2015).

The purpose of this research was to bring awareness to this concern, give voice to all stakeholders and work to create solutions. The research aimed to learn more about the unique experiences of Black female students who attend predominantly White institutions in the New England area, and the factors that negatively impacted their college experience and graduation rates. The goal was to provide institutions of higher education a better understanding of the unique needs that Black female students have, so appropriate resources and support can be provided. Current resources are not useful or known about by students, and as such colleges must assess the current programs and resources offered to Black female students to determine their effectiveness (Griffith et al., 2019).

The transition from high school to college is a major adjustment for all students. It is more challenging for Black female students, as they also must deal with racism and discrimination during their time attending college. Identifying as a Black female is an area in which not much research has been done to explore the unique obstacles that individuals must face. One of these obstacles is the treatment and relationship Black female students have with faculty members (McGee & Bentley, 2017). There are negative stereotypes that are associated with Black students, and these can hinder the academic experience of Black students. Professors can have a major impact on students' experiences, especially if and when the professor has lower expectations of Black students (Gershenson & Papageorge, 2018). There are misperceptions that Black students are not as engaged in their academic pursuits and/or are not as academically capable as other students (Blake, 2018).

In addition to faculty members, the campus culture also plays a role in the success of Black female students. Having a sense of belonging on campus and building connections with other students as well as the college is imperative (Grier-Reed & Wilson, 2016). Oftentimes students go on a college campus tour, but do not get an accurate idea of what college life will be for them. It is important for colleges to provide a truthful depiction of campus life, so potential students can select a college that is a fit for them. Because of the high cost associated with college, many students are selecting a college based on financial aid packages. But this is to the detriment to students as well as the institution (Destin et al., 2018).

Finances are another important aspect to investigate as not being able to afford paying for college is another major factor for the lower graduation rates of Black female students (Zhan, 2014). In 2014 Zhan conducted a study that showed that minority students with loans of $10,000 or more were less likely to graduate from college (Zhan, 2014). Paying for college can be a huge financial burden, and there needs to be more resources available for Black female students to assist in paying for college. There is a lack of knowledge around all the expenses associated with going to college, and how much obtaining a degree will actually cost. The cost of attending college provided by colleges and universities is not providing a realistic depiction of costs (Kelchen et al., 2017). It is also important for Black female students and their families to start saving for college much earlier and learn more about all costs associated with attending college.

METHODS

The site that I conducted my research at was Northeastern University in Boston, MA. Northeastern University is a predominantly White institution in the New England area with its main campus located in a city environment. Northeastern continues to expand and has campuses throughout the United States as well as abroad. The university's website states that 26% of their student population are students of color. However, they do not explicitly state the percentage of students who identify as a Black female. As such, data regarding the retention and graduation rates of Black female students attending Northeastern is not readily accessible. I selected Northeastern University to conduct my action step because as a staff member at the institution, I had established working relationships with key stakeholders and faculty/staff members who could assist in implementing a mentoring program. I had intimate knowledge of the university that was a benefit. I was able to discuss my research study with faculty and staff members who I already had connections with and could get their insight and feedback on my research and action step. I knew which colleagues to speak with who could provide valuable insight on how I should go about implementing the mentoring program.

PARTICIPANTS

Participants in Cycle 1 were Black females who graduated with a bachelor's degree within the past 5 years from a predominantly White institution in the New England area. Participants for Cycle 1 were recruited through several different avenues such as personal contacts and outreach to potential participants from colleagues at various other institutions. I recruited these participants through such methods like word of mouth and email communication. From my time working in higher education, I have met various students that would be interested in my research and were willing to participate in the study. I also recruited participants through contacting different professional organizations and reaching out to their members. I emailed participants regarding my research study to request their participation and provide a copy of the consent form, which provided an overview of my research study. While these participants did not serve as co-researchers, I collaborated with these insiders to gain knowledge from their experiences, as this will benefit my research (Herr & Anderson, 2015). I set up individual interviews with each participant to interview them and interviews were conducted at the date, time, and location of the interviewee's choice. These participants were interviewed and asked a series of questions to further understand the experiences they had during their time at college. Interviews were recorded with an audio recorder and then transcribed using the Temi transcription service.

For Cycle 2, student participants were Black female students who were incoming to Northeastern University during the Fall 2020 semester. Student participants were recruited with the support of internal stakeholders. A research study announcement was shared with potential student participants by other staff members at Northeastern. Interested participants were provided with my contact information to further discuss the mentoring program and answer any questions they had. Students who were willing to participate were required to complete an application form. This form asked for the student's contact information and their major. Students were also asked to share about their hobbies and special interests, what they wanted out of their mentoring relationship and the top three questions/concerns they had about coming to Northeastern.

Faculty/staff participants were Black female faculty and staff members at Northeastern University. Faculty/staff participants served as mentors and student participants were mentees. Faculty/staff participants were recruited through email outreach and word of mouth. Being a staff member at Northeastern I had connections with faculty and staff members that I had previously interacted with to see if they would be interested in participating in the mentoring program. I reached out to potential faculty/staff participants to provide an overview of my research study, discussed the action step of creating a mentoring program, and answered any questions/concerns that were brought up. Mentees' applications were reviewed and then they were paired with a faculty/staff mentor. Mentors were given the application of their mentee and provided with resources that could be used to reach out to their mentee as well as assist with building their relationship with their mentee.

DATA COLLECTION

Cycle 1 data collection consisted of individual semi-structured interviews. Each interview lasted between 45 and 90 minutes. The interview protocol focused on learning about the unique experiences these participants faced as Black female students. Among other areas of focus, participants were asked to share specific examples of the challenges they experienced as Black female students.

Cycle 2 data collection, during the action step, consisted of field notes from communication via emails with mentors and mentees as well as field notes from individual interviews with participants when they wanted to share their experience directly with me. Data collection, at the end of the action step, consisted of responses from two surveys, one for the mentors and one for the mentees. All participants were also provided the opportunity to meet with me one-on-one to discuss any reflections they wanted to share after completing the survey. The survey included open ended questions, multiple choice questions, and Likert-scale questions to help obtain an in-depth understanding of participants' experience.

DATA ANALYSIS

Data analysis for Cycle 1 was conducted using in vivo coding (Saldaña, 2016) and clustering. Themes that emerged from this process included financial challenges related to paying for the costs of college, parental pressure to select a major and career path that was deemed as profitable, a lack of awareness of campus resources, having to navigate ways of dealing with incidents of racism and discrimination faced while being a student, and concern for being considered an "angry Black female."

Data analysis for Cycle 2 consisted of an analysis of the survey items and field notes from communication with the participants. The analysis of the data showed the efficiency of a mentoring program and specialized resources for Black female students during their time at a PWI.

TRUSTWORTHINESS AND QUALITY ASSURANCE

As a person who identifies as a Black female, I come to my research study with my own perspective and insight. It is important to be mindful of one's own bias and subjectivity in action research (Herr & Anderson, 2015). I bring my own experiences to my research, but I am mindful of this. While I have my own assumptions regarding my research based on my bias, I was mindful to not let it lead my research. I made sure to let participants share their own experiences and perspectives. I determined potential solutions based on the data results from each cycle. Taking a critical look at the problem of practice and finding a concrete solution based on the research findings is essential (Ruona & Gilley, 2009). In both cycles of research, I conducted an unbiased review and evaluation of the research to ensure the credibility of data results. Participants in Cycle 1 were given the opportunity to review their interview transcript to ensure that their college experience was accurately captured. Cycle 2 participants were able to share their experience in the mentoring program through anonymous surveys and individual follow up meetings with me.

The study would be able to be transferred to other institutions of higher education. Cycle 1 can be easily transferred by interviewing Black female students who have recently graduated with their undergraduate degree. By working with key faculty and staff stakeholders, a mentoring program can be created to pair incoming Black female students with a Black female faculty/staff member. Faculty and staff will need to work with senior level administrators to get access to a list of incoming Black female students that could be contacted to provide the opportunity to participate in the mentoring program. Key stakeholders will need to be consulted to recruit Black female students and Black female faculty and staff members.

FINDINGS

Findings from Cycle 1 revealed that participants in this study faced many challenges including financial, parental pressure, campus resources, dealing with racism and discrimination, and fear of being considered an "angry Black female." The data analysis from Cycle 1 indicated that there was a need for more research to be done to learn more about the college experiences of Black female students. Some of the major themes identified in Cycle 1 were that students faced such challenges as having difficulties paying for college, knowing about campus resources, and navigating how to deal with incidents of racism and discrimination when trying to obtain their college degree. These factors negatively impacted their college experience.

While all the participants interviewed in Cycle 1 identified as Black females, they all came from different walks of life. They attended different colleges and universities, had varying amounts of support, and pursued diverse majors and career paths. Despite this, most of the interviewees shared very similar experiences while trying to obtain their bachelor's degree. One similarity that most of the participants shared was that they also identified as a first-generation student. This is significant because all the first-generation participants expressed a lack of knowledge on what they needed to be prepared for as their transition into college. "My mom was not a college graduate, so she didn't know about the process. I didn't know anything about it either. So, I was like the first to do it and we were trying to figure it out, but I saw that other people were coming so prepared" (D. McFarlane, 2019, interview). Many participants shared that they had to figure out how to navigate barriers that may come with going to college such as financial concerns, academic struggles, and acclimating to the college environment.

Financial difficulties were also a major theme that affected the college experience of the participants I interviewed. Many shared that they had many semesters where they had to struggle to figure out how to pay their tuition and other fees associated with attending college. "I made too much money from my FAFSA, or my parents made too much money at the time. So, it was like $60,000 without any financial aid. So, I was like wow, I can't afford it" (B. Noel, 2019, interview). Interviewees also shared that they did not have the knowledge on grant and scholarship opportunities that could have assisted with paying for college. Not knowing where the money would come from to pay for college adds an enormous amount of stress and pressure on a person, which inevitably negatively impacts one's mental health and academics.

Another major theme that was evident was the fear proving negative stereotypes about Black females to be true. There are several negative stereotypes associated with being a Black female, such as being depicted as angry when expressing oneself or being viewed as academically inferior and not being able to handle academics at the college level. "Like, cause when people think of like people like color and stuff like that, they're like, Oh they're not smart. They're not going to make it through college" (L. Bekoe, 2019, interview). Many participants also shared how they sometimes felt they had to be conscious about how they expressed themselves or had to hold in their feelings all together for fear of being called and labeled as an "angry Black woman." They provided examples of being passionate about a topic or being upset about a situation, and automatically being labeled as angry and aggressive. Participants felt that the choice of being considered an "angry Black woman" or not vocalizing their feelings, were both detrimental options.

To learn more about the factors that impact the lower graduation rate of this unique population, colleges must further investigate the experiences of this population of students as well as evaluate the specialized resources, or lack thereof, that are offered to assist them successfully earn a college degree. Research indicates that it is essential for Black female students to connect with other Black female students as well as Black female faculty and staff in order to successfully transition to college and feel engaged with the campus community (Grier-Reed, 2016). The analysis also showed that Black female students would benefit from resources and support specifically geared towards Black female students. Having access to role models and/or mentors was key to the success of Black female students (Biswas, 2019). The finding and research led to the creation of a mentoring program for Cycle 2. The aim being to create a mentoring program where Black female students have a Black female faculty/staff mentor will provide Black female students with the opportunity to connect with campus community members that they can relate to and that can help incoming students become more knowledgeable of other available campus resources.

In order to develop and implement the mentoring program, I met with various constituencies at Northeastern. I also contacted various Black female faculty and staff members that I had met and/or previously worked with to discuss my research study and action plan. I shared with these faculty/staff participants my objective and plan for the mentoring program and offered the opportunity to serve as a mentor for the program. Some participants provided the names of other faculty and staff who they thought would also be interested in being a part of the mentoring program. I created an application for student participants to fill out. The application asked students to provide some background information about themselves. This information was used to help pair students with a mentor. Once a mentee was paired with a mentor, I emailed both parties with the name and contact information of their mentor and mentee.

Mentors were also provided with additional resources such as a mentoring agreement and discussion prompts for each month, that the mentor could use to help mentors cultivate a meaningful relationship with their mentee. Mentees were asked to complete a brief application which asked for their email, phone number, major, and hometown. The application also asked mentees to include their hobbies and special interests, what they wanted to get out of their mentoring relationship, and the top three questions and/or concerns they had about coming to Northeastern. Mentors were emailed their mentee's application to help mentors know a bit about their mentee. Mentors were provided with a template initial email that they could use to email their mentee, as well as provided monthly talking points to help guide their monthly discussions with their mentee. Lastly, mentors were offered a mentor agreement that they could use in building their relationship with their mentee. The agreement discussed what both the mentor and mentee could expect of each other, a proposed plan for monthly meetings, and the mentee's short-term and long-term goals that could be discussed and updated with progress after each month.

To assess the effectiveness of my action steps, a survey was created for mentees and a survey for mentors to complete and provide their candid feedback. Participants were asked to share their reflection on their experience in the mentoring program. The surveys also asked participants to discuss what went well as well as what changes they would want to see implemented for future years. Participants were also offered the opportunity to meet individually to discuss how they thought the mentoring program went and provide any feedback on their experience.

In evaluating the Cycle 2 action steps, three findings were evident for mentees:

1. Most of the students wanted to join the mentoring program to have a mentor who was a Black female.

2. Periodic/recurrent meetings were helpful
3. Mentees valued the relationship they were able to form with their mentors.

Three findings emerged from the mentors. These included:

1. Mentors wanted to provide support to Black female students.
2. Mentors wanted to learn more about the current struggles facing Black female students. Mentors wanted additional resources provided to them.

MENTEES

To evaluate the experiences of mentees in the HERstory mentoring program, I reviewed each mentee's survey response. Mentees were asked to share about the rapport they had with their mentor and how helpful having a mentor was. Three main findings taken from survey responses of mentees.

Mentees Wanted Black Female Mentors

Students who identify as a Black female face unique challenges and experiences that are not always understood or relatable to individuals outside these identities. The HERstory mentoring program sought to intentionally pair incoming Black female students with a Black female faculty/staff member at Northeastern to provide these students with a person they could relate to in terms of their identities and shared experiences as being a part of these identities. Mentees shared that they wanted to participate in the HERstory mentoring program because they did not know how they would do in their first year of college. One participant shared that "having the opportunity to have a mentor, especially a Black woman, was something that felt really wonderful to have. I had no idea what to expect going into the fall semester so having someone who's been to Northeastern and could share similar experiences with was something I found to be amazing." Survey results also revealed that most participants wanted to join the mentoring program to have a mentor who was a Black female. As well as having a mentor who could support them as they navigated their first semester at a predominantly White institution (PWI). One participant shared that they did not know why they chose to participate but wanted to make sure they "established a strong support system at Northeastern." Based on survey responses, Black female students found it beneficial to have a Black female mentor as they transitioned into Northeastern.

Mentees Found That Frequency/Recurrent Meetings Were Significant

Out of the nine participants who completed the survey, eight shared that they were able to meet with their mentor at least once a month. Only one mentee said that they were not able to meet with their mentor once a month. Two participants shared that they communicated with their mentor on a weekly basis. Five participants stated that between their monthly meetings, they occasionally communicated with their mentor. When asked what were the barriers that impacted mentees meeting with their mentors, mentees shared that COVID-19 was a barrier and such things as work schedules and family events were sometimes a barrier. Most mentees expressed that they were extremely satisfied or somewhat satisfied with the frequency in which they met with the mentor, how often they communicated with their mentor, and the mentoring relationship they had with their mentor. As such, one finding from the survey was that periodic meetings with their mentor were helpful. One participant expressed that they were somewhat dissatisfied with the frequency in which they met with their mentor and the mentoring relationship they had with their mentor. Another mentee suggested change was having people with similar majors, so it is "a more aligned experience." Another suggestion was having mandatory bi-weekly meetings.

Mentees Valued the Relationship With Mentors

Another finding was that mentees valued the relationship they were able to form with their mentor. Survey results showed that mentees appreciated the relationship they were able to form with their mentor and were able to form a genuine relationship with their mentor. One mentee shared, "I found it very easy to confide in her and ask for help. She was very supportive and helpful throughout the time I was her mentee." When explaining their mentoring relationship, another mentee shared, "We often had discussions of my short and long-term goals as well as my progress within the semester. Receiving guidance really was influential to my beginning experience at Northeastern as a remote learner." The survey results showed that seven mentees planned on continuing to meet with their mentor during the Spring 2021 semester. The survey also illustrated that most mentees found it beneficial to have a mentor who identified as a Black female. Most participants shared that having a mentor helped them during their first semester at Northeastern and having a mentor helped them feel more connected at Northeastern. All mentees who completed the survey shared that they felt comfortable speaking with their mentor about any issues or concerns that arose during their first semester at Northeastern. The survey also asked participants to share what they gained from being a part of the HERstory mentoring program. One participant shared, "I gained someone in the Northeastern community who shares a similar background with me, who is there as a mentor, supporter and friend during the semester." Another mentee shared that "being a part of the HERstory mentoring program has allowed me to see that pursuing education at a prestigious university as a Black woman is extremely possible." Another key component to evaluating the HERstory mentoring program was to get feedback from the participants who served as mentors.

MENTORS

Having Northeastern faculty and staff members to serve as mentors was crucial to the execution of the HERstory mentoring program. As such it was important to get mentors' insight on their experience in the mentoring program. Mentors were given a slightly different survey to complete that sought to learn more about why they chose to participate in the mentoring program and what they hoped to gain from this experience. Questions also focused on asking mentor participants how helpful were the resources that were provided to them and what thoughts they had changes that could be implemented in future years to improve the effectiveness of the HERstory mentoring program. There were three main findings from the survey responses from mentors who completed the survey.

Mentors Wanted to Build a Support System for Black Women

Mentors were given a slightly different survey to learn about their experience from their perspective in the HERstory mentoring program. In addition to the survey questions mentees were asked, the mentor's survey included questions pertaining to the resources they were provided. Out of the seven mentors who completed the mentor survey, five found receiving their mentee's application helpful and two found their mentee's application somewhat helpful. Most mentors expressed that the mentoring agreement and monthly talking points were useful to them. Another mentor shared that they had "been a mentor in informal ways to many folks, and having a structured, supported program was what I have been looking for to support the development of a first year female-identifying Black student." In reviewing the mentor survey, most participants shared they were informed about the mentoring program from a colleague. Mentors were asked to elaborate on the reasons why they wanted to participate in the HERstory program. In their responses most mentors expressed that they wanted to support Black female students. One mentor shared that they wanted to participate in the HERstory program to help "build a strong support system for black and of color women on campus." Other participants shared that they had benefitted from a mentoring relationship and wanted to provide the same support to an incoming student as they understood the transition to college was challenging. One mentor responded that they joined to have the "opportunity to build a longitudinal mentor relationship with a Black female student before they enter the pharmacy program and helping to assist in her entry and retention in the program." In reviewing the responses from mentors, one finding was that mentors sought to build a support system for Black female students at Northeastern.

Mentors Gained Insight Into Struggle of Current Black Female Students

2020 was a challenging year for many reasons and brought with it unique obstacles that colleges and students had to navigate. Due to COVID-19 and the global pandemic, many institutions of higher education had to transition to virtual learning options. In addition, there were many incidents of police brutality against racial minorities that ignited protests and calls for reform against racial injustice in all areas of life. Incoming students had to navigate the challenges of 2020 in addition to managing the typical obstacles that come along with the transition from high school to college. Many mentors expressed that by being a part of the HERstory mentoring program, they were able to gain a better insight into the struggles facing current students. Mentors were able to hear first year from their mentee about the challenges they were having to overcome. One mentor shared, "I believe mentorship is important at every stage of life. I work with students in different stages of transition and wanted to give back to an incoming student—especially considering the challenges of 2020." One participant stated, "I often hear that being at Northeastern University as a Black student is challenging and I appreciate the opportunity to learn how it is this way and also be a resource for making it better." Mentors also shared that the first semester at college is hard and that they wanted to do their part to support young Black women and pay it forward.

Mentors Wanted Additional Resources

A few mentors shared that having an orientation meeting amongst the mentors to collaborate and network or having a bi-monthly zoom call with the mentors to see how things were going so that mentors could support each other would have helped. Participants shared that having the mentee's application include a mini self-assessment on wellness, their mentee's contact information, and the goals, aspirations, and weaknesses of their mentee would have been helpful. When asked what resources and trainings would be beneficial, a few mentors shared that having an orientation meeting amongst the mentors to collaborate and network or having bi-monthly zoom calls with the mentors to see how things were going so that mentors could support each other would have helped. Other suggestions included having a meet and greet with all participants and/or having an optional monthly check-in with mentees and mentors would have been beneficial. Another mentor shared that another resource that could be implemented in the future having "a short primer on mentorship, sistering relationships between Black women." Most mentors shared that they met with their mentees more than once a month to help build a rapport with their mentee. One mentor expressed that they had challenges when scheduling meeting times with their mentee and stated, "My mentee kept canceling our meetings even though she suggested the time would work for her. I was chasing her for most of the semester and I feel like I wasn't able to provide as much guidance as I wanted to."

DISCUSSION

Barriers to Success

Research shows that individuals who do not have a college degree are more likely to struggle financially in their life (Creusere et al., 2019). Individuals who have obtained a degree of higher education will earn 75% more money than individuals who have only completed high school (Long & Riley, 2007). Despite this, there are many obstacles that individuals seeking to obtain a college education must navigate to enroll into college. Research has found that Black female students must navigate several barriers when attempting to earn their college degree (Farmer et al., 2016). There are several barriers that Black female students have to overcome to enroll into college as well as successfully earn a degree. One challenge Black female students need to navigate is selecting the best institution that they can learn and be actively engaged at, while navigating financial struggles and readily having available the necessary resources to be prepared for success in their college setting (Griffith et al., 2019). As such, it is especially important for Black female students to take a critical look at the institution they decide to enroll at and learn about the resources offered. While finances do also have to be considered, it is most important for students to find the "right" college.

College Selection

Selecting a college can be a daunting task. Potential students need to consider many factors before selecting an institution that is best for them. Individuals need to look at the campus location and ratio of faculty to student. Diversity of the campus should also be considered, as well as campus resources and support offered to students. Housing options and even clubs and student organizations should be evaluated when selecting a college. Many students rely on the internet to research about a potential institution and do little to learn about the campus climate (Daun-Barnett & Das, 2013). Looking at all these various factors will help students get a true sense of the campus culture to see if the institution is a good fit for them. The cost to attend a college or university is steadily on the rise, and the increases in tuition and fees make gaining a college degree less attainable for many. As such, some Black female students select their college based on financial reasons alone and choose to attend the institution that offers them the most money (Destin et al., 2018).

Having to figure out paying for college and paying off student loans after college can be overwhelming. This can lead to Black female students selecting what college they should attend based on financial costs. Some colleges and universities use the tactic known as "tuition discounting," which entails having a higher tuition cost but then offering potential students a larger discount (Rine, 2019). Higher tuition costs lead potential students to think that the institution is of greater quality and believe that the institution's costs are directly correlated with the quality of education they will receive.

Prospective students also believe that when an institution provides a large amount of grants and scholarships, they see it as the college valuing them as a student (Rine, 2019). It can be detrimental for students to choose to attend a school that has offered the most financial aid and overlook the many other aspects of the institution. The campus culture and environment are also important to consider when selecting the college as a student's engagement with their college campus environment is directly related to retention and graduation rates (Museus et al., 2017). While financial struggles can't be overlooked, it is necessary for students to look at more than just financial support when selecting their college.

Financial Planning

Struggling to pay for college can have a negative impact on a student. When students deal with stress due to financial reasons, they are more prone to have psychological issues (Peters et al., 2011). Most schools have policies in place that prevent the student from registering for classes or even attending classes if their student bill is greater than a certain amount. There is a hold put on a student's account to halt their academic process and prevent the student from being able to obtain their student records, such as transcript. When students have a remaining balance on their student bill, they oftentimes will apply for student loans to cover the costs (Jackson & Reynolds, 2013). Some students may not be fortunate to have help with figuring out how to apply for student loans and/or help figuring out what student loan is the best one for them to apply for. While student loans can help a student pay for college, there are risks associated with taking out student loans (Jackson & Reynolds, 2013). Research shows that large amounts of college loans lead to greater debt and a likelihood to default on the loans. As such, it is important for students to think about how they will pay for college and should research scholarship and grant opportunities to help mitigate the needs for student loans.

Research shows that high student loan debt can negatively affect a student's graduation. Underrepresented students with large amounts of student loan debt were less likely to graduate from college (Zhan, 2014). Black female students and their families will also need to start preparing for college even before they are in high school. This will also include thinking about all the costs associated with attending college and starting to save for college earlier. Research shows that Black students are less likely to have access to school counselors in high school to assist them in preparing for college (Bryan et al., 2011). It is important for institutions of higher education and parents to educate their students on the topics of financial responsibility (Norvilitis & MacLean, 2010). Black female students and their families will have to be proactive about researching potential scholarships and grants that can help cover the costs of earning a degree.

CAMPUS LIFE

Transitioning from high school to college can be a difficult feat (Conley et al., 2014). Part of the reason behind this is because of the many changes that come with going from high school to college. Students are moving from home to a new environment, where most likely they will be living with other students who they are not familiar with. They also have to cope with being away from home and being in an atmosphere that they may not be used to, with people from various backgrounds and all walks of life (Conley et al., 2014). Students also have to traverse a different type of academic rigor and have to adjust to the different learning environment. As such, the campus environment is a key factor if a student will have a positive college experience (Museus et al., 2017). Students need to make connections with other community members and have a sense of belonging at their college. These connections are essential to a student's success.

SENSE OF BELONGING

One aspect of college that is significant in a student's success and the completion of their degree, is feeling a sense of belonging at their respective college. It is important that students feel that they belong and make connections with others. Studies show that students need to make a connection with their college within the first several weeks of starting school to have a successful transition (Woosley, 2003). This could be making a connection with another student, a staff member, and/or a faculty member. When students participate in campus activities and/or student organizations, they have a higher chance of graduating. Students need to make connections in the classroom setting as well. Professors should work to create a sense of community within their classroom. Building a sense of community amongst students provides the opportunity for students to learn more about each other, and also learn from each other (Bettez, 2011). Without having a connection, a student is more likely than not to have a sense of belonging and transfer to another institution or withdraw from the institution altogether.

It is important to have opportunities where Black female students can connect with other students of the same identity and affirm their experiences (Steele, 2017). This can be done by joining cultural student organizations and advocacy groups that their campus has to offer. Having an individual or group of people available to talk to and discuss issues and concerns, especially who can understand you and your feelings is crucial when adapting to a new environment such as college. Making friends and building connections during one's time at college is vital to a student's sense of belonging and their success during their time at college (Grier-Reed & Wilson, 2016). Joining cultural student organizations will allow opportunities for Black female students to share about themselves and their experiences with other students and build lasting relationships with other students.

It is also important for Black female students to connect with students of the same race and gender. Connecting with other Black female students and seeing individuals at their college who look like them in such roles as faculty and staff is valuable. It is crucial that Black women connect with each other so they can help each other when dealing with racism and other barriers (Henry & Glenn, 2009). Black female students will face challenging situations throughout their time at college. Having role models who are faculty and/or staff members are beneficial for students as they deal with academic challenges. Mentoring and receiving guidance from mentors is vital to Black female students' success in their academic as well as in the college experience (Biswas, 2019).

NAVIGATING BIAS AND MISPERCEPTIONS

There is a perception that racism and prejudice is an issue of the past. Unfortunately, this is not the case and individuals of minority groups still face discrimination in their lives. Racism is still a prevalent issue today and underrepresented groups still are dealing with the impact of this (West, 2003). Black female students must endure dealing with negative stereotypes and incidents of discrimination during their time at college (McGee & Bentley, 2017). Black female students also face bias and discrimination as both a woman and a person of color. Racial inequality still exists in our education system as a direct result of the slavery, and negative impacts on the lives of minority students (Bertocchi & Dimico, 2012). This bias can come from faculty and staff members, as well as interactions with other students. Dealing with racism and discrimination in regard to these tangible identities can negatively impact the college experience for Black female students (Bodkin-Andrews et al., 2010). Understanding the unique experiences of this group of students can better help inform college administrators and faculty/staff members of how to support Black female students, and what resources would be beneficial to their success.

STEREOTYPES IN CLASSROOM SETTINGS

Each year students from all over the world apply to institutions of higher education. They have diverse backgrounds and come from all walks of life (Wu et al., 2015). This is extremely important to note for professors and staff members working at these institutions, as these individuals can have a major impact on a student's college experience. Research shows that a teacher's expectations have a great influence on a student's outcome in college (Gershenson & Papageorge, 2018). The professors teaching students play a major part in a student's college experience as well as their graduation rates. Students who identify as a Black female student have to deal with stereotypes and bias based on their race and gender. They endure discrimination from students, faculty, and/or staff members. There are several negative stereotypes associated with individuals of color when it comes to education. Some people believe that Black students are less engaged in their academics than other students (Blake, 2018). Some also believe that Black students do not have the necessary aptitude to excel in an educational setting. There is a misperception that minority students are not as smart as other students and will not be able to be successful in the college setting. These stereotypes can be detrimental to Black students especially when coming from people who have power and influence over their academics and overall college experience. Misperceptions are detrimental to Black female students' success, especially in the classroom, as they oftentimes will internalize these stereotypes (Bir & Myrick, 2015). Professors get to determine grades for their students and college administrators govern policies and procedures for the institution.

As such, there needs to be more training for faculty and staff members regarding topics of diversity and inclusion. Colleges and universities must recognize and understand the importance of the identities of their students, especially when it comes to racial identity (Tatum, 2017). Many institutions provide minimal training for faculty and staff members regarding cultural sensitivity. Diversity and inclusion training would be for the benefit of employees at colleges and universities. It would help administrators and individuals working at institutions of higher education to have a better understanding of the diverse group of students they will be interacting with (Bezrukova et al., 2012). Professors and staff members have a major impact on a student's experience. Professors who have a negative preconceived of Black female students can make it harder for these students to be successful in the classroom (Parks & Kennedy, 2007). Professors with different expectations for Black students versus their other students can have a negative impact on these student's graduation rates (Gershenson & Papageorge, 2018). With more training on these subject matters, staff working at colleges can learn more about inclusion and how to have their course materials and teaching style be conducive to all students. Training would also provide the opportunity to individuals to be more open-minded and demystify certain preconceived notions and stereotypes.

ANGRY BLACK WOMAN

Another stereotype that Black woman combat is being considered angry and called an "angry Black woman." In movies and books, a Black woman can sometimes be portrayed as a person who yells and gets very upset when sharing their opinion or when addressing a situation. In Tyler Perry's 2007 movie *Why Did I Get Married*, throughout the movie, the character Angela is seen getting into arguments in almost every scene (Cannon et al., 2007). She is constantly yelling at her husband, workers, and strangers. In a store when shopping, Angela is seen confronting another patron when she feels the patron was rude to her. Her friends try to calm her down, but Angela continues to yell in a loud voice and causes a commotion in the store.

Angela is described as loud and aggressive by multiple characters in the movie. Viewers are made to see Angela as violent, hostile, and overbearing.

Angela and characters like Angela in other movies perpetuate this misconception that Black women are angry and ill tempered. Black women are stereotyped as being angry even without being provoked. These misperceptions initiated from historical events, such as slavery and segregation and have continued through current times contributing to the racial gap in our education system (Bertocchi & Dimico, 2012). Racial discrimination has helped to create negative depictions of Black women as angry and aggressive. Black females are sometimes labeled with these negative misperceptions and stereotypes, and this is detrimental to a student's experience in college.

Black women are depicted as confrontational and argumentative. They are shown to take small situations and escalate them by their hostile approach. This notion of the "angry Black woman" is still prevalent today and is something Black female students are mindful of (Walley-Jean, 2009). Some Black female students decide not to confront incidents of discrimination or unfair treatment for fear that they will be labeled as an "angry Black female." It can make it hard for Black female students to know who to speak with when dealing with issues that affect their academics and/or college experience. Black female students seek to not further enhance these negative stereotypes and have to be mindful of how they address situations during their time at college (Walley-Jean, 2009).

LIMITATIONS

One limitation to the study was getting access to a list of students that could be student participants in the mentoring program. I had to ask different offices to share my research study with incoming Black female students. I was not able to directly contact student participants myself. Emails were sent out to students informing them of my research study, but emails are not always the best form of communication for students. Because I did not have access to the list of potential student participants, I had to rely on other staff members to search my research study to students via email and hope that students would respond to me. I believe this impacted the number of student participants that signed up for the mentoring program.

As I reached out to potential faculty participants, another concern was brought to my attention. Some shared that Black female faculty members oftentimes get requests of a similar nature and are asked to provide additional support to minority students. Potential participants stated that most times they take on these additional initiatives on top of their standard job responsibilities without any recognition. Faculty members asked about what the time commitment would be if they decided to be a mentor as they were concerned with managing their workload as Northeastern was planning on reopening for the Fall 2020 semester and offering in-person and virtual classes.

COVID-19 and the global pandemic created several limitations to my research study. Due to COVID-19 the university shut down and Boston went on lock down. This meant that all meetings had to be conducted virtually and in-person events and gatherings were not allowed. The initial plan was to have participants meet in person to help get to know each other, but to also meet other mentors and mentees in the program. I was also hoping to have participants attend various events in person on campus to better get to know the campus and campus resources. All programming had to be held virtually. It was at the mentors and mentees discretion if they were comfortable meeting in person or to meet via video conference.

Another limitation was getting 100% participation in the survey. Due to COVID-19, I could not meet with participants in person to discuss their experience in the mentoring program. To evaluate the mentoring program and participants' experience during its first semester, I created surveys. I created two surveys, one for mentors and the other for mentees, to be able to share about their experience and provide any feedback in an anonymous manner. Since participants did not have to provide their name on the survey, I was not sure which participants completed the survey and which did not. As such I could not follow up directly with participants who did not complete the survey to get their insight and/or ask them to complete the survey. I had a 79% completion rate for the mentee survey and 50% completion rate for the mentor survey.

CONCLUSION

Consistent with other studies, this research showed that Black female students face a variety of challenges that can negatively impact their college experience as they seek to obtain their degree, such as dealing with racism and discrimination. While students who identify as a Black female student are continuing to increase their enrollment into institutions of higher education, these students are not showing the same increase in graduation rates (Farmer et al., 2016). The needs of Black female students are not being met by their colleges and universities, and this is having a negative impact on the college experience of these students (Ricks, 2014). Black female students must navigate transitioning to college in addition to dealing with bias and stereotypes. Black female students face a wide variety of challenges as they enroll into college and throughout their time at their college or university. As such, it is important for institutions of higher education to learn more about the experiences of Black female students, and to assist with improving this unique population of students' retention and graduation rates.

REFERENCES

Arao, B. (2016). Roles of Black women and girls in education: A historical reflection. *Listening to the Voices: Multi-Ethnic Women in Education,* 137–143. https://repository.usfca.edu/cgi/viewcontent.cgi?article=1012&context=listening_to_the_voices

Bartman, C. C. (2015). African American women in higher education: Issues and support strategies. *College Student Affairs Leadership, 2*(2), Article 5. https://scholarworks.gvsu.edu/cgi/viewcontent.cgi?article=1020&context=csal

Bertocchi, G., & Dimico, A. (2012). The racial gap in education and the legacy of slavery. *Journal of Comparative Economics, 40*(4), 581–595. https://doi.org/10.1016/j.jce.2012.04.001

Bettez, S. C. (2011). Building critical communities amid the uncertainty of social justice pedagogy in the graduate classroom. *Review of Education, Pedagogy, and Cultural Studies, 33*(1), 76–106. https://doi.org/10.1080/10714413.2011.550191

Bezrukova, K., Jehn, K., & Spell, C. (2012). Reviewing diversity training: Where we have been and where we should go. *Academy of Management Learning & Education, 11*(2), 207–227. https://doi.org/10.5465/amle.2008.0090

Bir, B., & Myrick, M. (2015). Summer bridge's effects on college student success. *Journal of Developmental Education, 39*(1), 22–28, 30. https://files.eric.ed.gov/fulltext/EJ1106091.pdf

Biswas, S. (2019, March 13). Advice on advising: How to mentor minority students. *The Chronicle of Higher Education.* https://www.chronicle.com/article/advice-on-advising-how-to-mentor-minority-students/

Blake, M. (2018). All talk and no action? Racial differences in college behaviors and attendance. *Sociological Perspectives, 61*(4), 553–572. https://doi.org/10.1177/0731121418777237

Bodkin-Andrews, G., O'Rourke, V., Grant, R., Denson, N., & Craven, R. (2010). Validating racism and cultural respect: Testing the psychometric properties and educational impact of perceived discrimination and multiculturation for Indigenous and non-Indigenous students. *Educational Research and Evaluation, 16*(6), 471–493. https://doi.org/10.1080/13803611.2010.550497

Bryan, J., Moore-Thomas, C., Day-Vines, N. L., & Holcomb-McCoy, C. (2011). School counselors as social capital: The effects of high school college counseling on college application rates. *Journal of Counseling and Development, 89*(2), 190–199. https://doi.org/10.1002/j.1556-6678.2011.tb00077.x

Cannon, R., & Perry, T. (Producer), & Perry, T. (Director). (2007). *Why did I get married* [Motion Picture]. Tyler Perry Studios.

Conley, C. S., Kirsch, A. C., Dickson, D. A, & Bryant, F. B. (2014). Negotiating the transition to college: Developmental trajectories and gender differences in psychological functioning, cognitive-affective strategies, and social well-being. *Emerging Adulthood, 2*(3), 195–210. https://doi.org/10.1177/2167696814521808

Creusere, M., Zhao, H., Huie, S., & Troutman, D. R. (2019). Postsecondary education impact on intergenerational income mobility: Differences by completion status, gender, race/ethnicity, and type of major. *The Journal of Higher Education, 90*(6), 915–939. https://doi.org/10.1080/00221546.2019.1565882

Daun-Barnett, N., & Das, D. (2013). Unlocking the potential of the Internet to improve college choice: A comparative case study of college-access Web tools. *Journal of Marketing for Higher Education, 23*(1), 113–134. https://doi.org/10.1080/08841241.2013.805708

Destin, M., Destin, M., Svoboda, R. C., & Svoboda, R. C. (2018). Costs on the mind: The influence of the financial burden of college on academic performance and cognitive functioning. *Research in Higher Education, 59*(3), 302–324. https://doi.org/10.1007/s11162-017-9469-8

Farmer, E., Hilton, A., & Reneau, F. (2016). Variables that contribute to retention and graduation of Black American females at an historically Black university. *Negro Educational Review, 67*(1–4), 133–148, 169. https://www.proquest.com/docview/1926455426

Gershenson, S., & Papageorge, N. (2018). The power of teacher expectations: How racial bias hinders student attainment. *Education Next, 18*(1), 65–70. https://www.educationnext.org/power-of-teacher-expectations-racial-bias-hinders-student-attainment/

Grier-Reed, T., & Wilson, R. (2016). The African American student network: An exploration of Black students' ego networks at a predominantly White institution. *Journal of Black Psychology, 42*(4), 374–386.

Griffith, A. N., Hurd, N. M., & Hussain, S. B. (2019). "I didn't come to school for this": A qualitative examination of experiences with race-related stressors and coping responses among Black students attending a predominantly White institution. *Journal of Adolescent Research, 34*(2), 115–139. https://doi.org/10.1177/0743558417742983

Henry, W., & Glenn, N. (2009). Black women employed in the ivory tower: Connecting for success. *Advancing Women in Leadership, 29*, 1–18. https://doi.org/10.21423/awlj-v29.a271

Herr, K., & Anderson, G. (2015). *The action research dissertation: A guide for students and faculty* (2nd ed.). SAGE Publishing.

Jackson, B. A., & Reynolds, J. R. (2013). The price of opportunity: Race, student loan debt, and college achievement. *Sociological Inquiry, 83*(3), 335–368. https://doi.org/10.1111/soin.12012

Kelchen, R., Goldrick-Rab, S., & Hosch, B. (2017). The costs of college attendance: Examining variation and consistency in institutional living cost allowances. *The Journal of Higher Education, 88*(6), 947–971. https://doi.org/10.1080/00221546.2016.1272092

Long, B., & Riley, E. (2007). Financial aid: A broken bridge to college access? *Harvard Educational Review, 77*(1), 39–63. https://doi.org/10.17763/haer.77.1.765h8777686r7357

McGee, E., & Bentley, L. (2017). The troubled success of Black women in STEM. *Cognition and Instruction, 35*(4), 265–289. https://doi.org/10.1080/07370008.2017.1355211

Museus, S. D., Yi, V., & Saelua, N. (2017). The impact of culturally engaging campus environments on sense of belonging. *The Review of Higher Education, 40*(2), 187–215. https://doi.org/10.1353/rhe.2017.0001

Norvilitis, J. M., & MacLean, M. G. (2010). The role of parents in college students' financial behaviors and attitudes. *Journal of Economic Psychology, 31*(1), 55–63. https://doi.org/10.1016/j.joep.2009.10.003

Parks, F., & Kennedy, J. (2007). The impact of race, physical attractiveness, and gender on education majors' and teachers' perceptions of student competence. *Journal of Black Studies, 37*(6), 936–943. https://doi.org/10.1177/0021 934705285955

Peters, R. J., Jr., Ford, K., Lin, M.-T., Meshack, A. F., Johnson, R. J., & Essien, E. J. (2011). The relationship between perceived psychological distress, behavioral indicators and African American student financial aid attainment difficulty. *American Journal of Health Studies, 26*(3), 131. https://www.thefreelibrary .com/The+relationship+between+perceived+psychological+distress%2C+ behavioral...-a0349488843

Ricks, S. A. (2014). Falling through the cracks: Black girls and education. *Interdisciplinary Journal of Teaching and Learning, 4*(1), 1–12. https://files.eric.ed.gov/ fulltext/EJ1063223.pdf

Rine, P. (2019). The discounting dilemma: Institutional benefits, unintended consequences, and principles for reform. *Christian Higher Education, 18*(1–2), 16–23. https://doi.org/10.1080/15363759.2018.1543242

Ruona, W. E., & Gilley, J.W. (2009). Practitioners in applied professions: A model applied to human resource development. *Advances in Developing Human Resources, 11*(4), 438–453. https://doi.org/10.1177/1523422309344719

Saldaña, J. (2016). *The coding manual for qualitative researchers.* SAGE Publications.

Steele, T. (2017). "Retaining Black female college students: The effects of meritocracy on their ideas of success." *College Student Affairs Leadership,* 4(1), Article 7. https://scholarworks.gvsu.edu/csal/vol4/iss1/7

Tatum, B. D. (2017). *Why are all the Black kids sitting together in the cafeteria? And other conversations about race.* Basic Books.

Walley-Jean, J. C. (2009). Debunking the myth of the "angry Black woman": An exploration of anger in young African American women. *Black Women, Gender & Families, 3*(2), 68–86. https://doi.org/10.1353/bwg.0.0011

West, C. (2003). A genealogy of modern racism. In L. Cahoone (Ed.), *From modernism to postmodernism* (pp. 298–309). Blackwell Publishing.

Woosley, S. A. (2003). How important are the first few weeks of college? The long term effects of initial college experiences. *College Student Journal, 37*(2), 201–207. https://www.researchgate.net/publication/288265346_How_important _are_the_first_few_weeks_of_college_The_long_term_effects_of_initial_college _experiences

Wu, H.-P., Garza, E., & Guzman, N. (2015). International student's challenge and adjustment to college. *Education Research International, 2015,* 1–9. https://doi .org/10.1155/2015/202753

Zhan, M. (2014). Education loans and college graduation: Differences by race/ethnicity. *Social Development Issues, 36*(2), 17–34. https://link.ezproxy.neu.edu/ login?url=https://www.proquest.com/scholarly-journals/education-loans -college-graduation-differences/docview/1655246265/se-2

ABOUT THE EDITORS

Sara B. Ewell is the associate dean of faculty affairs for the College of Professional Studies and Teaching Professor in the Graduate School of Education at Northeastern University. She previously served as the assistant dean of the Graduate School of Education and director of the Doctor of Education which was awarded the Carnegie Project of the Education Doctorate 2022 Program of the Year Award under her leadership. Dr. Ewell's research interests include social justice, educational leadership, urban education, teacher preparation and retention, and qualitative research. Previously, Dr. Ewell taught at the University of North Carolina, Stonehill College, and as K–12 classroom teacher.

Joan Giblin is an associate teaching professor in the Graduate School of Education at Northeastern University. She serves as the dissertation lead for the EdD program and has served as faculty lead for the MEd in Higher Education Administration program. Prior to Northeastern, Dr. Giblin held leadership roles in residence life, orientation programs, first year seminar, academic support programs, and academic advising, as well as provided strategic leadership for student support and retention initiatives. Her research interests include academic self-regulation, intentional instructional design, and the field of higher education. In addition to teaching in both the doctorate and masters' programs, she also serves as an elected official on her local school board.

Taking Action, pages 215–216
Copyright © 2024 by Information Age Publishing
www.infoagepub.com
All rights of reproduction in any form reserved.

Joe McNabb is a full-time faculty member in the Graduate School of Education. Prior to joining the faculty, he completed an 11-year term as president of Labouré College. This position followed a 17-year tenure as professor and dean of faculty. He served as a commissioner, a six-year term, on the New England Commission of Higher Education (NECHE). He also chaired, or served as a site visitor, for many accreditation teams throughout the United States and several in Europe. He has also served on many boards, including teaching hospitals, community educational agencies, and several non-profit organizations.

ABOUT THE CONTRIBUTORS

Emily J. Bauer, EdD, is a mental health advocate who has spent two decades serving students across various higher education institutions. Emily currently serves as a clinical coordinator for a trauma-informed behavioral health agency. She has volunteered as a mental health first aid instructor and serves as a volunteer crisis counselor for a national organization. Emily wishes to assist educational institutions in addressing mental health issues including suicide, depression, and anxiety. Emily holds a Bachelor of Science from the University of Nevada, Las Vegas, a Master of Education from Oregon State University, and a Doctor of Education from Northeastern University.

Jen Bevins, EdD, serves as the director of data analytics and student engagement for the Watts College of Public Service and Community Solutions at Arizona State University. Her research interests include first-generation students, trauma-informed practice in higher education, hidden student populations, the impacts of financial aid, and inequalities in access to higher education. She holds a BA in religious studies and classical and near eastern archaeology from the University of Minnesota, an MA in divinity from the University of Chicago, and an EdD in leadership and innovation from Arizona State University.

Joe Castelot, EdD, is an organizational strategist working to untangle systems with the goal of improving organizational culture, community, and sense of belonging. He is an educator, researcher, and innovator with a pas-

Taking Action, pages 217–220
Copyright © 2024 by Information Age Publishing
www.infoagepub.com
All rights of reproduction in any form reserved.

sion for fostering a positive sense of community and belonging on college campuses. His professional experiences cross the areas of student center operations, campus and student life, orientation, admission and retention, academic evaluation and support, safety, and wellness—most recently at the Ivy League level. He is a graduate of Northeastern University's Doctor of Education program, concentrating on organizational leadership studies. His doctoral dissertation focused on improving student community engagement and belonging on college campuses.

Jeff Cheng, EdD, is a full-time faculty member in the business department at Community College Aurora in Colorado. With over a decade of experience in Higher Education, he has actively engaged in various campus initiatives, such as serving as president of Faculty Senate, volunteering on committees, and serving as a faculty advisor. Additionally, Jeff also serves as the contact advisor at Phi Theta Kappa International (PTK) Honor Society on campus since 2016. As a scholarly practitioner, he is deeply committed to making a positive impact on students' lives through his research and knowledge in higher education. He holds five college degrees, including an MBA from Oklahoma City University and a Doctor of Education in higher education administration from Northeastern University.

Christopher Collins, EdD, serves as the director of recruitment initiatives and student excellence at NC State University's College of Natural Resources. With over 10 years of experience in enrollment management and undergraduate admissions, Christopher has a passion for helping students and their families along their educational journey—especially those taking a nonlinear path. Christopher earned a Bachelor of Science in plant and soil science from the University of Kentucky, a Master of Science in instructional technology from the New York Institute of Technology, and a Doctor of Education in higher education administration from Northeastern University.

Kathleen A. Dilks, EdD, is a current higher education professional and educator with over 30 years of progressive experience spanning student affairs, enrollment management, teaching, and advising within private and public institutions. As an administrator, action research practitioner, and educator, Kathy focuses on fostering growth-minded change-agency and collaborations to affect positive trainee and student-centered support. Problem solving and removing institutional barriers are strengths that she couples with kindness, enthusiasm, and respect for everyone serving the mission of the institution and profession. Kathy earned her doctorate from Northeastern University. She and her husband are the proud parents of two boys.

Lars Farabee, EdD serves as the associate vice president for Graduate Admissions at High Point University, working directly with students seeking advancement in a variety of fields. During his 20-year career, Lars has guided students at the undergraduate and graduate level in finding the college experience that "fits" them best. Lars earned a Bachelor of Arts degree in English from the University of Maine at Farmington, a Master of Arts degree in liberal and global studies from the University of North Carolina at Greensboro, and a Doctor of Education in higher education administration from Northeastern University. He resides in Greensboro, NC with his wife and their two children.

Brandon G. Gross, EdD, has focused his career and research on leadership development. He serves as director of strategic engagement supporting the office of the president and office of the provost at Michigan State University. He earned his bachelor's and master's degrees at the University of Miami and his doctoral degree at Northeastern University. Throughout his career in higher education, he has served in various roles with student affairs, enrollment management, and academic affairs at the University of Miami, Arizona State University, and Michigan State University.

Nicole Johnson, EdD, currently serves as the inaugural director of educational equity and justice for the Massachusetts Department of Higher Education (DHE). Nicole comes to this work with the aim and passion to challenge the status quo and consider the voices and experiences of underrepresented and minority students. Through her professional and personal endeavors, Nicole seeks to learn more about the experiences of minority students and advocate for change to eliminate the challenges and barriers racially minoritized students face in the public postsecondary education system. She holds a Bachelor of Science in management from Bentley University, a Master of Art in peace and conflict studies from University of Massachusetts Lowell, and a Doctor of Education in higher education administration from Northeastern University.

Lindsey Plewa, EdD, is a seasoned career coach with over a decade of experience, guiding thousands of graduate students and professionals in finding meaningful work and navigating successful job searches. Currently serving as the deputy director of career advising at the Zicklin School of Business at Baruch College in New York City, she ensures that MBA and MS students receive comprehensive career guidance through coaching sessions, workshops, and online resources. Lindsey's expertise extends to areas such as navigating career changes, conducting assessments like the Myers-Briggs Type Indicator (MBTI) and Gallup Clifton Strengths, and salary negotiation. She holds a Doctorate in Higher Education from Northeastern University and a Master of Arts from New York University, and her research focuses on the challenges faced by international students when searching for jobs in the United States.

Thomas Tressler-Gelok, EdD, is a change agent, leader, and administrator. He specializes in the administration and oversight of student affairs and student services functions—especially residence life and student life. His research interests include leadership development, organizational culture in higher education, and the professional development of student affairs and student services practitioners. He holds a Bachelor of Arts from Siena College, a Master of Education from the University at Buffalo–SUNY, a Master of Business Administration from Wagner College, and a Doctor of Education from Northeastern University.

Mike Urmeneta, EdD, is an accomplished researcher, educator, and data scientist with over 2 decades of experience specializing in student success and institutional effectiveness. Leading organizations including the Association for Institutional Research (AIR), the National Association of College and University Business Officers (NACUBO), and EDUCAUSE have recognized his major contributions to several academic institutions. In his most recent role with AIR's Data Literacy Institute, he prepares university leadership teams to adopt a culture of data-informed decision-making. Before that, he served as the director of analytics at the New York Institute of Technology, where he provided strategic guidance to the provost and president. Mike holds a BS in mechanical engineering, an MS in management from NYU, and a Doctor of Education degree from Northeastern University. He received the Dean's Medal for Outstanding Doctoral Work for his research on first-generation college students.

Milton Keynes UK
Ingram Content Group UK Ltd.
UKHW020955021123
431778UK00005B/56